WANDERING IN WALES
AND THE BORDERLAND

Wandering in Wales
and
the Borderland

by VERONICA THACKERAY

author of

Tales from the Welsh March

Foreword by Francis Neville Chamberlain

Photographs by David Mitchell

CRESSRELLES PUBLISHING COMPANY LIMITED

Malvern

First published in 1995 by
Cressrelles Publishing Company Limited
10 Station Road Industrial Estate, Colwall, Malvern, Worcestershire

ISBN 0 85956 070 8

Printed in Great Britain by
BPC Wheatons Ltd, Exeter

Dedicated to
ROMA CHAMBERLAIN
and CLARE MORE
whose enthusiasm has been such a joy
and whose encouragement has helped me so much

Acknowledgements

By its very nature a book such as this owes much to a great many people and it is not possible to mention them all for they are legion. However, I must record my gratitude to the following who were so generous with their time and knowledge and, in several cases, the loan of precious documents.

Mr and Mrs J Baker, Mr and Mrs Tom Baker (whose expertise and help with the index was invaluable), Mr Rupert Bowater, Miss Emma Bullock, Mrs Mary Cadwallader, Mrs Ailsa Corbett-Winder, Mr and Mrs Jeffrey George, Major and Mrs Harwood Little, Mrs Hood, Mr Peter Hood, Mrs Jarvis, Mrs P. Jobson, Mrs Hugh Jones, Mrs V Jones, Mrs Lewis, Mr and Mrs Sam Meredith, Mr Robb Morgan (who kept my elderly Traveller, now in its fifth decade, fit and flourishing and well able to deal with Arthur Bradley's 'kill horse' hills), Mr and Mrs Mottram, Mr Bernard Pugh, Mr and Mrs John Roberts, Miss A Richardson, Mr and Mrs Thom, Mr and Mrs John Wheeler, Mrs Michael Williams, Mrs A Woodward and Mr Christopher Woodward.

and, above all, I must thank the late Geoffrey Bowater who came with me on so many of my wanderings up and down the lanes of the Borderland and over the hills of wild Wales. He was indeed the very dear, the very beloved companion.

My thanks are also due to the Editor of *The Shropshire Magazine* and the Editor of *The Country Quest* for permission to include excerpts from my articles in their publications.

Contents

Photographs and Drawings

Sketches by Veronica Thackeray

Foreword

This is no ordinary guide to the people, places and tales of Wales and the Borderland. Miss Thackeray deftly touches upon the ambiguous and haunting quality of that beautiful country. She summons up for us a vivid gallery of adventurers, farmers, noblemen and countrymen of all descriptions; some eccentric, some ordinary. Their stories are full of such vitality that they stamp indelibly on to our minds the personality of the places they inhabit.

Once read, who will forget the story of Captain Leslie Woodward, seen walking up the drive of Hopton Court the same day that he was killed in France? Or that of the Martin brothers, their appearances so affected by the trenches of the First World War that they returned on the same train, from Southampton to Whatshill, without recognising each other? Many of us will envy the very British fortitude of Henry, father of the adopted Prince Falanisi of Tonga, who consoled himself upon the loss of his leg at sea by reflecting that he was 'happy to say that his leg had been buried at sea in very good company because it had been placed in the same canvas sheeting and sewn up together with the body of a beautiful girl who had died on the voyage'.

Those of us who are privileged to know Miss Thackeray will recognise in this fascinating and invaluable book all the qualities that we most admire in her; her genuine and consuming interest in people of all kinds, her capacious memory, the sense of humour which enlivens all it touches and her intuitive feel for time and place. We could have no better companion on our journey.

Francis Neville Chamberlain

March 1995

Chapter 1

Bitterley & the Clee Hills
&
William Nash of Ludlow Town

Oh, come you home of Sunday
When Ludlow streets are still
And Ludlow bells are calling
To Farm and lane and mill.

In my last book, *Tales from the Welsh March*, I wrote mainly of the Middle March and parts of Wales and my starting point for the various peregrinations was Ludlow. However, in this book I will be wandering further up the Border in the Northern March and a good deal more into Wales. A large part of my journeying, as before, will be following in the footsteps of Arthur Bradley, who scampered up and down the Border and over much of Wales in his pony and trap more than a hundred years ago. However, before travelling northwards, I hope I may be forgiven for a little further wandering in the Middle March in order to visit people and places I bypassed before.

I cannot leave the Ludlow area without remembering William Nash who, for almost half a century, was sexton to Saint Laurence's Parish Church in Ludlow. So beloved was he by the entire town that the Ludlow Town Council presented him with a framed "address of appreciation from the Townspeople of Ludlow".

I first met him about fifteen years ago. I had been examining a silver buttonhook and a long-handled shoehorn in a Ludlow auction rooms and, as I handed them back to the porter, I said 'Imagine having to fasten dozens of little boot buttons before going out, no time for that in this age

1

of zips and slip-ons, those were the days indeed.' I looked up to see a pair of very blue eyes smiling at me, 'I could tell you quite a lot about those days', replied the porter, taking the items from me and placing them carefully back in their velvet-lined case. 'I used to be a gentleman's gentleman, I went right through from hallboy to first footman, and what's more,' he added almost defiantly, 'what's more I enjoyed my years in service.' There was a sudden scuffling and scraping of chairs around us and at the back of the hall little knots of dealers were murmuring together. Mr Talbot, the auctioneer, mounted his rostrum and, reluctantly, I left the porter, William Nash, to his work but not before I had scribbled his name and address on my catalogue.

A month later I called on him at his Tudor cottage in Ludlow. He led me into a room with a blue painted wainscot and a delicious scent of primroses coming from a bowl of spring flowers on the table. A kettle was singing on the hob by a brightly burning coal fire and the only other sound was the steady ticking of a cuckoo clock. The cottage wrapped itself around us like a cosy eiderdown.

'Mr Nash,' I broke the silence, 'have you lived here for long?' 'Nigh on forty-seven years,' he replied. 'I was born in Ludlow, 1898 that would be, and I went to a little school run by a Mr and Mrs Baker. When I was twelve-years old I stopped attending full time and worked for Mr Collins, the baker, for part of the day. Early in the morning I used to fetch the big wooden trays from the bakehouse and take them to the shop in the High Street. Then I would get a bucket of ice from Papa Lowe, the fishmonger, everyone called him Papa I can't think why. I would put the ice in a compartment around a huge caldron of custard and turn a handle to make it into ice cream. After that it was off to school with me.

'After I'd been with Mr Collins for about a year my uncle, who was a butler, suggested I go into service, so I left Ludlow with him and started work as a hallboy. My duties were to fetch in the coals, pump up the water, clean all the shoes, lay the servants' table and carry the meals from the kitchen to the servants' hall.

'I always had to put the joint in front of my uncle, the butler, and the vegetables in front of the cook. I had to call my uncle 'sir' for you had to be very careful that there was no favouritism shown in the servants' hall'. 'You were kept very busy Mr Nash,' I said. 'Busy and happy,' he replied. 'It was my life and I thoroughly enjoyed it you know. I've always done everything I've had to do in life as well as I possibly could. It's a wonderful thing the satisfaction of a job well done.'

'You had a certain amount of free time I expect,' I said. 'Oh yes indeed and I well remember on one of my days off going with my uncle to the Derby. We had to bike the twenty-odd miles to Epsom. It was 1913, that was the year when the judges announced a dead heat for the two leading horses. We saw them coming up the straight as if they were bolted together, that was a sight I can tell you. It was on that day,' he added, 'that a young woman, suffragettes they called them, threw herself under a horse and was killed. Of course, when it was all over we had the twenty-miles to bike home but what a day it was, I'll never forget it. ,In 1914,' he continued, 'in order to better myself I took a job as second footman to a Major Allen. He owned an island off the west coast of Scotland and he would hire a train every year to take most of us servants and mountains of luggage up there for the season. In 1914, we'd got as far as Crewe when we found everyone rushing round saying 'War has been declared'. However, we carried on and we stayed on the island for the usual three months.

'It was just like paradise, we swam and fished and caught rabbits. Everywhere else in the world things were topsy-turvy but we never felt anything of it. At last, at the end of the season, we left the island and the Major went off to the war and I took a post as footman to a Viscount Valeport in Sloane Square. He was second in command of the Duke of Cornwall's Regiment and in 1916 I joined the regiment and went to France as his batman. Lance-Corporal William Nash, that was me.

'He was Lord Mount Edgecombe by then, his father having died. He survived the war but when he died the title went to an Australian. They had no children you see. Great tragedy. She was a lovely lady, very tall and frail.

'After the war, I applied for a job as footman to Lord Cheylesmore at Prince's Gate. I asked for sixty-pounds a year all found. Her Ladyship said to me, "That's a bit expensive isn't it?" But I had good references and she took me on. She was a very big lady, strange sort of person,' he added thoughtfully. 'Very suspicious that there were goings on among the servants. They had some very grand parties at Princess Gate, like the time when Princess Alice, Countess of Athlone, came to dine. I waited at table. The ladies wore the most beautiful gowns and you've never seen such jewellery. Their tiaras flashed and sparkled like stars. The tableware was snow white and covered with shining glass and silver. They knew how to do things in those days you know.

'Lord Cheylesmore always gave a luncheon on the last day of Bisley

3

and I would go down to valet him and wait at table. One year the guest of honour was His Royal Highness, Prince Arthur of Connaught. There were about fifty people at the luncheon and a veal and ham pie had been made for the occasion. Huge thing it was, about two-feet high. I had about twenty-yards to go to the kitchen to fetch the food. Well, everything was going well until I got to his Lordship, he being the last one to be served, and I had to tell him, "The veal and ham pie has run out, my Lord". "Well," he said, "bring me the ham and tongue". So off I goes to the kitchen but it was the same story. "The ham and tongue has run out my Lord". So he looks at the menu and says "Well bring me the cold beef", but that had run out too. Do you know I went four times to the kitchen only to tell him the veal and ham, the ham and tongue, the cold beef and the

William Nash as a footman, before the first world war

lamb had all run out, but he took it very well. "You go back to the kitchen William," he said "and catch me a chicken before that runs out too!" You should have heard the laughter, they laughed their heads off.'

There was a sudden shift and splutter from the coals in the grate and, still chuckling, he busied himself with the poker. 'When were you married Mr Nash?' I queried, as he resumed his seat. 'Oh, early in the twenties, I left Lord Cheylesmore to marry and I brought my wife back to Ludlow with me. I first met her you know when I was second footman to Major Allen and she was house parlour-maid at the place opposite. I would be scrubbing the steps every morning and she would pop out sometimes and that was it. Lady Cheylesmore didn't allow followers so I would go to my fiancée's home in the country and we would meet there.

'In Ludlow I joined my father in his business of restoring antiques and we settled in Saint John's Lane, one-up and one-down, two-shillings and nine-pence a week. Then, in 1931, I got the job of sexton to the parish church and we moved to this place. When I left Ludlow as a lad,' he said, his blue eyes shining, 'never did I think in my wildest dreams, that I would eventually become sexton to Saint Laurence's Parish Church, Ludlow! By rights I ought never to have come back at all, I had some narrow squeaks in the first world war, I can tell you and then, in the 1939 war, I went into munitioning down at Hereford. I was the only one allowed to put the charge on the two-thousand-pound bombs. Big as this room they were, phew! Every time I sat on one of those things while I was drilling I used to think, 'If a spark should come now . . . '

'One morning, when I was helping to move the twenty-five pounders, all hell was let loose. When the dust had cleared, we found one of the bombs had exploded, killing four people. One of the fellows had been swapping jokes with some friends and, for some reason, that morning I didn't join in. If I'd paused for one second to listen to his tales I'd have been blown to bits along with the rest of them.'

A sudden cheerful 'cuckoo, cuckoo' from the clock on the wall shattered the little pool of reflective silence. 'Mr Nash,' I said, 'I believe you have been the time keeper and chief bell-ringer at the parish church for a very long time.' 'Yes,' he replied 'when I was a lad of eight I used to go up with my grandfather and ring the curfew every evening from Michaelmas to Candlemas. When I became sexton, I took up bell-ringing properly. One particular time I remember well was when George V was dying. The reports were coming through on the wireless. "The King is sinking fast". The Mayor of Ludlow, old Tommy Bryant, said to me, 'I don't think there's much hope William. If anything happens, day or night, I want you to ring the tenor bell half muffled. I'll pay for it'.

'Very good sir', I said, and that particular night in January 1936, I waited up until midnight and when Big Ben had struck, I heard the announcer say "The King is sinking fast". I'd got my grandfather's lantern with a candle in it ready and my eldest lad, he was about fifteen at the time, was waiting to go up with me. When Big Ben struck the quarter-past midnight the announcer quietly began, "We regret . . . " I didn't wait for more. "That's it," I said, "come on Bill we've got to go." We lit the lantern and we went out. The streets were covered with ice, just like a sheet of glass, you never saw nothing like it in your life.'

'We climbed up the tower and put a half muffler on the tenor bell. Then, as it struck half-past midnight, we started him ringing - boom - boom. As soon as they heard it, folk knew what had happened, they didn't have to wait for the morning papers to tell them.'

He was leaning forward, gazing into the fire, seeing once again perhaps the man and boy on a bitter winter's night, slipping and sliding, by the light of a candle lantern, up the hill to the church, to climb the tower and muffle the bell so that it could send its sad message over the sleeping town.

A little shiver frisked down my spine, 'Mr Nash,' I said, interrupting his reveries, 'did you ever see any ghosts in the church when you were there at night on your own?' 'Well,' he replied, 'I must say you do hear some very strange noises at times, they seem to rush out and hit you and you wonder who the devil's that? Sometimes I've seen some very strange shadows, too, but ghosts, no I've never seen a ghost.'

'Going out on such a night to toll the bell on the death of a King makes me think you are a Royalist,' I said. 'Yes,' he replied. 'I am a Royalist. When I went to Hereford Cathedral to receive the Maundy money from the Queen in 1976, why that was one of the best moments in my life. That there Willy Hamilton - they should have cut off his head long ago!' I had a brief vision of Willy Hamilton's head on a pike at the Ludlow Broadgate and hastily changed the subject.

'This is interesting', I said, indicating what appeared to be a framed address hanging on the wall. He took it down and handed it to me and I read. 'Ludlow Town Council, address of appreciation to Mr T W Nash from the townspeople of Ludlow on the occasion of the silver jubilee of Her Majesty, Queen Elizabeth II, 1952 - 77. In sincere appreciation of his loyal and devoted service in that he has wound the clock and chimes for a period of no less than forty-six years, in the tower of the Parish Church of St Laurence, Ludlow. Such dedication as this sets standards of Christian and public service that the citizens of Ludlow would do well to follow.' The address was signed by the Mayor and other prominent citizens of Ludlow, 'For and on behalf of the townspeople of Ludlow'.

'It's a wonderful thing to have from your own townspeople, wonderful thing,' he said, his rich warm Shropshire voice filled with pride. A wonderful thing indeed, I thought as I left his cottage and walked up the hill, and a wonderful thing for those citizens of Old Ludlow Town to be able to claim William Nash, timekeeper, bellringer, sexton and citizen *par excellence* as their own.

Without a doubt the best view of the Clee Hills is from the Whitcliffe a large area of commonland to the west of the old town of Ludlow. To reach it we leave Ludlow by crossing Ludford Bridge. This ancient packhorse bridge leads onto the A49. Almost at once a turning right takes us past the Charlton Arms and the little cottage, with the diamond panec windows, which sits so snugly by it. Continuing up the hill for a short way we find the road has widened to include a long parking space on the right. The view from here is surely one of the most fascinating and spectacular in the whole of the Border Country.

The green turf falls gently away to where, far below, the meandering Teme glimmers through the trees and the mellow-roofed old houses climb from its banks up the slope of the ridge on which the town is built, to cluster round the walls of the once mighty castle and line the streets which were laid out in a grid pattern by the Normans, a pattern which is still plain to see nearly one thousand years later.

Away to the right soars the slender spire of the Parish Church of St Laurence, the largest parish church in the Border Country and probably in England, built by those war-thirsty border barons who made the Marchland their home. Rising up behind the town are those guardians of its Eastern flank, the Clee hills, 'Those mountains of Command' as the poet Drayton called them. On the early summer afternoon when I last saw them from the Whitcliffe the westering sun was gilding their summits and scudding clouds made long purple shadows on their backs so that they formed an ever changing and splendid backdrop for the town.

Looking at them from the Whitcliffe, it is very surprising to learn that the rounded slopes of Brown Clee are higher than the more conical top of Titterstone Clee, but those who know about these things assure us that while Brown Clee is 1,792 feet high, Titterstone Clee is a mere 1,749 feet high. Both the hills are extinct volcanoes and both are covered with a thick cap of basalt. This was quarried for stone which was called dhustone, dhu being the Welsh for black. The stone was an excellent hard material for the roads of the past, but now-a-days a surface with more give in it is required for modern vehicles, however, a certain amount of quarrying still goes on for curbs and such things. Beneath the basalt cap was coal and this was mined extensively, as was iron ore. The mining scars have been softened and in many cases obliterated by nature and time and now the area has been designated as one of 'outstanding natural beauty'.

We reach these hills by carrying on to the end of the parking space and turning right down a very steep incline. This will take us round to the back of the castle. Pause for a moment and look across the river to the castle walls rising sheer to an immense height and ponder how anyone in the days before aircraft could contemplate assaulting such a fortress, and yet it did change hands on many occasions, by treachery or marriage.

Carrying on past the castle and over Ludlow's second bridge, crossing

7

the Teme, we turn sharp left averting our gaze from the modern swimming baths at the bridge and glancing instead to the right at the old houses built into the very stone of the outer bailey walls. At the end of this road another turn left takes us onto the A49 and very soon we take a right hand turn over a small bridge. Keeping to this road as it curves round under a railway bridge we find ourselves on the A4117 which crosses the Clee Hills.

The third turning on the left, a mile or so out of Ludlow, leads to the very heartland of the Clees. On the right of the A4117 as we turn, at the end of a long avenue, stands Henley Hall, built by Thomas Powis in the seventeenth century. In 1907 the mansion was bought by Thomas Wedgwood Wood, who made a great many alterations to the place, and it is now owned by Captain Lumsden. The left hand lane down which we are trundling seems like a tree-lined extension to the Henley Hall avenue bisected by the road over Titterstone Clee. About two miles along this lane is the village of Bitterley. There is an old saw which runs, 'Bitterley, Bitterley under the Clee the devil take me if I ever come to thee.' The rhymester probably thought the name Bitterley was cold and uninviting, as did Arthur Bradley when he trotted along these lanes for he wrote 'Set among green summer foliage Bitterley village looks attractive as we traverse its one quiet thoroughfare, but in winter time, as the name suggests, the district is bleak and chilly.' In fact it got its name because in Saxon times it was considered such a lush and fertile spot that they called it Butter Lea or Butter Meadow, and this has been corrupted into Bitterley.

The lane to Bitterley leads on over a small ford with a little white painted footbridge, past an old farm, nicely settled down at the roadside, an immense yew tree peering over its chimneys, past some attractive timber-framed houses where I stopped to ask two pretty schoolgirls the way to the church. They were so brightly chatty that I asked their names. 'Clementine and Elizabeth', was the reply. Lovely old fashioned names, befitting the dwellers in this peaceful backwater, tucked in a hollow beneath the Clees. Following their directions, I drove past the village green and the little stone school, founded in 1712 by John Newborough, a past head master of Eton, then across a bridge over another stream and past an old stone wall, mercifully hiding a complex of battery hen cages. Then, having driven through what appeared to be an extension of a nearby farmyard, complete with hens, I arrived at the white-painted wicket fencing and the kissing-gate leading to the church.

8

A kindly soul passing by advised me to call at a nearby cottage, the home of the church warden, and get the key for, as with so many of our country churches these days, in order to lessen the risks of thieves and vandals, it was prudently locked.

All was hustle and bustle at the cottage when I called. Another visitor arrived almost simultaneously with me and Mrs Howell, the church warden, whisked us in and then answered the telephone, which was ringing incessantly in the background. Having dealt with the other visitor and the telephone, Mrs Howell gathered up a large key and we crossed her garden to the church. Apologising for the bats which were 'coming out of hibernation and making a dreadful mess', she opened the door.

Bitterley church was the first place of Christian worship around the Clee Hills area but the only thing remaining of the original church is the font. The present building, built in the reign of King Stephen, is transitional Norman. It is a beautiful building and well suited to be the mother church of Christianity among the Clee villages. At the right of the altar there is an interesting memorial to Timothy Lucye. His statue kneels in prayer. He was the nephew of Sir Thomas Lucye of Charlcote, in Warwickshire, and must have spent much of his life in that area because he was MP for Warwick in 1571 and again in 1584. When his uncle died at Charlcote, he walked behind him with the chief mourners.

The story goes that when Timothy's uncle, Sir Thomas, was the owner of Charlcote the young Will Shakespeare, from nearby Stratford-upon-Avon, was caught together with some of his friends poaching deer in his park. Sir Thomas ordered them all to be beaten and fined. Later in life Shakespeare had his revenge and sent Sir Thomas down to posterity as Justice Shallow in *The Merry Wives of Windsor*. With a further twist of the knife Shakespeare changed the white luces or pikes on Sir Thomas's coat-of-arms to white louses. (See *The Merry Wives of Windsor* Act 1, Scene 1, Evans, referring to Justice Shallow's arms. 'The dozen white louses do become an old coat well.')

Another Charlcote-Lucy connection in the area comes from the little town of Church Stretton, a handful of miles from Bitterley. Here lived, until her death a few years ago, the genealogist and historian, Vere Hodgson. She too was a member of a branch of the Lucy family and her ancestor, another Thomas Lucy, made an unsuccessful claim to the Charlcote estates. It was in the year 1772 that, after consulting family papers, he felt certain he was the rightful heir to Charlcote. Sir George Lucy, the then owner, was in his fifties and unmarried. Accordingly,

Thomas set off from Slimford in Sussex to stake his claim. It was high summer and Thomas was not a young man so by the time he had ridden the many miles to Charlcote he was travel stained and very weary. However, George Lucy received him with great courtesy and listened to his story. He was undoubtedly very impressed by Thomas Lucy's claim for he settled a large sum of money on him. Thomas renounced his claim and with the money built the Lucy Mill in Stratford-upon-Avon. Vere Hodgson maintained that this was a pay-off to avoid litigation but the Lucys at Charlcote felt it was more likely to be a philanthropic gesture, at all events his arrival at Charlcote must have given a certain young Mr Hammond, who was Sir George's secretary-companion and his heir, a nasty jolt.

After that little digression, I must go back to Bitterley and the church and to another interesting memorial in the church, that to John Walcot. His coat-of-arms is shown emblazoned with three chess rooks. These replace a cross and fleur-de-lys and the alteration was made by command of his King, Henry V. This came about because one day, when King Henry was playing chess with his friend, John Walcot, John checkmated him with a rook, a move placing himself in a situation of extreme delicacy one would suppose, but what red-blooded man could resist giving the coup-de-grâce in chess when in a position to do so? Happily all passed off well. Henry merely insisted that his friend replace the cross and fleur-de-lys on his arms with three rooks as a permanent reminder of the day he trounced the King. John Walcot rose from the table no doubt vastly relieved albeit with a change of arms.

The Bitterley church bells are quite remarkable in that they are all pre-reformation. The tenor bell, which was cast at Worcester Monastery in 1414, has an inscription in Norman French, 'Jesu le seigne seynt Anne per le oudynsunce Aleis Sturye que Dieu asoile pur sa gaunt mercee'. - ('Dedicated to Jesus the Lord and Saint Anne, by the appointment of Alice Stury whom God pardon by his great mercy'.) According to the Reverend Prebendary J R Burton writing, in the *Woolhope Transactions*, the use of Norman French for a bell inscription is unique in Britain, all other church bells being inscribed either in Latin or English.

Alice Stury lived at Droitwich near Worcester, quite a distance from the Clee Hills, and it seems strange that she should be such a great benefactress to Bitterley church. She was, however, Lady of the Manor of Hampton Lovett near Droitwich. The rector there, from her childhood on, was Sir William Hugford who owned two manors in Bitterley parish and no doubt that was the reason for her generosity to Bitterley. For nearly thirty thousand Sundays, this old tenor bell has rung out over Bitterley parish, calling the faithful to worship in their church.

The second bell is just a little younger than the tenor bell, having been cast in the Worcester Foundry sometime between 1450 and 1500, and it has a much briefer inscription. 'Sancts Jacob ora pro nobis'. - ('Saint James pray for us'). The baby of the bells is the treble bell and when this was cast in 1520 the tenor bell was already more than a century old. This bell is the Angelus bell and is inscribed 'Hic sono que Helis camans vocor Gabrielis'. - ('Here I sound who am called the angelus bell of the hymn of Gabriel'.) In the morning, at midday, and in the evenings, the angelus bell would ring out calling the workers in the cottages and farmsteads and in the fields around to prayer.

Jack Baker, a former church warden of Bitterley church, has compiled a fascinating booklet on the history of Bitterley and from it I learned that of the 1,016 church bells in Shropshire there are only forty which have come down from mediaeval times. Of these Bitterly is 'almost unique in having all its bells in sound condition and untouched for five-hundred years'. Mr Baker is a most interesting man with a fund of stories about Bitterley but more of him soon.

Bitterley churchyard contains another great treasure, a mediaeval stone cross, considered to be the best example of an ancient churchyard cross in Britain. Erected in the early fourteenth century, tall and slim, about twenty-feet high, it stands on four

John Baker in front of the mediaeval stone cross, Bitterley

11

hexagonal stone steps surrounded by lichen covered gravestones grouped and leaning together, as if they are listening to a sermon. Among them, poignant reminders of man's inhumanity to man, stand several new headstones commemorating young men who fell in the 1914-18 and 1939-45 wars. Behind the cross, past the dark yews, stretch the green meadows where sheep quietly graze. Standing at the wicket gate looking at this scene of pastoral tranquillity, snippets of Gray's *Elegy in a Country Churchyard* fluttered through my mind. It must have been scenes such as this that inspired him to write such verses as:

Oft did the harvest to their sickle yield,
Their furrow oft the stubborn glebe has broke;
How jocund did they drive their team afield:
How bowed the woods beneath their sturdy stroke:

I left Bitterley church thankful that no trendy vicar would seem to have passed that way and organised the removal of all the grave stones to stand them 'dressed by the right' around the churchyard walls, leaving smoothly mown stretches of grass, where no primroses or daisies or other wildlings would dare to show their heads.

Near to the church, almost cheek by jowl, are the grounds of Bitterley Court. This old mansion is said to date from the early seventeenth century. It was bought jointly by Thomas Walcot, a member of a branch of the Walcot family at Lydbury North, and the Littletons of nearby Henley Hall. Thomas took his bride, Anne Littleton, to live at Bitterly Court and it remained in the possession of the Walcot family for 244 years until 1889, when it was sold to James Volant Wheeler of Worcestershire. It has remained in the Wheeler family for nearly a century. John Wheeler, the grandson of James Volant Wheeler, is the present owner.

In 1796 Charles Walcot employed the Shrewsbury architect, Thomas Farnoll Pritchard, to make the various alterations to the Court. Many examples of Pritchard's work can be seen in houses along the Border. Croft Castle near Leominster had extensive work carried out by him. Until fairly recently Pritchard was a little known Shrewsbury architect, however, some fascinating detective work by Robin Chaplin, a lecturer in the Extra Mural Department at Birmingham University, has changed all that. Now a great deal more is known about Pritchard's work and many of his designs and buildings have been identified.

With the help of James Dawson, the librarian at Shrewsbury School, Robin Chaplin set off, as he put it 'In pursuit of Pritchard', and what a harvest he reaped. He told me that the voyage of discovery began some years ago, when he was working with Sir George Trevelyan at Attingham Park. He was curious to know who had built the place but no-one seemed to be sure. He consulted endless papers belonging to the family and was finally able to show that the architect of the present building had built around a previous one called Tern Hall. Much of this previous building was by Thomas Farnoll Pritchard, but he was dismissed when the place was only half completed. This may not have been entirely due to pique on the part of his patron, since Tern Hall was not one of Pritchard's most successful designs, indeed he had arranged things so that the windows were set too high for any Georgian landowner to sit in satisfied contemplation of his parklands.

Filled with enthusiasm to discover more about the man, Robin Chaplin has, over the years, spent countless hours researching through innumerable papers and his efforts received a tremendous boost when Pritchard's record book was discovered in the library of the American Institute of Architects near Washington DC. This contained numerous designs for carved decorations in the houses along the Border. There are also several drawings for chimney pieces and door cases at Croft Castle, Bitterley Court and other great Border houses, including the names of the carvers, Alexander van der Hagen and John Nelson of Shrewsbury. Their work, crisp and spirited and deliciously elegant can be seen at Croft today.

In 1765 Pritchard also refronted and made many improvements to Croft Castle. The improvements were, in effect, the virtual insertion of a 'gentleman's residence' of manageable size into part of what was once an open courtyard. The style he chose was gothic with a K, and the gothic staircase in the 'new' house within a castle soars up, surrounded by the airy, gothic frivolity of the plaster work on the walls and ceilings.

At Bitterley Court, alterations made by Pritchard also included a new staircase and hall and two very beautiful chimney pieces carved to his design. Some of the panelling at Bitterley Court is said to have come from Park Hall nearby but John Wheeler has no record of this.

A short distance from the church and Court, bordering the main thoroughfare as it leaves Bitterley, there is a meadow where, smothered in grass, a few stones remain of an ancient mansion that once housed the mother of a King's son. When the author, Thornhill Timmins, came upon it in the year 1888 he wrote in his book *Nooks and corners of Shropshire* that with its 'Crow stepped gables smothered in ivy, the mullioned windows agape to every gale and roof and chimneys tottering to their fall, the old place looks like a haunted house.' Over the years, I gleaned snippets of the romantic history of this once proud dwelling but never enough to satisfy my curiosity until, by chance, I came upon a paper written by the Reverend Prebendary J R Burton, B.A. and dated 1919, thirty years after Mr Timmins wrote his melancholy description.

Oh, those parsons of yesteryear! What a debt we owe to them and how much they have enriched our literature and our lives. Diarist parsons such as Francis Kilvert who wrote so lyrically of the Border country and its people; dear old parson Woodforde who left such a fascinating record of every day life in a country parsonage in the late eighteenth century; Gilbert White, the great naturalist; and even poor Parson Skinner with his diaries of unremitting gloom and despond; and so many more, all providing a rich vein of history into which those of us with a sense of the past may delve. Parson Burton of Bitterley was one such for over the years I have found various papers written by him crammed with information of the parish he served and loved and which would, no doubt, be lost but for him.

Sixty-three years ago another author, Byford Jones, while wandering among the Clee villages, called at Bitterley rectory. He was informed that both the eighty-three-year old rector and his eighty-six-year old wife were far too busy to see him, however, their daughter, he writes, 'entertained me in the rambling old rectory. She said that her father and mother had just received a letter of congratulations from the former Prime Minister, Mr Stanley Baldwin, on their golden wedding, she thought this rather funny as their golden wedding took place seven years ago!'

Parson Burton attributes the building of Park Hall to Sir John Blount in the reign of Henry VII. In 1485 Sir John received a splendid appointment from the monarch, that of the Keepership of the Park, a vast area of the Clee Hills. He and his wife seem to have been much in favour at the court, maybe because her father, Sir Hugh Pershal, fought so well for his King at the Battle of Bosworth Field that he was knighted on the field of battle. At all events, in the ensuing years, their daughter Elizabeth was chosen by Queen Catherine to be one of her ladies-in-waiting. Sir John and his wife had eight children with a slight overdose of daughters, five in all. The Queen's action in removing Elizabeth from the fold and taking her to court, must have brought a little relief of the pressure on her parents for, apart from being an honour, there would be one less daughter for whom to find a suitable husband or convent, not to mention dowry.

Elizabeth was a very lovely girl and, indeed, Lord Herbert wrote of her as 'Ye beauty and mistress piece of her time' and it was not long before the king was enamoured of the delightful creature. The inevitable happened and in 1519 Elizabeth became pregnant by him. Hastily Cardinal Wolesley, that adept smoother of unseemly ripples round the royal barque, was called in to resolve the matter. A word in the ear of the Mother Superior of a religious house in Essex and the good Cardinal, discreetly whisking Elizabeth away from the court, placed the young girl under her wing. Elizabeth gave birth to a son and the boy was christened Henry Fitzroy. The Cardinal, ever ready to oblige, was made his godfather. Happily, Elizabeth's fate was not to spend the rest of her life in a nunnery. Instead, Henry bestowed on her a great deal of Crown property and armed with this and her undoubted physical charms she very soon married, first to Gilbert Lord Talbois and after his death, to Lord Clinton and Say. She died when she was forty-years old, leaving three small daughters.

When he was six years old, Elizabeth's son by the king was created Earl of Nottingham and Duke of Somerset. As he grew, more honours were heaped upon him by his father and he was made Lieutenant-General Warden of the Scottish March and Lord High Admiral of England. His playmate as a boy was Henry Howard, Earl of Surrey, whose sister Mary he eventually married. With so much largesse showered upon him, it is obvious that the King was very fond of him and, indeed, intended to make him his heir. Alas it was not to be, at the age of seventeen, he died childless.

Parson Burton, pondering the affairs, thrills to the thought that the King's beloved Elizabeth was baptised in the old Saxon font at Bitterley by one of his predecessors, Parson Pemberton, and later, still in romantic mood, he visualises Elizabeth running up and down the stairs at Park Hall. Those stairs were still in the Hall in his day and describing them he writes, 'Huge blocks of solid oak in imitation of the spiral staircases of older castles and churches, the material was changed but the design persisted.' It was from Parson Burton's writings that I learned of the removal of 'The fine oak panelling in Park Hall to Bitterley Court' by his predecessor. Another glimpse of the Old Hall is left to us by James Herbert Green, who was Headmaster of Bitterley village school in 1807. James's father and grandfather were, each in turn, headmasters of the school and his father told him that he remembered when Park Hall had two drawbridges over the moat and the road through Bitterley passed over these and then under a spacious archway and through the hall. This archway divided the hall into two, each side having its own octagonal tower. On Sundays, James's father recalled, as many as four coaches-and-four would rattle through the archway and over the two drawbridges, on the way to church, thus ensuring that any morning lie-a-beds in either hall archway were jolted into action.

In the seventeen hundreds, when James's grandfather was headmaster of the school, a chestnut tree was ceremoniously planted in the school playground and all the boys in the village contributed from their treasured store of marbles to mark the occasion, as many as one thousand marbles were buried with the young tree. The chestnut grew and flourished and became one of the focal points of the village and, weather permitting, all special celebrations were held in the shade of this mighty tree. Sadly, in the nineteen thirties it was discovered that the crown was dangerous so 'All that crown and tower of leaves was levelled to the ground'. One wonders what future archaeologists will make of it if dozens and dozens of marbles turn up near the place where the old tree once stood.

Parson Burton wrote that the oldest family in Bitterley was the Nott family. He also recorded 'Nott says if the church clock strikes when the congregation is singing the first psalm there is always a funeral before the next Sunday'. When one of their number died, in 1830, Headmaster James Herbert Green wrote an epitaph on him which I have included in the chapter on Bedlam..

Along a lane, running beside the village school, there is on the left a small cottage with diamond-paned windows and a garden bright with flowers. This is Spout Cottage so called because, I was told by a villager, 'Until recently there was a spout of good, clear water there, a lovely spring, then someone built a fishpond nearby and the water just drained away', but the cottage name goes on and perhaps one day, when the fishpond owner has gone, the 'spout of good spring water' will return.

Just past the Spout Cottage there is a blue gate and a short drive leading to the house of Jack Baker who, until two years ago was church warden of Bitterley church. It was a brisk sort of morning with a rather penetrating wind when I called on Mr Baker and the hot coffee, which his wife Bessie had awaiting my arrival, was more than welcome. As I sipped it, his blue eyes regarded me quizzically from under bushy eyebrows and a thatch of snowy hair. 'So', he said, 'you want to know more about Bitterley?' I nodded. 'Well,' he continued, 'I was born in Angel lane in a nearby village and I came to live in Bitterley in 1922. We all made our own entertainment then, little concerts and sing-songs, one village community helping another. Bitterley had no village hall so everything had to be done in the village school, that was until after the First World War. Then everyone clubbed together and bought an army hut, but then Mr Wheeler from the Court bought another one. He kept half for his cattle and we had the other half. My father owned a small farm in those days and when I left school I worked for four years - part of the time on my father's farm and the rest of the time keeping the gardens in order at Bitterley Court. I remember Park Hall,' he said, 'it was a great moated place and one of the orchards in my father's time was called the Moat Orchard. The Hall had a round tower at one side and in this was a winding staircase made of huge oak blocks. In 1915 the kitchen was still in great shape for my father kept his tools there. Windsor Court had a lot of bits from Park Hall, you know. It's all gone now though'.

'The first bus in Bitterley was after the 1918 war and the Motor Company in Ludlow bought a W.D. wagon and put steps in it and that was it. Everything until then had been by horses and even the vet went round on horseback too. There were a few bicycles later but it was a great day when the W.D. wagon came. The first post office we had was in the black and white cottage you passed when you came into the village. It was the telegraph office too and Bessie's aunt, although crippled, was the first post mistress. The only telephone in those days was in the pub on Angel Bank about two miles away. Two of Bessie's brothers died of diphtheria, and when she told me this I remembered as a child in the nineteen twenties seeing two stretcher-bearers emerging from a house in a Plymouth street, a bright scarlet blanket covering the patient. "Scarlet fever or diphtheria", said Nanny in hushed tones as she hurried us away.' 'Yes', said Bessie, 'I remember the red blanket well, but my brothers never came back.' Bessie's remaining brother and two women named Bowser, who were sisters, all lived in a tiny cottage in the village, one sister was the postwoman and the other did the baking and kept house, while Bessie's brother was a pig butcher who always wore a bowler hat.

Jack Baker began bell ringing in 1922 and only gave it up in 1990, when he could no longer climb the twenty-four steps on the steep ladder leading to the belfrey. 'The trouble was', he said, 'even if I managed the steps, when I got to the top I had to climb through a trap door. Daunting to someone half his then eighty-seven years. Even now, as he approaches his ninetieth birthday, he still rings the bell which calls the people to worship, as he has done for close on seventy years.

Bell ringing meant Jack Baker travelled round quite a lot with the

Diocesan Guild of Church Bell Ringers. Knighton, Tenbury Wells, Hereford and a host of other places, all heard Jack and his friends ring out their peels. He gave up his churchwardenship in 1992, but he loves the old church which has been part of his and Bessie's life for so long and still spends many happy hours there. Lucky Bitterley to have such parishioners as these. Will there still be people ninety years hence like Jack and Bessie Baker of Bitterley or that dear old Royalist, William Nash of Ludlow Town who, having given a lifetime of service to their beloved church will still, when bordering on nonagenarianism teeter up and down steep ladders and squeeze through trap doors to send a peel of bells ringing out over their parish? I wonder.

i. *Slipping and sliding by the light of a candle lantern. (See page 6)*

Chapter 2

More Villages of the Clee Hills

When lads were home from labour
From Abdon under Clee,
A man would call his neighbour
And both would send for me,
And where the light in lances
Across the mead was laid
There to the dances
I fetched my flute and played.

Who could resist the signpost on the outskirts of Bitterley announcing Bedlam one mile? Although I was on my way to Blackford I could not and soon my ancient motor was puffing and spluttering its way up the steep hill to the tiny village. On my left the way was heavily wooded, but on my right the trees were spaced at intervals along a low hedge revealing a glorious view of meadows, woods and distant hills. Near to the top of the hill, past a small farmhouse nestling cosily down in a fold, a neat little terrace of cottages perched high on a bank to the left, looks out over the open country. These are dwellings of quarry workers of the past, for Bedlam was a stone quarrying village. A war memorial stands sentinel at the end of the row and next to it a little white house with pointed windows proclaims its new lease of life as 'The Old Chapel House'. Driving on past the flower-bright gardens of Ivy Cottage, I found myself at a deadend, the gates of the old quarry facing me firmly locked.

Bedlam certainly belies its name now, for the whole village seemed deserted, and the only noise was the distant barking of a dog and the excited clamouring of a gaggle of geese which required shooing out of the way so that I could proceed. No doubt, when work in the quarry on its doorstep was in full swing, 'bedlam' might well have been a suitably descriptive adjective to use for the place.

In the days when the horse was the only means of transport, other than Shank's pony, this little community high above the valley villages would have had to be self sufficient and, if the winter was a long and hard one, they could have been snowed up for weeks on end. In the year 1830 one of the inhabitants of the village, a certain William Nott, met his death in these hills in one such cruel winter. He was the local shoemaker, as well as being Parish Clerk and rate collector for the parish of Bitterley, and from 1805, for good measure, he became Church Warden. Parson Burton of Bitterly mentions in his many notes on the area that the Nott family lived in the district longer than any other family. He also supplied a somewhat macabre little statistic. 'Nott', he wrote, 'has stood by seven-hundred and forty-four open graves during his time as church warden.'

William Nott was obviously a respected and well-liked member of the community for, in February 1830 when he was seventy-three years old, the parish wishing to show their 'Approbation of his honest and faithful service in those parochial offices he has filled for nearly forty-seven years', collected enough money to buy him a 'handsome piece of plate'. Alas, he was never to receive it for, in that same month, in bitterly cold weather, he set off to collect the rates. It was almost dark when he started on his return journey, but he would have been quite confident of finding his way, for had he not lived in the area all his life and countless times made the same journey? However, as he trudged along the snow began to fall, steadily and softly at first but then a stiff wind sprang up whipping the flakes into skirling whirls and soon the old man found himself struggling through a blizzard. Unable to see clearly, he missed his way and stumbled into a brook. Somehow he staggered out and scrambled on, limbs numbed by cold, sodden garments flapping round him like icy whips. Gasping for breath and buffeted from one side of the lane to another, he finally reached a familiar field gate. He managed to open it and crawled along by the hedge to the corner of the field, but he could go no further and, crouching down in the lea of the hedge, he waited for the morning. When it was realised that he was missing a search party set out from Bedlam early the following day. They found him at noon, still crouched in his makeshift shelter under the hedge, frozen to death.

The money collected for his 'handsome piece of plate' was used instead for his monument and Mr Herbert Green, the headmaster of Bitterly School, wrote the following clever and amusing epitaph.

He was NOTT born of womankind
And so it may be said
Although within this grave he lies
We know he is NOTT dead

No one possessed a better SOLE
When death gave him a call
He to the LAST was firm and strong
And calm gave up his AWL

To church he regularly went
Upon the Sabbath day
It was his duty so to do
As clerk and NOTT to pray

Foolish or mad he never was
And yet it strange appears
He lived a very quiet life
In Bedlam forty years.

Then underneath this verdant sod,
We'll let him now remain
For sure and confident we are
WILL NOTT will rise again.

Alas, I am told there are no longer Notts in the area.

Carefully, down what seemed an almost perpendicular lane, I retraced my way and, when safely at the bottom, I set off once more for Blackford, another little hamlet clinging to the coat tails of Bitterley. Blackford is in the Parish of nearby Stoke Saint Milborough. The story of this parish is most beautifully told in an erudite booklet *A Quart in a Pint Pot* written by Maureen Thom and Margaret Pearce. In their introduction, they agree that Blackford is difficult to find and record that, in order to remedy this, everyone living in Blackford at the time of the Queen's jubilee, planted a copper beech in their gardens. The area is certainly very tree girt but not knowing the significance of the copper beeches I did not look out for them when I called on Mrs Thom. However, I had been given some excellent directions and so I crossed the ford out of Bitterly, drove past the Three Horse Shoes Inn and up the hill until, just past the letter box, I came upon red-roofed Holly Cottage overlooking a terraced garden falling steeply down the hillside. The vista from these flower decked terraces takes in thirteen counties and on a clear day it is possible to see Sugar Loaf Hill near Abergavenny.

Mrs Thom's enormous bearded collie rushed out to greet me dragging Mr Thom in tow. More or less simultaneously, Mr Thom's sister rushed in with some tomato plants. When this little up-to-do had died down, Mrs Thom and I sat in the window overlooking the terraces, burgeoning with colour, and I learned from her a great deal about the district. It never ceases to amaze me how unselfish are so many people who research the history of their area and how willing and even anxious they are to share their knowledge and finds with others. I left Holly Cottage my head spinning with information and Mrs Thom's booklet firmly tucked underneath my arm.

Long years ago, when, having marched out of their military station at Leintwardine, 'The Roman stood on Clee', the villages and hamlets were duly subdued, but the only evidence of Roman occupation are traces of a settlement at Stanton Lacy. In due course the Saxons took up residence and it is from them that the village of Stoke St. Milborough derives its name, Stok being the Saxon word for fortified manor, or some think it was stoc from the early English for a daughter settlement. Eventually the name became Godestoch, and finally, Stoke Saint Milborough after the beautiful and saintly Christian granddaughter of Penda, the warrior king of Mercia, great champion of the heathens and slayer of the Christians.

When she was a girl, Milburga's father King Merewald and her mother, a Kentish princess, separated. Her mother returned to Kent taking her three daughters, Mildred, Mildrith and Milburga with her. Once back in her homeland, she entered a nunnery on the isle of Thanet. Surprisingly she was already abbess of this establishment. Although it was not unusual for the daughters of rich and influential people to be given such exalted positions, one does not often hear of them taking 'French leave' as it were to marry and produce three daughters.

Two of her girls, Mildrith and Milburga were bundled off to a convent just outside Paris where they were miserably unhappy, for the abbess was a sadistic woman who devised cruel punishments for any small misdemeanours. Eventually, their mother listened to their pleas to be allowed to leave and they were brought back to England not, however, to interrupt mama's religious life for they were promptly sent across country to Much Wenlock, a village in Shropshire and part of their father's kingdom. Here in 680 Milburga founded an abbey and herself became abbess.

22

As well as being saintly she must also have been a very beautiful young woman, for much of her early life seems to have been spent fleeing from ardent and rejected lovers. On one occasion, while journeying among the Clee villages, she realised she was being pursued by her erstwhile betrothed who, furious at being jilted by her for the religious life, was thirsting for revenge. He had with him several men and a pack of baying hounds. The terrified girl at last arrived at Godestoch and here, utterly exhausted, she slipped from her horse to the ground, where she fainted. Some villagers sowing barley nearby rushed to help her. After recovering, she ordered the seed they had just sown to sprout. Then told the villagers that, if anyone should come that way looking for her, they were to indicate the waving barley shoots and tell them that the abbess had indeed passed that way but it was when they were sowing the seed of the crop they could now see flourishing around them. Before continuing her journey Milburga ordered her horse to strike the ground with his hoof and as he did so a spring of crystal clear water gushed up. This spring has never died and you may see it to this day near the church, still bubbling forth. It is known as Milburga's Well.

It was not possible to enter Stoke Saint Milborough Church when I arrived at the pretty village on the slopes of Brown Clee. It appeared to be being re-roofed. I peered through the doorway to find all was draped in sheeting. I ventured a little further in and, looking up, saw that large areas of sky were visible. It was while gazing at these that I was suddenly showered by what looked like plaster dust, or perhaps it was just the dirt of ages. Prudence, I decided, must be the order of the day and I did not wait for further contributions. As I walked down the church path brushing bits of debris from my clothes and hair, I heard a familiar voice and looking up I spotted Mr Morris, the roofing contractor from Bucknell, 'Morris the roof', as he is known locally. I have met Mr Morris many times but hardly ever on terra firma. He pops up in the most unlikely places, doctoring and preserving the roofs, old and new, of the Border Country. I have seen him three stories up, when a north wind was freezing the blood, the snow was lying thick on the ground and on the roof, on which he was working, icicles twelve inches long hung like cruel spears from the gutters. His cheerful hail, from whatever slippery slope he happens to be perched on, never fails to warm the heart.

On another occasion when the sainted Milburga was once more riding in the foothills of the Clee Hills - a practice which in view of her previous experience might well be considered akin to tempting providence - she realised that she was again being pursued. She urged her horse on and managed to ford the River Corve near Ludlow . Realising her pursuer, a hot-blooded young Welsh prince, was almost upon her, she dismounted and, falling on her knees, prayed ardently that she be delivered from her would-be lover's princely attentions, vowing that if she were, she would build a church on that very spot. At once the gently flowing, shallow River Corve rose to a mighty roaring torrent, impossible to cross, and the frustrated princeling had to abandon the chase. Milburga kept her word and founded a church on the river bank in the village of Staunton which latterly became known as Stanton Lacy.

The village of Stanton Lacy near the banks of the River Corve is a picturesque mix of timber-framed Tudor and stone and brick Georgian houses. The Lacy part of the village name comes from the de Lacey family who held the manor of Stanton for several centuries. Walter de Lacey was one of the Norman knights sent to the border by William the Conqueror and he was given the manor of Stanton. Some years later it was his son Roger who began the building of that mightiest of border bastions, Ludlow Castle.

The church, founded by Milburga, is dedicated to Saint Peter and much of the original Saxon work remains. Opposite the church is the Old Vicarage. A cattle grid, very necessary in view of the working farm next to the church, protects the drive. A few feet away in a weathered stone wall is a friendly little wicket gate. It looked so inviting I pushed it open and found myself in what appeared to be a small copse and facing me was an archway cut into the tall hedge bordering the drive. I peered through it and there in the dusk stood the Old Vicarage bathed in the soft evening light. Nothing stirred, no little breezes bending the grass stems and shivering the leaves, no evening bird song, just silence with an expectant quality almost as if all activity was suspended waiting for 'The sly shade of a Rural Dean' to glide over the lawns. All the villages in the Clee Hills have this tranquil quality about them, perhaps it is because they are so tucked away in the wooded dips and hollows, keeping the noisy twentieth century at arms length.

A finger post on the edge of the village proclaims Village Hall. Following the direction indicated, I travelled on for what seemed quite a few miles and then found myself back in the village. There was no one around to ask directions so off I set again, determined to be more observant. The second time round was more productive. I noticed a second finger post almost hidden by an overgrown hedge and turning right, as it directed, I avoided making the full loop back to the village. I found the village hall at last. It must be two or three miles from Stanton Lacy. I understand from Mr Baker, of Bitterley, my 'Font of all Wisdom' in these parts, that it is so far from the village because it was once the Haytons Bent school. When the school ceased, the building which looks very like a stout little Victorian or Edwardian one, was just what Stanton Lacy had in mind for their village hall.

I suppose everyone gets together with proffered lifts if there is anything on at the hall and if there is an overflow then its a good healthy scamper and fingers crossed that it does not rain. Standing proudly erect in the forecourt of the hall was a maypole, the red and white ribbons tightly wound round it waiting to be unleashed for the mayday jollification's.

A mile or so from the village hall is Hopton Cangeford. I had heard that there was a church there with a squire's pew complete with a fireplace and red velvet curtains so I set off down another lane. I found the church, a red-brick Georgian one but, alas, it is another redundant church and is now the home of a pewter worker and his wife a potter. I did not meet them although I called twice. The door was ajar and on a chain and a very indignant and noisy dog rushed out. He flew into a frenzy every time I tried to attract the occupants attention. His snarls were so alarming on my second visit that I left in a hurry and nearly fell down the steps which are, indeed, in a very dangerous state and need to be treated with respect.

Not far from Hopton Cangeford is Middleton. This seems hardly more than a hamlet with a pleasing scattering of houses and farms along the lane. Middleton Chapel is a small ivy-clad building. To the left of the lych-gate, which is topped with a cross, is a great mound resembling a barrow. Through the trees can be glimpsed the long windows of Middleton Court. The path to the church porch is lined with eight ancient yews and the interior of the church has a surprisingly sumptuous air. Four elegant brass electroliers hang overhead and there is a rich royal-blue carpet underfoot. Bringing one down to earth, however, a notice on the wall requests the flower ladies to vacuum the carpet after their ministrations.

It is very difficult not to include more and yet more of the villages which honeycomb the slopes of the Clees. For one thing they have such fascinating names and for another, in the tangle of lanes that wind in every direction, one comes upon them unexpectedly and each one seems so intriguing one is loathe to pass it by.

Barely a mile north of Stoke St Milborough is the village of Clee St Margaret. This is a very picturesque place where the old stone houses crowding, together along the main street, flank a fast flowing water-splash or ford. This is the Pie Brook, or at least it is nearer to its source. In Clee St Margaret, I understand, it is known simply as the Clee Brook. At least fifty or sixty yards of it scampers jauntily down the street as if well aware of its superior status as the longest ford in England. This village, so peaceful now, was once of bustling importance, for above the steep lanes leading out of it are the remains of the Roman Camp of Nordy Bank, where Roman legionnaires were stationed in order to keep an eye on the surrounding countryside.

Wandering in the lanes around the village with a companion, searching for that jewel in the crown of the Clee Hills, the Heath Chapel, we came upon Broncroft Castle. As we drove along, we became aware that the high hedge on one side of the lane had given way to an immensely long wall. It had a rather suburban air about it, possibly because it was bordered with manicured verges and flowers dressed by the right. When we reached the gateway we fully expected to see some pseudo-Tudor or neo-Gothick pile, country retreat of a city magnate. Far from it! Facing us at the end of the drive was a great red sandstone castle complete with crenellations and massive tower. We were gazing at this surprising find in the middle of the lanes, when a small group of people approached, two men and a woman with three dogs. I asked them if they lived at the castle. No, they said, the place was for sale and they were waiting their turn to be shown round by the housekeeper, who was then busy with another lot of viewers. As it was their second visit to the place we asked them what it was like inside. 'Ghastly', was the reply. All the same I suppose it was not beyond redemption or they would not be making a return visit. Not wishing to join a queue we left them to it. I discovered later that Broncroft Castle was built in 1320. During the Civil War, it was garrisoned first for the King and then for the Parliament. Finally, in 1648, the Roundheads set about demolishing it. Fortunately, it proved rather a hard nut to crack and much was left, including the massive fourteenth century tower. Early in the nineteenth century it was restored and used as a private house. When Leland passed this way, in the reign of Henry VIII, he wrote that it was 'A very goodly place like a castell, longing to the Earl of Shrewsire.'

We found the Heath Chapel. It is a perfect little Norman building standing alone in a field. Desecration and restoration have passed it by and it is virtually unchanged since those Norman stonemasons completed the building of it in 1090. A notice outside the chapel tells one to call at a nearby farm for the key, so off we set down the hill but we were pipped at the post by a very jolly roly-poly woman who was swinging an enormous key, about nine or ten inches long, which she had just collected. We walked back to the chapel together during which time she told us that she and her husband were great walkers and that they were on a walking holiday and had spent the night at a farm in the district. They walked everywhere, she said, miles and miles, they'd seen everything and done everything and always on foot. One had to admit she was in very good condition, for in spite of being so chubby, she chattered away without pausing for breath the whole way up the hill which was quite steep.

3   *The Heath Chapel*

We arrived at the chapel. She turned the key in the lock, the great door swung open and whoosh, the centuries peeled away and we were back in yesteryear. Outside the sun shone brightly down on fields busy with sheep. The air was full of farm noise, the hum of a distant tractor, the barking of dogs and the occasional cheerful shout, but in the little Norman chapel all was cool and quiet in the soft grey light which filtered through small windows, some of them narrow enough to be virtual arrow slits and set in stone embrasures many feet deep. The place had an extraordinary charm. The simplicity of the white-washed walls, looking down on two rows of ancient gated pews in the miniscule nave divided from an equally tiny chancel by a Norman arch and the massive Norman font at the west end, almost rough hewn and quite innocent of the stone carvers art, had an atmosphere of timeless continuity which was quite spellbinding. Even Mrs Chatterbox was quiet but, alas, not for long. This time her subject was 'rights of way'. My companion had judiciously moved to the far end

27

of the chapel and appeared to be lost in contemplation of a scrap of old linenfold panelling on one of the pews so I was subject to the full torrent of her indignation over the local 'rights of way.' She and her husband, she informed me, were from Lancashire where they had been very active in a campaign to open up rights of way and did I realise that there was a right of way behind the church? She had discovered it and she had spoken to the farmer who owned the field but he had refused to open it. She was going to take it up with the Rambler's Association and they would 'soon tell him what was what'. She seemed quite oblivious to the atmosphere of the church and in the end I just let her ramble on about her Rambler's Association, a worthy body no doubt, but how true is the old injunction 'There is a time and a place for everything'.

4   *Norman Interior of The Heath Chapel*

Notices on the walls of the chapel warn one not to touch the plaster, as mediaeval paintings underneath are awaiting uncovering. This plastering over was the work of Cromwell's men. They were very busy in the area undoing any attempts to beautify the churches and having hacked about the poppy heads on the choir stalls in Ludlow Church they then turned their attention to the smaller churches around. At Pipe Aston, a hamlet a few miles from the Heath Chapel, the wall paintings have recently been uncovered in the little church and now the whole interior looks as if it has been wallpapered with a very attractive design, complete with frieze, giving the place a delightfully cosy atmosphere.

Our loquacious Lancashire lass was still chattering on, so we decided to call it a day and come back another time to this little chapel which has weathered the snows and suns of close on a thousand years and in which countless people, from knights before battle to peasants praying for their crops or just innumerable families praying for each other, had come to kneel and seek benediction. As we walked to the car, our chatterbox called after us 'You want to get yourselves some stout shoes to start you walking.' Humph, thought I in my mediaeval frame of mind. How about a scold's bridle to stop you talking.

In spite of the beckoning villages with intriguing names, I felt the time had come to leave the Clee Hill district and wander on up the border and into Wales. However, before finally doing so there was just one more village I wished to visit because at one time it was part of the estate of a certain Boriah Botfield. There's a name to conjure with and one not likely to elude the memory!

I first came upon it a few years ago in the Clun Forest uplands. In this wild and lonely scrubland there stands a handsome stone cross, erected at the instigation of Boriah Botfield in memory of a pedlar named William Cantlin. In the seventeenth century the pedlar was found dead in this desolate spot. His brass bound box, which had been broken open, was lying empty beside him. The neighbouring village of Bettws allowed him to be buried in their churchyard and a stone was set up to mark the place where he was found, it was inscribed 'W.C. deceased here buried at Bettws.' Nearly 200 years later Boriah Botfield arranged for the memorial cross to mark the spot.

I wrote about this kindly action in my first book on the Welsh March and subsequently learned from a descendent of the benevolent Boriah, who had read the book, that the village in which he lived was Hopton Wafers on the slopes of the Clee Hills and I was invited to visit his house, Hopton Court. Accordingly, I set off on the A4117 the main highway over the Clees, this time avoiding the ramification of the lanes and the beguiling villages hiding in the folds of the hills.

The turning to Hopton Wafers is on the far side of the hills just before The Crown Inn, a comfortable looking hostelry with a green lawn running down to the water's edge. A lane winds up from the inn to the heart of the place where most of the houses are clustered round the church. Opposite the churchyard, with its fine old yew trees, the road widens so that it might almost be dignified by the name of a square. Bordering it, facing the church, is a row of old cottages, their frontages a pleasing mixture of plaster, mellow brick and timber-framing. One end of the row is flanked by the village post office and shop and the other by the arch leading to the stable yard of the Manor house.

On the left of the church path there is an immense mausoleum surrounded by iron railings. On top of a vast stone plinth rests a sarcophagus very reminiscent in shape, if not in size and material, to that of Napoleon Bonaparte at Les Invalides in Paris. Here lies Thomas Botfield, grandfather of our Boriah. It is a splendidly befitting resting place for a great iron master, who rebuilt the Parish Church at his own expense. The Botfields were an ancient family connected with the Thynnes of Longleat (Marquess of Bath) and descended from two knightly brothers, Geoffrey and Oliver Boteville, who came to England from France in the thirteenth century in order to help King John in his fight against the unruly barons.

The founder of the modern Botfield fortunes was the father of the Thomas Botfield lying in his stately tomb in Hopton Wafers churchyard. Like his father before him, Thomas of the tomb was an ironmaster and he succeeded his father in the management of the Clee Hill quarries. He died in January 1843, leaving no heir and his nephew, our Boriah Botfield, inherited his estates.

Boriah, an MA, was a most scholarly man. He was a fellow of many learned societies and the author of numerous erudite publications. He was High Sheriff for Northamptonshire, where he owned another estate, and was Member of Parliament for Ludlow for a number of years. He was decorated by Leopold of the Belgians and Frederick Augusta, King of Saxony. The life of this very important landowner must have been so fulfilling and busy that it is all the more intriguing to ponder on what caused him to make such a generous and quixotic gesture to an itinerant pedlar who had been dead for close on two hundred years.

5   *Boriah Botfield of Hopton Court*

Boriah also died without heirs and the estate passed to Thomas Woodward, whose father was a nephew of Mrs Thomas Botfield, and has remained with the Woodward family to the present day.

By the year 1825 the old Norman church was in a very sad condition and Thomas Botfield had it demolished and rebuilt at his own expense. There are many tablets and monuments in the church to various Botfields and Woodwards. On one wall a collection of memorial tablets has a space left for the addition of a tablet in memory of the next Woodward to join the merry throng. 'That', said my hostess who was showing me round, 'that space is for me.' One hopes it is not visible from her pew for surely, to use the well worn phrase, looking at it must 'concentrate the mind' wonderfully.

Soon after crossing a small stone bridge leading out of the village a drive turns off on the right to Hopton Court. This is a fine and elegant house with two great pillared porticos. It was Nash designed and around it the land rises in rounded hills and then falls away in green glades and woodlands only to rise again in gentle slopes. The grounds of the court were laid out by Humphrey Repton and the present owner, Christopher Woodward, is gradually restoring the house, doing much of the work himself and this includes repainting in the original delicate colours, vestiges of which can still be seen, the intricate ceiling friezes.

The Woodward family have a great many naval and military connections and Christopher has a fascinating collection of old uniforms belonging to his forebears. These he has displayed in glass cases and among them is that of his great uncle, who was awarded the Croix de Guerre during the first world war. One day during the war, members of the staff at Hopton Court saw him walking up the drive. Excitedly, they rushed into the house crying, 'Captain Leslie's home, he's coming up the drive.' Alas, when the family hurried to welcome him he had vanished. They learned later that it was on that day that he was killed in France.

Christopher noticed me looking at a naval uniform, resplendent with gold braid. 'Ah', he said, 'that was my great-grandfather Woodward. He was the family gaolbird. While he was at sea, chasing slave traders, a seaman was extremely rude and started swinging his arms in an insolent manner. Great-grandfather, who considered they were on active service, decided that he was entitled to put the man in the brig'. This was frowned on by the civil authorities and his great-grandfather was fined. He refused to pay and went to prison. This so embarrassed the Admiralty that they paid the fine for him. However, in due course the time came for his retirement, he was then an admiral and hoped he would be given a nice juicy morsel such as the governorship of Jamaica. Alas, this was not to be. The Civil Authorities got their own back by offering him a much less attractive position, that of Governor of the Island of St Helena. However, this sturdily independent man indignantly refused the offer and came back to England to run his estates.

Walking back to the car with Christopher and his mother, we paused to chat with David Martin who popped out of his cottage as we approached. David's father was the Hopton Court Estate's mason for many years and David told us a curious story about him in the first world war.

His father and uncle both enlisted in the Shropshire Yeomanry, one at the age of seventeen and the other only fourteen years old. During that war it was often some years before home leave was granted, but eventually David's father found himself disembarking at Southampton and on his way home. He and five other soldiers shared a carriage on the train for London, Birmingham and then Bewdley. As the journey progressed the men one by one, having reached their destination, left the carriage until there were only two remaining, David Martin's father and another soldier who asked David's father where he was going. 'Oh, I'm heading for a little place you've never heard of', was the reply. 'Place by the name of Whatshill.' 'Yes, I've heard of it right enough', said the other, 'that's where I live.' Both men regarded each other closely for a while, Whatshill being so small a place they felt they must know each other, then suddenly one of them spoke, 'You ain't our brother Ben', he queried. Sure enough brother Ben it was. The dreadful conditions in the trenches on the Western Front had so changed their appearance that they had travelled together from Southampton to the Border Country without recognising each other.

Saying good-bye to the Clees without exploring every one of the delightful villages that hide in the skirts of the hills is very difficult indeed. A whole book could be devoted to this area so rich in beauty and interest, perhaps one has already been written, at all events I shall return one day and wander once again in this forgotten arcadia.

32

Chapter 3

Bedstone, Bucknell and Stowe

The week in which I had arranged to explore Knighton and the surrounding district Aunt Christina decided to pay me her annual visit. Living on the south-east coast, most of her jaunts had been across the channel, but when she heard I was due to visit Wales she was quite excited. 'Splendid,' she said, 'I shall come with you.' This suggestion was not received with enthusiasm. Although very sprightly for her ninety-five years, I did feel that having her with me might slow my trundles round quite a bit. 'Oh, but you wouldn't enjoy it.' I assured her. 'On these expeditions I'm forever hopping in and out of the car, prowling round old buildings and churches and holding long conversations with the locals, you'd have to wait in the car, it would be dreadfully boring.' I got no further. 'Utter nonsense, I shall certainly come with you,' she announced, 'and I most certainly do not intend to sit in the car the entire time.' Experience had taught me that to argue would be quite useless, after all was she not the aunt who, before the turn of the century, having managed to get herself accidentally locked into the cathedral in Freiburg at dusk, thereupon knotted her long frilly knickers and petticoat together and hung out of the belfry waving them and shrieking to attract the attention of the startled strollers in the square below. And did she not frequently row her sister out into the middle of the lake so that they could indulge in a few quick puffs of the forbidden cigarettes? Such determination on the one hand to be noticed and on the other not to be, particularly in view of the social mores of the time, must command respect. So, contenting myself with sprinkling a few muttered clichés about of the 'Don't say I didn't warn you' and 'Don't blame me if . . . ' variety, I set about preparing the picnic.

33

As I slapped the tomatoes between the slices of bread and filled the thermos, I glanced out of the window. Hopton Titterhill had completely disappeared and in its place was a thick grey, enveloping mist and overhead the pale blue, early April sky had given way to ominous slate coloured clouds. Within minutes the rain was lashing down, as it can only lash in Wales and along the border, great sheets of relentless unremitting water, bouncing off the thatch, flattening the flowers in the beds and in no time at all churning the lanes into a muddy mire. 'Well', I said, not without a feeling of relief, 'that's put paid to our little sortie, we'll just have to cosy up and hope for a better day tomorrow.' Something akin to a snort came from the aunt. 'Not go! Why on earth not? Surely we're not fair weather travellers.' Bowing to the inevitable I brought the car round, stowed picnic and aunt aboard and off we set.

Housman certainly knew what he was talking about when he called this area 'The valley of springs and rivers'. Every sodden lane had a gushing torrent criss-crossing its length, but on we ploughed sending up great wings of water on either side of the car. The modest windscreen wipers of my elderly traveller were finding the deluge very difficult to deal with and, eventually, even the intrepid aunt conceded that there was not much point in continuing a journey where nothing and no one could be seen through the driving rain. We drove home munching our sandwiches as we went and arrived in time for an early tea by the fireside.

'Just for once,' I said, as I drew the curtains against the monotonous rain and the dripping landscape, 'just for once I wouldn't mind being on a cruise in the South Seas, think of all that heavenly sunshine.' 'Mmm,' replied Aunt Christina, helping herself to a crumpet, 'Mmm. That's all very well, but when Franz was living in Tonga, he always said that, in spite of looking such a paradise with all that lush green vegetation and all those gorgeous flowers, not to mention dusky maidens, it was, so hot that life was only bearable if most of it was spent in the water. 'Franz?' I queried, 'Cousin Franz living in Tonga?' 'Oh yes, didn't you know? He lived there for some years, in fact, the Tongan royal family adopted him and made him a prince, Prince Falanisi of Tonga.

Replete with crumpet and Earl Grey and not unaware of the effect created by this last seemingly throwaway remark, Aunt Christina settled back in her chair to indulge in one of her favourite pastimes, reminiscing, happily certain that I was 'all ears'. This is not a tale from Wales or the Marchland but, since it was told to me in the heart of the March, I am going to cheat a little and tell it to you because it is a tale worth the telling

'We grew up together,' said Aunt Christina, 'our families lived near each other and Franz's father, Uncle Henry, was our favourite uncle. He had a wooden leg. When he was a young man he lost a leg at sea, gangrene you know. They just filled him with rum and sawed it off', and she added, pausing dramatically, 'they dipped the stump in hot pitch to stop the bleeding. Poor Uncle Henry,' she continued, 'he was so brave, he wrote to his people telling them that he was very happy to say his leg had been buried at sea in very good company because it had been placed in the same canvas sheeting and sewn up together with the body of a beautiful girl who had died on the voyage.'

Aunt Christina was obviously warming to her subject and, if I was to hear about cousin Franz in Tonga, must be headed off wooden legs and back to the South Seas. 'Did Uncle Henry go to Tonga to see Franz?' I asked. 'Good gracious no! Aunt Elske would never have allowed that', she replied, safely on course again. 'Franz always wanted to travel. As soon as he was 21 years old, off he went with his sketchbook to see the world.'

'It was about the turn of the century and I was seventeen at the time. I can remember how excited we all were when his letters started to arrive. We never knew where they would be from, Canada, America, Africa, India, Australia - they were such magic names to us in those days. He wrote from them all and then, about three or four years after he left, we received a letter from the South Seas, the Tongan Islands. From the first he was fascinated with the place although he told us that in spite of the name 'The Friendly Islands', given to them by Captain Cook, it was only a few generations ago that the people were cannibals. He spent his time on the islands drawing and painting. He drew everything he saw, people, trees, flowers, boats, dwellings, everything. He often enclosed little

sketches with his letters and when he became a well known artist he would send us prints of some of his pictures.'

'When he had been on the islands for some months he received a summons to the royal palace. He wrote that he was just a little apprehensive in case there had been a relapse into former habits, thoughts of 'long pig' and missionary pots, he said, did cross

Kata Lahi - a Tongan beauty sketched by Franz Stelling

his mind. However, he was received with great courtesy, the King was very friendly and very interested in his drawings, indeed, he offered Franz apartments in the royal palace. Franz accepted them and a few months later he was told that the Princess Vike Veriogo Toufou wished to adopt him. He wrote that although he did not wish to upset his parents it was a very delicate situation and he felt that it would be politic to agree since he was not really certain of the position on the missionary pot front. He was made a member of the royal family and given the name of Prince Falanisi of Tonga. He was also given the position of Kamoto. This was a top job in the Tongan hierarchy but with it went a rather doubtful privilege. The Kamoto always sat at the right hand of the King, on feast days and ceremonial occasions, and it was his duty to taste the Kava, a very potent liquor made from pepper, and eat from the various dishes before the King drank or ate. This was to ensure that they were not poisoned.'

'Queen Salote of Tonga, who came to England for the coronation of our Queen Elizabeth II, was only five years old when Franz first met her. Over the years of their friendship, he grew to love and respect her very much indeed and we were not surprised when she came to London to hear that, in spite of the pouring rain, she alone rode in the procession with the hood of her carriage down so that the people might see her. She was magnificent, the people cheered themselves hoarse.'

Aunt Christina's voice was trailing away and her eyes were closing. Outside it was now quite dark. I put another log on the fire and with a few judicious kicks coaxed it into a blaze. The leaping flames lit up the tea table with its bowl of first primroses and danced over the copper jugs on the dresser and I thought how remote those islands in the tropic seas, with their long, languorous days of sun, seemed from the cosy cocoon of light and warmth in the dripping Marchland.

Aunt Christina stirred and pulled a rug across her knees. 'What happened to cousin Franz in the end?' I said. 'Oh, he married a girl from New Zealand', she replied. 'Then he settled in Australia. He became a very famous artist. As well as painting, he loved to work in silver and I believe some of his silver work is in the Kensington Museum. He continued to visit the islands almost every year and always took his place as Kamoto when the need arose. In 1957 at Queen Salote's request, he designed a coat of arms for the Tongan royal house. He was an old man then and did not travel so much. However, he went to the islands again in 1964, but it was for the last time. Soon afterwards Queen Salote died and her son, Prince Taufa 'ahau Toupou, was crowned king. Franz was about to go to Tonga to carry out the duties of Kamoto but he died a week before the coronation. The new king is modern, and times have changed. No one has been appointed to take Franz's place.' Aunt Christina's eyes were closing again. I crept out of the room and left her dreaming down the long years to the days when she was a young Victorian girl excitedly reading of far away places in those eagerly awaited letters from her cousin Franz, the last of the Kamotos.

The weather behaved very badly during the rest of Aunt Christina's visit so the Knighton expedition was not attempted again. Thus it was sometime before once more I set off for the little Welsh town.

There are many roads which cross the border in these parts and lead to Knighton and probably the A4113 from Leintwardine is the most direct. My route, because my starting point was Hopton Castle, was part lane and part road, wandering through the villages of Bedstone and Bucknell before joining the A4113 about three miles out of Leintwardine.

The lane between Hopton Castle and Bedstone, like so many lanes in the area, burrows along between high banks reminiscent of those old Celtic ways in which people might flit silently from place to place, unseen by members of neighbouring warlike tribes. To the right, as one turns into the lane, stand the gaunt ruins of Hopton Castle, an old Norman Stronghold. At dusk, when those grey stones loom out of the shadows and the rooks fly in and out of the sightless windows, passing along Bedstone lane never fails to produce a frisson of fear and one can well understand how it gained the reputation of being the most haunted castle on the Border.

During the Civil War, the castle was the scene of a cruel massacre, when a party of Parliamentarians defended the castle which was being besieged by Royalist soldiers. The beseigement lasted for three weeks during which time one-hundred and fifty Royalists were killed. When, at last, the garrison was forced to surrender, the besiegers, thirsting for revenge, killed them all with the exception of Colonel More, their leader. Their bodies were pushed into a pool at the back of the castle which from then on was known as the Bloody Pool.

Past the castle and a few yards further along, bordering the lane, is Park Cottage. Timber-framed with diamond-paned windows and a profusion of honeysuckle and roses clambering over the wicket fence, it would seem the very antithesis of the mayhem and bloodshed that took place in the meadow adjoining the garden. The inhabitants of the cottage not a bowshot away from the castle were no doubt evicted by the soldiery, if they had not already fled, and more likely than not their menfolk were among the besieged, for Colonel More gathered together all the able-bodied local men to help defend the castle. Their little world was turned upside down in that long ago summer time.

In later years Henrietta Rodney, a descendant of the great Admiral Rodney, lived in the cottage and she lies buried in the little church across the fields.

About half-a-mile on past the cottage, we come to Hollybrooks where, in early spring, the apple orchard waves pink and white banners over the hedge. Roger Hadfield, the gamekeeper, lives here and many a brace of pheasant have I enjoyed from him, dropped off on his way home from the shoot. A few hundred yards further on from his cottage, we pass Old Manor Farm on our left and then slip down into the pleasant village of Bedstone. Until 1956 Bedstone and Hopton Castle and many other surrounding villages made up part of the five-thousand acre estate belonging to the Ripley family. Sir Henry Ripley, the first baron, bought the estate in the 1880's. He was a Yorkshire man and a descendant of the last Wakeman and first Mayor of York. The family fortune was founded on wool and the manufacture of cloth. They also invented industrial dyeing. His grandmother was known as 'The Flower Lady of York' because she had a stall in the market, where she sold cloth and flowers.

Sir Henry must have been a very accomplished and extremely busy man because, as well as being Chairman of the Bradford Chamber of Commerce, he was also a distinguished politician in Disraeli's government. It does seem strange that such a 'dyed in the wool' Yorkshire man, forgive the pun but it was irresistible, should wish to settle in the remote borderland, but perhaps he was captivated by its beauty and felt that it would be a relief to distance himself, from time to time, from the hurly-burly of the Bradford or London scene. At all events, he built himself a great black and white mansion in the village of Bedstone. It is a Calendar house and, as such, has three-hundred and sixty-five windows, fifty-two doors and twelve chimneys.

The second Baron Ripley, also a Henry, was a typical hard drinking, fox hunting country squire. Many are the stories told of him, and not always to his credit, but then saintliness was never considered a necessary attribute of English Country Squires. William Ripley, his grandson, has a fund of Grandfather Ripley anecdotes. He told me that at one time his

Grandfather, finding that a modest glass or two of after dinner port was not sufficient for his needs, but fearing to make this known to his wife, would pop back into the dining-room later in the evening for a few top-ups. Lady Ripley, however, noticed that the port decanter needed refilling much more frequently than formerly and promptly reported the matter to him. Sir Henry at once ordered all the servants into the library and, without more ado, accused the butler of drinking his port. Jackson, the butler, was a man of great propriety, very smart and very correct. Horrified at the accusation, he protested his innocence but, deny it as he would, it was no use. Sir Henry suspended him from his duties and, to Jackson's great mortification, ordered him to do a spell of cleaning out the chicken house and furthermore to wear an apron while doing so. One can only hope that poor Jackson, the whipping boy in his pinafore, was properly compensated in private by his feudal lord.

Another tale of this particular Lord of the Manor, also told to me by his grandson, was of the occasion when he and Lady Ripley set off on horseback for Clun about seven miles distant. Arrived at the Buffalo Inn in the little square, he dismounted and strode into the bar only to find several people drinking after hours. In his capacity as magistrate, he ordered them out and told them to appear the next day before him on the bench at Bishop's Castle. He then settled down to a cosy afternoon of after-hours imbibing. Presumably Lady Ripley left him to it. Arriving home some hours later, he learned that the Bishop had been invited to conduct the service that evening in church. Dutifully Sir Henry turned up for the service but, alas, his afternoon's indulgence got the better of him and the Bishop preached his entire sermon to the accompaniment of loud snores from the Squire's pew.

Those rip roaring carefree days did not last for long, however, and the long shadow of the second world war was reaching out. Sixteen young men did not return to this tiny village and among them two of Sir Henry's sons. A little over a decade after the end of hostilities the old squire died and, mainly due to heavy death duties, the estate was broken up, reducing it to five-hundred acres. Sir Henry's great mansion is now a school, but there are still Ripleys in the village. Sir Henry's son, Sir Hugh Ripley, owns several properties in and around Bedstone and his daughter, Susan, and grandson both live in cottages on the estate. When the contents of Bedstone Court were being sorted for sale, Sir Henry's sister noticed an old prayer book in a pile of rubbish that was waiting to be thrown out. She rescued it and although a little battered it was of great interest. The cover was ivory and gold and on the fly leaf was inscribed 'Admiral Rodney 1782, to his wife Sarah'.

The little church, in which Sir Henry snored the service away after his Buffalo frolic, has a timber-framed steeple with a shingle roof, topped by a cockerel weather-vane. There are fifteen windows, some no bigger than an arrow slit, in this small church and they are very deeply set in embrasures of at least four feet if not more. A large marble tablet on the wall records the 'Expressions of affectionate regret by the officers of the Royal Oak' for the death of Arthur Ripley who was eighteen years old when his ship, HMS Captain, turned turtle in the Bay of Biscay with the loss of eight- hundred men. He had served on HMS Royal Oak since he went to sea at the age of fifteen and had only been on HMS Captain for four days when she capsized. He must have inspired great affection in his former comrades for them to erect such a memorial. Sir Henry's two sons are remembered on simpler plaques, as is another young man, William Garnett, who was killed in Ypres in 1916.

Walking down the short drive from the church, I caught sight of a heron teetering on the ridge of a thatched cottage opposite, looking for all the world as if he was about to take off over the green meadows and hills beyond; but no, he was just a merry thought of the cottage owner and made of reed, so he must stand forever yearning to soar away.

Like all self respecting villages Bedstone has a village shop and post office. Annie Morris and her husband, Jim, have run them for thirty-five years. Annie told me that a certain Mrs Langley, after a great deal of effort, finally persuaded the authorities in 1908 that Bedstone should have a post office to combine with the village shop. Ever since a Morris has run it. First came Jim Morris, the local blacksmith. With the aid of his womenfolk, he was able to keep things running smoothly and still continue his shoeing. He died in 1938 and his son, another Jim Morris, took over although he used his second name, Geoffrey. When he died his son, Annie's husband Jim, took up the reins, nearly one-hundred years of the same family running the village post office and all with the same name.

A signpost in the centre of the village points to Darky Dale with one arm and with the other to Bucknell. Darky Dale is aptly named indeed for it lies in the heart of Hopton Titterhill or Tittrell as it is locally known. This heavily wooded hill overhangs Bedstone and Hopton Castle. Long leafy paths, overshadowed by trees whose branches reach out to each other across them, wind through it and in a clearing, at the end of one of them, is an old cottage once the home of a gamekeeper. Here lives Alan

Beamond and his family. Alan is the local builder and he combines this with a spot of farming. His sheep graze in the meadow at the end of my garden. Alan's wife breeds Yorkshire terriers and it was from there, deep in the woods, that my little Sam came and brought me such joy until she died two years ago. Peppercorn or Peppi as he is known, lives with me now. He is curled up at my feet as I write this and, of course, he is very special, a dear little long-haired dachshund with a coat like softest velvet; but nothing can take the place of Sam, with her bright button eyes and butterfly ears. But this is digressing and we must leave Bedstone and take the road to Bucknell.

Bucknell is a much larger village than Bedstone and a few years ago it suffered an outbreak of bungaloiditis around the outskirts. However, the heart of the village is undisturbed and now that the new buildings have mellowed and pretty gardens have sprung up among them the impact is not so disturbing. Nevertheless, it is a good example of how not to develop a centuries old village. Around the church all is as Bradley found it when he came past in his pony and trap and wrote that he 'paused for a moment in the peaceful hamlet of Bucknell which spreads itself along the banks of the River Redlake as it babbles joyously towards the Teme'.

To the right of the Sitwell Arms a wide path borders the village green. This is for pedestrians, not cars, and provides a delightful walk to the church. On our left an ancient black-and-white cottage looks out across the green to where groups of ducks clamber in and out of the water or waddle around preening themselves under an old tree by the water's edge. This is a cameo truly redolent of all that was best in English villages long ago. The path widens towards the end and groups of pleasing houses among them The Hall, with its mellow brick and sporting a delightful Georgian fanlight - lead to the church. The Church of Saint Mary's Bucknell is part Norman and part Early English. It was heavily restored in 1870 and it stands in a wide and spacious graveyard on the perimeter of which crowd many attractive and ancient houses. As I walked up the path, I was greeted by a tall man with a pleasant wind-tanned face. He was busily cutting the grass between the gravestones. His name is Brian Whittall and he told me that his father and grandfather before him had all tended the churchyard and cut the grass. All on a voluntary basis. His grandfather cut the grass with a scythe. Brian said, 'Until we got this contraption', indicating the electric mower, 'it was all done by hand, almost the whole village would turn out and help, but they don't seem to want to do that now. The only thing is, when you have one of these

41

contraptions you don't get the flowers, it takes them all away you see. I don't know why that is, perhaps its letting the grass lie when it's cut so that it smothers them, but you can't have it both ways can you? Then again we do get the anemones now, strange that, we never had them before we introduced this machine, now we get big patches of wood anemones.'

Near the church porch is a tree that looked to me vaguely like a weeping ash. 'Ah, no,' said Brian, 'that's the devil's pear tree, it has some lovely blossom, smothered it is, but it only lasts a short time, see, these are the pears.' He picked a small, hard, green pear-shaped fruit the size of a large pea and handed it to me. 'Do they grow any bigger?' I asked. 'Oh no', he replied. 'Well', said I, 'that's not much good'. 'No', he said smiling, 'but you can't expect much good from the devil's tree'.

Looming up behind the village is Coxall knoll, the hill on which Caractacus is said to have made his last stand against the Romans. According to Tacitus, the little river babbling along at the foot of the hill ran red with blood, after that ferocious battle, and it is to this day called the River Redlake. Caractacus escaped after the battle and fled from the scene, seeking the protection of his stepmother, Queen Cartismandua Queen of the Brigantes, a northern tribe. She, perfidious creature promptly handed him over to the Romans; perhaps she was the source of all those wicked stepmother stories.

Bucknell has a railway station with a pretty little grey stone stationmaster's house, now in private occupation. Built in 1860 with curly white-painted barge boards and Tudor style chimneys, there is a strong whiff of the cottage ornée. Crossing the line here to leave the village, the road winds on over Bucknell Bridge, spanning the Teme, and a little further still and we are at a T-junction, a right hand turn will take us straight into Knighton. The cottage on the right of the turning is Turnpike Cottage and here lived, for many years in his retirement, the Reverend Hodges formerly vicar of nearby Brampton Bryan. One of his sons, Christopher Hodges, has written the definitive story of the Battle of Mortimer's Cross which took place about three miles away. The battle between the Yorkists and Lancastrians was fought on Candlemas Day in 1461 and afterwards the victorious young Duke of York rode to London and was proclaimed King Edward IV.

But I am wandering again and we must continue our journey to Knighton. Very soon we pass the sign Croeso y Cwmry - Welcome to Wales - and we have crossed the border. A few hundred yards on our left is the romantically named farm, Heartsease. The entrance, flanked by yews and a long stone barn, leads to a large courtyard where, on the far side, an old ivy clad farmhouse surrounded by stone and timber-framed farm buildings, dozes on time. A scene of great charm and peacefulness and yet here, on the very border between England and Wales, fierce skirmishes were the order of the day in the battle torn past.

John Watkins who farms the land, as did his father and grandfather before, told me that one of his fields has a name which is said to be a corruption of Gallows Tree. And no doubt many a Saxon or Welshman in those more turbulent times 'danced upon the midnight air' as the poet so delicately put it. There is an old tradition that Heartsease was so called because when some Welsh raiders were being chased back across the border the pursuing Saxons found that they were on the right road near Knighton which set their hearts at ease. A little bit wobbly that one but, whatever the reason, it is a lovely name and suits this idyllic scene.

A mile or so further along the highway is a country hotel named The Milebrook. In the days when this was a private house, Hailie Sallassie, the Emperor of Ethiopia, spent part of his time in exile there. He stayed in various houses on the border and I have met people in Clun who remember seeing him quite often crossing the town square. For anyone living in that hill-girdled fastness half-a-century ago and who had rarely, if ever, seen anyone from the African continent, the sight of that erect and elegant little figure must have seemed strange indeed.

Just past the burgeoning rhododendrons of the hotel Milebrook a finger post on the right hand side points to the village of Stowe. About half a mile along a very up-hill and

7 *The rushing River Teme at Stowe*

43

down-dale lane, across a little bridge spanning the rushing Teme, overhung by the Holloway rock, the tiny hamlet nestles into the side of Stowe Hill. Towards the end the lane becomes so steep as to be almost vertical, two or three pretty cottages are sprinkled around the final huff and puff up to the church which, with its wooden bell cot, is built into the hill which towers over it. The churchyard, which falls steeply away down the hillside, is oval. Over the dog roses climbing through the hedge, there is a wonderful view of pastureland and hills.

At the far side of the church path, a gate leads to the Old Vicarage, which snuggles neatly down into the hillside, the garden behind it rising up in waves of gentle colour. I called at Glebe Cottage, opposite the lych gate, in the hope of getting the key to the church. A single green wellie stood a forlorn sentinel in the middle of the cottage path and a great clump of yellow Welsh poppies waved a welcome from beside the door. There was no reply to my knock until, just as I was turning away, it was opened by the owner, petite, dark haired and a little out of breath. 'I was decorating', she said, apologising for the delay in answering. Hoping I hadn't brought her down from her ladder, I asked where I could get the key to the church and was directed to a cottage lower down the hill. Before leaving I mentioned the lonely wellington boot on the path. A smile flitted across her vivid face, her eyes sparkled even more and then she was gone I walked down the garden path, carefully skirting the wellie. At the wicket gate I turned, but it had vanished and, if the cottage with its two little gables and charmingly tangled flower beds had vanished too, I should not have been surprised, for the whole hamlet, with not a soul to be seen save the elfin creature who had appeared at the cottage door, had a dreamlike quality bordering on the unreal.

No-one answered the door at the 'cottage lower down the hill' so my next port of call was The Old Vicarage. Here I was in luck for both Valerie and Jeffrey George were at home. Jeffrey George, who is an historic buildings consultant, is a great enthusiast for Stowe and trundled me round various points of interest, generously sharing his knowledge.

Stowe in the past was a place of some importance, for it was the crossing point of an early drovers' route and an even earlier mediaeval road from Knighton. However, the village declined in importance when it was by-passed by an eighteen-twenties enclosures road and this decline was accelerated by the opening of a turnpike road on the southern side of the River Teme. All these old routes can be traced on an ordinance map. From the tall arched windows of The Old Vicarage, the drovers road and the mediaeval sunken road are plainly visible, as is the site of the mediaeval Stowe village, now just a number of grassy humps and bumps.

A few yards from the porch, a yew lined path takes us to a gate into the churchyard and here a wide grassy path, travelling on the one side from the Old Vicarage gate, and on the other from the lych-gate, leads up to the church porch. This broad sweep of green is regularly mown by Jeffrey George who shrugs deprecatingly and says, 'May as well do it when I do my own lawns.' The result of this labour of love is a wide ribbon of verdant green running in front of the church and acting, as it were, as a mount for a delightful picture.

When a churchyard is an oval one as at Stowe, Jeffrey George told me, it usually means it was a very early sacred site. The Norman church at Stowe is therefore probably built on the site of many former places of worship, some of them very likely pagan. George is not a common surname and yet Jeffrey George showed me, under an ancient yew, the graves of three Georges - John, George, and Fanny George. They were no connection of his but I could see that for him it was a pleasing coincidence that he should come from far away to settle in this remote village and then find these namesakes on his doorstep as it were.

The church has a mediaeval roof in remarkably good condition and some very beautiful stained glass. There are also a number of very colourful and interesting memorials of the Art Nouveau period.

The searching wind sent us back to The Old Vicarage to join Valerie George and warm up with a pot of steaming coffee. This old building, with its pretty gothicised Victorian frontage masking a wonderful mixture of earlier periods within, was enlarged and extensively restored in the eighteen-sixties by John Rogers, the then incumbent. Valerie George is a professional dress designer and has small residential classes in the Old Vicarage for people who wish to learn something of her art. We have long had artists, potters and weavers and even sculptors in our border hills and valleys and now we have haute couture too!

All around this village are steep hills that swoop and dive into deep valleys, only to soar again, and the views must be exactly the same as those which Parson Rogers saw, as he walked up the garden path to the church or did the rounds of his little flock, nearly a hundred and fifty years ago.

Stowe is a place of great tranquillity and one in which to linger, however, the time had whizzed by and Knighton beckoned but, for travellers on the way to Wales, it is only a small detour off the Knighton road and a gem not to be missed.

8   *Stowe Church*

Chapter 4

Knighton

We still had sorrows to lighten,
One could not always be glad,
And lads knew trouble at Knighton,
When I was a Knighton lad.
A. E. Houseman: *A Shropshire Lad*

Many writers have likened Knighton, or to give it its Welsh name, Tref y Clawdd, the town on the Dyke, to an Alpine town. There is no question about it, the alpine flavour is there, from the encircling hills rising to heights of one thousand four hundred feet and the dark sweep of forestry commission firs marching over them, to the little grey stone houses clinging to their slopes and the clean streets that clamber up and down to meet the clock tower in the centre of the town. There is, too, something vaguely Germanic about this particular clock tower, something reminiscent of those clock towers which seem to be an indispensable adjunct of every snow girt little town in the Austrian Alps.

Knighton can be snow girt too. I remember one winter in the 1980s, when the snow lay so thick on the ground and the drifts were so deep, that John Garmon, the local doctor, having set off to bring an expectant mother down from the hills, lost the road and ended up in the ditch. The intrepid doctor struggled on foot to the nearest farm and he and the farmer set off in a tractor to retrieve his vehicle, only to find it had completely disappeared under the snow and could not be found, nor was it, for several weeks. Doctors in these parts are resourceful souls, so John Garmon commandeered tractor and driver, garnered up the patient, stowed her aboard and off they all trundled to the cottage hospital in Knighton.

This was the winter when helicopters circled overhead searching for any cut off farms and in our hamlet, and many others, the water supply froze and the electricity supply ceased for some weeks. The only thing that worked was the calor gas stove and this poor thing never recovered from the scratchings it received, when called upon to melt bucket after bucket of snow. It was amazing how many buckets of snow had to be melted to obtain one bucket of water and even more amazing to watch the water in the bucket begin to freeze as one carried it out to the paddock, where Poppy the pony was anxiously waiting. Poppy wore a tiara for days during this great freeze up, her breath had frozen into brilliantly shining six-inch spikes, which encircled her head so that she looked a veritable pony princess.

If much of Knighton resembles an Alpine town, then surely the most

9   *Knighton Clock Tower*

quaint and attractive of its streets could have been lifted straight from a Cornish seaside townlet. Winding up from Broad Street and yet so different in flavour, it is known as the Narrows and is another street which climbs so steeply out of the town that, I doubt, if even the determined Arthur Bradley in his pony and trap would have attempted it. Old houses nudge each other on either side many of them hiding sixteenth and seventeenth century interiors behind later facades. Walking down the Narrows it is always a surprise to me to find the clock tower and the busy bustling shopping centre waiting at the bottom instead of fishing smacks in a little Cornish harbour.

Offa's Dyke, part of which runs through Knighton, marked the Anglo Saxon frontier with Wales. It was built in the eighth century by Offa, King of Mercia, and is the oldest frontier in Europe. The present border between the two countries still follows the general line of the Dyke. In Saxon times any Welshman found armed on the English side of the Dyke had his ears, and in some cases hands, cut off but, in spite of this rather discouraging arrangement, cross border raiding by the Welsh continued for centuries.

In 1971 the Offa's Dkye long distance footpath, all one hundred and sixty-eight miles of it, was formally opened at a point on the Dyke in Knighton, by Lady Green-Price, Sir John Hunt and Mr Noel Jarman. A commemorative stone was set up in the riverside park. Soon after the opening of this walk, the newspapers carried stories of angry hikers who had been chased by bulls along the Dyke, where it ran through or near farmland. Letters to the press grew quite heated, but eventually a compromise was reached and farmers, through whose land the Dyke ran, agreed to make sure that if a bull was out he would have other temptations with him in the form of accommodating cows, so that chasing hikers would be low on his list of priorities. The plan must have worked because the protests have long ceased.

In Norman times, Knighton was a walled town and had two castles. Bryn-y-Castell, the earlier one, was to the east of the town and was probably only a superior motte and bailey affair, for an earth mound is all that remains. The later castle was of stone and was built by William de Braose in the twelfth century. The site he chose was high over the town at the top of The Narrows. Eventually the castle was acquired by those mightiest of border barons, the Mortimers. This was an honour Knighton could have well forsworn since the name of Mortimer seems to have been synonymous with battles; battles to seize properties and battles to retain them. Their history was long and bloody and in 1260 when, true to form, they were hotly engaged in a war with Llewellyn the Last, Knighton was attacked by the Welsh and castle and town were burned. Nearly a century and a half later, in 1402, Owain Glyndwr was ravaging the country and Knighton castle was again burned and Edmund Mortimer defeated in a great battle at nearby Pilleth.

From that time on law and order broke down in the area. The hills and woods provided shelter for numerous outlaws and robber bandits and the Welsh, never slow to seize the opportunity, stepped up their raids across the border, so that the whole district became one of ill repute and was avoided by all but the foolhardy.

It was during this time that the Lollards sought hiding places in the area, particularly in the Deerfold Forest up above Wigmore. Among them was the great Lollard martyr, Sir John Oldcastle. The Deerfold

Forest was an old hunting forest of the Mortimers and there is still a fourteenth century farm, known as Chapel farm, in this wild untrammelled place and it was in this farm that many of the Lollards hid and held their services. Up until sometime after the second world war, a great medieval oak table stood in this farm and it was traditionally said to have been used as the altar for the Lollard services. According to a previous owner, it winged its way to America.

Sir John Oldcastle's family were Lords of the Manor of Almley near Weobley and as a young man he was a 'trusted servant' of the crown and a great friend of the future King Henry. In 1406 he was made Sheriff of Herefordshire and in 1409, after his marriage to Joan, Lady of Cobham, a new barony was created in his favour. From then on he was known as Sir John Oldcastle, knight and Lord of Cobham and for some years he divided his time between London and Kent, leading a very fashionable life under the wing of his friend the King. What made him forsake all those delicious fleshpots and embrace so fervently Lollardism is not known, but it is a fact that in the last decade of the fourteenth century, Herefordshire, particularly around the Welsh border town of Knighton, was a hot bed of Lollardry and many brave followers were imprisoned or burned for their beliefs. The earliest evidence of Sir John's Lollardism was in the year 1410 when he preached, without license, in three churches, on his Lollard convictions. Another three years pass before we hear of him again, when in 1413 a chaplain was denounced as a heretic at the first meeting of a convocation set up to 'Examine the heretical beliefs of the Lollards'. He was accused of celebrating the communion in the Lollard's chapel in Sir John's presence. Thanks to various informers an illuminator's shop in Paternoster Row in London was searched and several Lollard tracts were found which belonged to Sir John. After this discovery the outlook seemed very bleak for him but his friend, the King, begged the Bishops for clemency, until he had time to make Sir John see the error of his ways.

All was to no avail, however, and the exasperated Henry upbraided his friend for his obstinacy, whereupon Sir John stormed out of the King's presence without his leave. The Archbishop immediately sent a citation requiring Sir John to appear before the magistrates at Leeds Castle. Messenger and citation were sent packing. The citation was then nailed to the door of Rochester Cathedral, only to be torn down by Sir John's friends. After this outrage Sir John was promptly excommunicated. This box-and-cox went on for some weeks until, finally, Sir John was arrested by Royal writ.

He was brought before the Archbishop and the Bishops of London and Manchester. During his examination, Sir John said he believed most of the doctrines of the Roman Church but he could not accept the power of the Popes, Cardinals and Prelates to forgive sins. The court met a second time with reinforcements in the shape of the Bishop of Bangor and twelve doctors of divinity. The arguments grew very fierce. Sir John most impudently denounced the Pope as the head of Anti-Christ, the prelates as his limbs and the friars as his tail. For good measure, he turned to the onlookers, who were certainly getting their money's worth, and told them that anyone believing the judges would surely be dispatched to perdition. This was too much for the Archbishop who rose in wrath, declared Sir John a heretic, and handed him to the secular for sentence.

By now Lollards from all over England were rising and declaring themselves ready to fight for Sir John; twenty-thousand of them were heading for London and the fields of Saint Giles. The King was forced to act and ordered the city gates to close, cutting them off from the London Lollards. Without their London contingent and confronted by the King's armed and trained men, the rebels disbanded and fled.

Sir John, who had somehow eluded his captors, most wisely made haste for his homeland and, with a price of one-thousand marks on his head, spent several years in hiding in Wales and the Border country. Alas in the year 1417 his then hiding place, a secluded spot overlooking the Vyrnwy near Meifod, was discovered by the Lord of Powis and some of his henchmen who surprised Sir John and his followers. There was a tremendous fight during which a vitriolic old beldame, wielding a wooden stool, broke Sir John's leg. He was captured and taken to London on a horse litter, his injuries being so grave he could not ride. Immediately on arrival, after what must have been a nightmare journey, he was brought before Parliament and condemned as an outlaw, a traitor and a convicted heretic. He was then drawn on a horse litter to the tower and the same day placed on a hurdle and dragged to the newly erected Lollard gallows in Saint Giles field. Here this stout-hearted, outspoken, Herefordshire knight, who had inspired such affection in his King that he fought desperately to save him from the clutches of the Bishops and showed such loyalty to his fellow Lollards that he so often risked a grisly death was finally 'hung and burned hanging'. A gruesome picture of the times shows him suspended horizontally in chains over a glowing fire.

One hundred years later in 1517, a young German named Martin Luther, nailed to the door of a church in Wittenberg a list of ninety Papal indulgences which he and his followers refuted, chief among them being the right of the Pope to forgive sins, thus beginning the period of the Reformation, the seeds of which were sown by such men as Sir John Oldcastle of the Border Country more than a century before.

The deer, the wolves, the boars and even the heron have long gone from the Deerfold Forest and, near the Chapel Farm, a few crumbling low stonewalls are all that remains of the Limebrook nunnery, which flourished in the forest, when the Lollards were fugitives there. But there is still one living reminder of those days long past for, on a grassy bank a bow shot from the nunnery, grows that rarest of herbs, the Asarabacca, a remembrance of the herb garden tended by those medieval nuns.

Curious to know what usage the Asarabacca had in the world of herbs, I hunted it up and discovered that among other things it was considered a splendid cure for a hangover. Hangovers and nuns do not normally go together but at one time the Lymebrook nunnery had a very bad name, though not perhaps equal to that of Port Royale near Paris, which became a superior brothel for the local aristocrats. One hopes that the fate of the Mother Superior was not akin to that of the Abbess of nearby Leominster; she, poor thing, was seduced by Sweyn, the son of the Saxon Earl Godwin, for which novel choice of mistress he was banished to France for four years. Nevertheless, the 'goings on' at Lymebrook were sufficiently worrying for the Bishop of Hereford to order the vicar of St John's in Ludlow to make all speed for the Deerfold Forest and investigate the nunnery. During these times, a good supply of Asarabacca anti-hangover brew would surely be most useful.

The Act of Union in 1556 ended the state of near anarchy in and around Knighton. The lands of the former great war lords, the Marcher Barons, were welded together and a new county, called Radnorshire, was formed. The inhabitants were given the same rights, privileges and responsibilities as the English.

In the year 1230 Henry III had granted Knighton the right to hold a market every Thursday and somehow the town authorities had managed to cling on to this privilege during the dark years after the defeat by Owain Glyndwr. After the Act of Union, when things became more stable, Knighton grew into a flourishing market town and by the eighteenth century it was an important corn and sheep market which, with the coming of the railway in 1861, became nationally known.

Sheep and corn were not the only things to be sold at the market for, up until the middle of the nineteenth century, husbands could auction their wives there too. The last recorded sale of a wife was in 1854. These hapless creatures were led by a halter round their necks to the market place to be sold. The cost of a divorce was far too high for the poor to afford and this method of 'off with the old and on with the new' cost nothing. Indeed, it was quite remunerative for the husband and certainly a great deal quicker than a divorce. One can only suppose that any wife treated by her husband in such a cavalier way would feel she was well rid of him and perhaps she fared better the second time round. Thomas Hardy, in his novel *The Mayor of Casterbridge*, describes an auction of a wife by her husband and then goes on to tell the story of what happened to them both in future years. It is a grim but fascinating read.

Like every self respecting town, Knighton had a whipping post and one of the regular market day entertainments was to see petty criminals being whipped from the bridge to the market hall and back until the 'back be bloody'. Women were treated the same as men and Knighton was by no means singular in this. In Ludlow there are records of women being stripped to the waist and tied to a cart's tail and being whipped round the town until, as in the case of Knighton, the 'back be bloody'.

During the Civil War, Knighton was for King and Parliament and very fiercely so for when, after the execution of Charles 1 in 1652, Cromwell sent six excise men to collect taxes from the town, the three town constables waylaid them 'Having first disarmed them, bade the people fall upon them, and thereupon the whole town rose against them with clubs, bills, weapons, and stones . . . and threatened that though they brought one-hundred men with them to collect the excise they should all be beat.' The excise men fled for their lives and demanded of Cromwell a military escort for any further incursions into 'Those parts'.

In a trim little house on the Offa's Dyke road lives Mary Cadwallader. I was fortunate indeed to have an introduction to her, for there is little she does not know about Knighton past and present. It was an early spring morning when I walked down the crazy-paved path to her door and rang the bell. Silver haired, fresh as a daisy in a flower print blouse with a pussycat bow, she led me into a room looking onto her garden where, through a rustic arch flanked by two ancient and gnarled flowering cherry trees, I could see the slopes of the Garth Hills. Mary Cadwallader told me that her father, a builder, built her house and three other similar ones in 1925. They were known as 'Subsidy houses' because the government gave a seventy-pound subsidy for each house. Mary has lived in her house ever since and has had the same neighbour for sixty-seven years.

For twenty-five years she was deputy head at the Knighton Primary School in West Street and as a child she herself was a pupil there. The school has closed and the building now houses the Offa's Dyke Association. Mary is the secretary. 'When I was a girl,' she said, 'Knighton was a nice, neat little self-contained place. Everyone knew everyone else. There were only one or two cars; the doctor had one called Scuffle. Then there was the town charabanc, but most vehicles were horse drawn. On market days the buying and selling was done in the streets and in the September sheep sales there were thousands and thousands of sheep in the streets - they were everywhere.'

Mary Cadwallader's great uncle was William Hadfield whose book on Knighton, now sadly out of print, is eagerly sought. Writing and a deep love of the town runs in the family for Mary's cousin, Mona Cadwallader, wrote a delightful booklet called *Teme Valley Touches*. It deals with her childhood memories, in and around Knighton, and fascinating they are.

The Parish Church of Knighton is dedicated to St Edward, an English saint. This is very rare in Wales. In his book on Knighton, William Hadfield writes that at an earlier time it was dedicated to St Lawrence and, before that tradition says to St Michael. Altering, restoring and in some cases entirely rebuilding churches is not unusual, but almost always the name remains the same down the centuries. One wonders what caused the chopping and changing at Knighton. However, the town does seem to have settled for St Edward because this has now been its name for many generations.

Most of the church was rebuilt in the nineteenth century and only the lower part of the original Norman tower remains. The church suffered a long period of decay until 1756, when it finally became unsafe. A few years before that, the condition of the church had become so bad that a Mr Steele wrote, after seeing it, 'The parish church of Knighton and the two chancels thereto adjoining, being very ancient buildings, are by length of time becoming very ruinous and decayed and in so bad a condition that the inhabitants cannot without great hazard and danger of their person attend Divine Service therein.' Eventually the church was demolished. The rebuilding began in 1876 and continued in fits and starts, as the money became available. It was completed in 1897. Nevertheless, one wonders whether such a drastic dose of restoration was necessary. *The Hereford Journal* of 1877 stated of the proposed new church at Knighton, 'There will not be the slightest likeness to the old one, scarcely a vestige of which will be left. It appears to be intended to allow the solitary remnant of the old Norman tower to remain but that is all.'

10   *Old cottage by the Clock Tower, Knighton*

W.H.Howse, in his book on Radnorshire, writes or rather pens from the heart, a cry of despair, 'Again and again on reading of restoration work which was in reality church destruction we are led to exclaim "If only you had left us the shell of the building and some of the old oak and spared us from your pitch pine and varnish and kitchen tiles" but no appeal would have reached those deaf ears.' Writing of the architect who restored Michaelchurch, another Border church, W.H.Howse tells us 'The architect employed was Thomas Nicholson, the Hereford Diocesan Architect, who was unfortunately entrusted with much 'restoration work' and left a trail of destruction through the diocese, one of this architect's ideas was to 'Sweep away the old ramshackle pews' and substitute seats of varnish and pitch pine. He varnished all the woodwork of the church, including the screen. Supplied an elegant new pulpit and paved the sanctuary and chancel with black and red tiles.'

Every century has its despoilers and the twentieth century is no exception. We had the horrors of the sixties, the time when the planners and their Councils caused so much havoc and changed the face of so many of our towns and cities. Countless numbers of beautiful old buildings were demolished to make way for hideous, soul destroying and often, so it later proved, dangerous high rise flats. It was the era of the juggernaut. On they ploughed, leaving devastation in their wake, all over the country. Everywhere groups of people got together and formed societies to try and stem the flow of destruction but, to echo W.H.Howse's words 'No appeal would have reached those deaf ears.'

Knighton is one of the gateways to Wales and so we will leave it and, following the Pennybont Road, head for the interior.

Chapter 5

Monaughty, Pilleth, Bleddfa and Abbey Cwmhir

Radnorsheer, poor Radnorsheer,
Never a Park and never a deer,
Never a squire of five hundred a year,
Save Richard Fowler of Abbey Cwmhir.

Leaving Knighton on the A485, the road climbs high over the hills before a making a rushing decent into the valley of the Lugg. About four miles out of the town, set in a hollow a little back from the road so that one looks down on its gables and chimneys, is a magnificent Elizabethan manor house. This is Monaughty, a name said to derive from the Welsh Mynach-ty, meaning the Monk's House, for Monaughty was built on land which belonged to the monks of Abbey Cwmhir, a Cistercian abbey near Llandrindod Wells.

It was in 1565 that a certain James Price, a descendant of the Welsh princes of Maelynidd, decided to celebrate his second marriage by building a great manor house. When finished, it was by far the largest house in Radnorshire at that time. Two enormous rooms, the Great Chamber on the first floor and the Great Hall below, are at the heart of the house and these are surrounded by numerous spacious, albeit smaller, rooms. The huge fireplace in the Great Hall would accommodate a young tree and on the walls are paintings of the Royal Arms and the arms of Sir Henry Sidney, who was the patron of the Prices of Monaughty. Sir Henry, as Lord President of the March, lived at Ludlow Castle the seat of the Lord President. It is not unreasonable to suppose that he stayed with the Prices of Monaughty, for they would certainly have invited their patron to visit them, especially as they were only a handful of miles from Ludlow. Sir Henry's wife was a lady of the bedchamber at Queen Elizabeth's court and one can imagine the latest court gossip going round the table with the wine flagon, in the Great Hall at Monaughty.

No doubt there were a number of favours James Price could expect from his patron, but financial assistance would not have been one of them, for Sir Henry had spent a vast sum on improvements at Ludlow Castle, but could not get the Queen, whose property it was, to reimburse him. This was because of his tolerant attitude towards the Roman Catholics in the area, an attitude much frowned upon at court. Indeed his friend, Sir Thomas Walsingham, sent him a letter warning him that he was very out of favour in high places. 'Your doings are narrowly observed', he wrote, 'and her Majesty is apt to give ear to any that shall yll you'. Sir Henry kept his head but he lost his fortune and in a letter to Sir Francis he wrote 'The Queen will not be moved to reward me, I have not now so much ground as would feed one mutton'. In addition to this, he was five thousand pounds in debt.

Alas, by the year 1639 James Price's great-grandson was in the same situation as Sir Henry in his time. Like Sir Henry, he spent enormous sums on improving his property. There was a final flourish, just before his death, when the last of his inheritance went on an ornamental staircase, which to this day bears his initials, and the addition of a delightful, small half-timbered room, a perfect place to sit with a decanter of wine at his elbow, viewing his beautiful estates. It was known then and still is as the Prospect Room.

Twelve years after the death of James's grandson, Monaughty was sold to a cattle dealer and drover. He had two daughters and both made very good marriages, one to a Vaughan of Hergest near Kington, and the other to a member of an old Breconshire family. However, by 1722 the place had changed hands again, this time it was sold to a London merchant named Chase. Mr Chase employed a Knighton lawyer to collect the rents on his estates, a man named John Price but no connection with the Prices who built Monaughty. Lawyer Price most prudently married his employer's daughter, thus gaining the Monaughty estates. The Prices eventually became Green-Prices and Monaughty remained with them until 1973, when it was bought by the present owner.

The Price/Green-Prices did not use Monaughty as their principle seat; it was occupied by a succession of farming tenants. No further work was done on the place after the original Prices died out and so it has remained dreaming down the years, a perfect example of an Elizabethan manor house unscathed by nineteenth and twentieth century improvements. The original features and amenities remain: the beautiful ceilings, the panelling, the great fireplaces, and the garderobes (lavatories) adjoining most bedrooms. One of these, in a guest bedroom, even has flushing arrangements managed by a series of ducts carrying rainwater off the roof and down through the garderobe into a stone cesspit. The kitchen, too, has mediaeval 'mod cons' in the form of a hatch leading to a shute which used to carry the kitchen refuse down into an adjoining pigsty.

A team of local craftsmen have been working for several years on the restoration work and when the beautiful plaster work of the ceiling in the Great Chamber was being restored a local man made fifty-two tools with which to do the work. I was told that the old plaster in the ceilings contained a great deal of cow hair and cow manure and I was reminded of an old plasterer, named Rigden, who lived in a Kentish village near Sandwich. Many years ago, when he was a boy, he helped his father repair the ceiling in the dining-room of the house of the Dean of Canterbury Cathedral. Remembering the occasion, he said to me 'That there Dean 'ad no notion 'ow many cow pats was 'anging over 'im when he eat 'is bacon and eggs'.

Queen Elizabeth did not sleep at Monaughty but Jean-Jacques Rousseau very nearly did. Lawyer Price's second son was an MP and a great friend of John Wilkes, the radical reformer, and between them they thought they had persuaded Rousseau to visit Monaughty. A bedroom was 'done up' in 1776, ready to receive the great man. 'The best laid plans' are often changed and so it turned out and Rousseau never came.

The Great Chamber has a giant four-poster found, I was assured, in a pigsty at Sudeley Castle. Most of the old Monaughty estate has been sold over the years but it is still possible to sit in the Prospect Room and absorb a green and tranquil outlook, the same view that the unfortunate James would have enjoyed, before his financial collapse.

Outside, traces of the original Elizabethan garden have been found, some feet below a cabbage patch, and a careful work of restoring old paths and planting beds has been carried out. The planting followed the original design and now this most romantic of old houses dozes gently beside a garden unchanged in essence since the first James Price had it laid out to welcome his new bride.

A few yards past Monaughty, there is a left-hand turn signposted Pilleth and although we are on our way to Bleddfa and Abbey Cwmhir this is a little diversion we must make for one of the most significant battles in the history of Radnorshire took place at Pilleth. When Arthur Bradley came to Pilleth he wrote of it as a 'Somewhat lonely place, unless indeed the stormy day on which I paid the field a visit left too sombre an impression of it'. It is still a lonely place but, with the sun shining and the autumn colours glowing, none the less attractive for that.

11   *A general view of Pilleth*

It was in the year 1402 that the green slopes of Bryn-Glas, the hill of Pilleth, rang with shouts and cries and the clash of swords on armour, for it was here that the men of Hereford and Radnor, under Edmund Mortimer, fought with the men of Owain Glyndwr commanded by Glyndwr's most able and ruthless lieutenant, Rhys Gethin, Rhys the terrible. This was the battle of which Shakespeare writes in *Henry IV*, 'When all athwart there came a post from Wales laden with heavy news'. The English were routed and over 1,100 of Mortimer's men were killed. After the battle, it was said that their hatred of the English was such that gangs of Welsh women, beside themselves with fury and armed with knives, swarmed all over the battlefield mutilating the corpses, in the manner of the tribal women of the North West Frontier after English battles fought much later in that far continent. For many years after the battle, the bones of the fallen were constantly being turned up by the plough until, in the nineteenth century, the land where the bones were found was removed from cultivation and Sir Richard Green Price planted a grove of trees to mark the spot.

The thirteenth century church at Pilleth was burned by Glyndwr, along with the neighbouring churches of Cascob, Bleddfa and the abbey at Cwmhir. However, the building was restored. In 1894 the church was again gutted by fire. This time the fine rood-screen and the pews, some of which were enriched with beautifully carved poppy heads, were lost. This second conflagration was due to an overheated iron chimney which set fire to the roof.

The little church stood a desolate and burned out shell for eleven years and then, thanks to the generosity of Edward and Agnes Whitehead of Nantygroes, it was once again restored. A temporary roof, with a very shallow rake, was put on and this gives the church the appearance of being rather squashed down or of someone wearing a flat cap on occasions when he should be sporting a top hat. The interior of the church is charming and has an air of great peace. In mediaeval times this church at Pilleth was a place of pilgrimage, for to the north of the tower is a well the water of which was said to be a cure for eye diseases. There was also a remarkably fine statue of the Virgin Mary and this drew pilgrims as well, so that the church became known as The Chapel of Our Lady of Pilleth.

The bones of the English Commander, Edmund Mortimer, do not lie among the slain on Bryn Glas. Sir Edmund was taken prisoner at the battle. However, running true to form with former bearers of that illustrious name, he knew on which side his bread was buttered. He managed to quell any patriotic feelings he had towards England and his King and made yet another of those judicious marriages for which the Mortimers were so renowned and by which they had so enriched their coffers. His bride was one of the daughters of Owain Glyndwr and, in order to seal the bargain, he actually espoused his captor's cause, sending proclamations out in his own name to the people of Radnor and Presteigne commanding them to follow suit. What the families of his followers who fell at Bryn Glas thought about this history does not recall.

I came to know that long drive up to Pilleth Church almost too well, for I traversed it three times in one afternoon. It was about six months after my visit to the church that my companion and I were driving past and I suggested he might like to see it. It was a miserable day, overcast and very windy, with rain in every gust, and the drive up to the church was a mass of squelchy mud. However, we turned on to it and, with much jerking and wheel spinning, we got about three-quarters of the way up before deciding it would be prudent to abandon the church viewing and reverse back to the road.

The drive is really a long wide shelf cut into the hillside so that, when going towards the church, the hill rises up on the passenger's side, while on the driver's side there is a drop varying between five and eight-feet, after which the land slopes very steeply down to the fields below. All was well at first, then suddenly the car began to slide away from the comforting mass of the hill towards the drop. It seemed inevitable that we would go over, but miraculously, we came to a halt on the very edge. Very gingerly indeed we clambered out of the car on the passenger side and surveyed the scene. Teetering on the edge, it looked as if the slightest push would be the end of the matter.

Down in the valley below we could see the white walls of Pilleth Court, so off we plodded through the mud, hoping to be able to use their telephone. At the bottom of the church drive a car had just turned in from the road. We flagged it down and warned the occupants of the worsening mud higher up the drive and told them of our little calamity. They were farmers, Mr and Mrs Meredith, and they had been following the Teme Valley Hunt as guests of the Hunt. The weather was so awful they decided to leave early and look at Pilleth Church on their way home. We were bundled into their car and off they drove to Pilleth Court.

There was no reply from the Court although we walked all round it, knocking on every door we came across, so we then tried nearby Pilleth Lodge. Here the key was in the front door but there was no reply to our knockings. Sam Meredith said that he had noticed a roadside cottage, about half-a-mile back, so off we scampered. Here again the key was in the front door but no reply to our knocks. It seemed a truly Alice in Wonderland situation. Our farmer, having his feet planted on the ground, then said, 'Well, I came to see Pilleth Church and Pilleth Church I am going to see, then we can drive you into Knighton and find a telephone.'

Off we set, up the church drive, this time on foot. The Merediths, wise virgins, had wellies ready in the car; we of course did not. As we passed our stranded vehicle, Sam Meredith, eyeing it with a knowledgeable look, pronounced that it was 'a job for the A.A. or R.A.C'. He had thought that if we could have got hold of a tractor from a neighbouring farm that might have been the answer, but having seen the situation, decided that it was far too dicey and must be left to the experts.

It was dusk as we made our way down from the church, but far below in the valley, Sam spotted a figure outside Pilleth Lodge. This remarkable man somehow scrambled down the drop at the edge of the drive and then, still wellie clad, ran down the slope, climbed the fence and continued running across the field, shouting as he went to alert whoever it was outside Pilleth Lodge. When we all met again at his car, he told us that Mrs Hood who lived in the Lodge would be happy for us to use her telephone. He drove us there and, after we had telephoned the R.A.C., Sam and Doris Meredith, those truly good Samaritans, set off at last for home. In no time at all, Mrs Hood produced a pot of tea and some shortbreads. She told us she had been watching the racing on television when we called and had been too engrossed to hear us. Luckily for us, she had popped out to see how her husband was getting on with the lambing and that is when Sam Meredith's sharp eyes spotted her.

By the time the R.A.C. man had arrived, it was dark. We climbed into his vehicle and set off once more up the church drive. When he saw the car, he told my companion to get into the driving seat, while he fixed the tow rope. To my horror Geoffrey obeyed and was just crawling in from the passenger side when, down the path from the direction of the church came a Range-Rover, horn blowing and headlights flashing furiously. Almost before it came to a halt just short of the marooned car, a man tumbled out and rushing over shouted, 'get out, get out!' With much relief and very carefully, Geoffrey crawled out. The man, who turned out to be Mrs Hood's son, Peter, was returning from a shoot, when he came upon what he felt was an impending disaster. After consulting with the rescue man, he virtually took over the operation. Standing on the passenger side of the car to prevent it toppling , he directed the R.A.C. man who was manoeuvring with the tow-rope. Incredibly, unbelievably, the car swung round, its two front wheels hanging over the drop and then was dragged back onto terra firma.

When Mrs Hood telephoned later to see whether we had arrived home safely, she said that her son told her he was aghast when he came on the scene to find someone trying to get into the driving seat of a car about to topple over the drop. 'Thank God, I arrived in time to stop him', he said. Thank God indeed. In mitigation, the R.A.C. man was young and had probably never seen a car in such a pickle on such unstable ground.

There is a service in Pilleth Church on the last Sunday in every month and that will be my next visit to that lonely church. A prayer of thanksgiving for our rescue would not go amiss for, while lamenting the fate of those many soldiers killed at the Battle of Pilleth whose bones lie buried on Pilleth Hill, neither I nor Geoffrey had any wish to join them.

A mile or so back up the lane and we are once again on the highway and bowling along to Bleddfa, a little over two miles distant. This minuscule hamlet on the northern edge of the Radnor Forest has a rather dramatic name, for Bleddfa means 'The place of the wolf'. The English often suffer a little frisson when it comes to the pronunciation of Bleddfa, but it is really quite simple if one remembers that double D in Welsh is TH and F is pronounced V, thus making it Blethva. Some say it was named thus because the last of the wolves in Britain were killed there. That may well be as there is a strong tradition that the wolves being hunted in the Radnor Forest and the hills around were driven to this valley to be killed.

I always think that 'The place of the wolf' is rather a contradiction in terms - 'place' seems such a peaceful sounding word and 'wolf' certainly is not. A very dashing and romantic friend of mine, Claudia Burgoyne, lives on a mountain in Spain. Her house is called Huerta del Jabali which, she tells me, means 'The lair of the wild boar.' It is a name which always sends a little shiver frisking down my spine. I doubt whether 'The place of the wild boar' would have the same effect. Lair is a splendid word, much more suitable for savage beasts such as wolves and wild boars. It can be used to effect in conjunction with humans too. A few years ago my brother sent me a picture of Castle Rising, on the back he had written 'The last lair of the She-Wolf of France'. Isabella, the French Queen of Edward II of England, spent the last twenty-seven years of her life as a prisoner there. She was the evil queen who connived with Bishop Orleton in the unspeakably brutal murder of her husband, the King, in

Berkeley Castle, and she well deserved her fate. She was known to her husband's subjects as 'The She-Wolf of France'. Lair is a perfect word for her habitat. The last place of the She-Wolf of France sounds far too tame.

Enough of this, for here we are at Bleddfa and anything more peaceful it would be hard to imagine.

The thirteenth century church with its sturdy defensive tower and timber bell-turret stands cheek by jowl with the old school building. Facing them, a few paces away, is The Hundred House Inn, an ancient, white-painted hostelry as cosily old-fashioned with its polished wood tables and blazing fire as one could wish. In former times it was quite a place of importance for the Petty Sessions were held there. However, in 1867 this modest feather was removed from its cap and given to Pen-y-bont and later to Llandrindod Wells. The church has a fourteenth century king-post roof and a Jacobean pulpit and communion rail balusters. The tower is built on raised ground which was thought to be a Bronze Age burial mound until fairly recently. Doubt was cast on this theory following some excavations which revealed that a previous tower had collapsed and its remains might well be the mound.

The church, the school and the Inn on the other side of the lane form a sort of gateway to the sprinkling of old houses and farmsteads which make up the rest of this small hamlet, in its tranquil hollow beneath the encircling hills.

About twenty years ago, in 1974, The Bleddfa Trust was formed and became a registered charity aiming to provide, in the words of its founder, James Roose-Evans, 'A centre for those seeking through prayer, through the arts and through encounter with others, a deepening of spiritual understanding.' Exhibitions are held in the Old School Gallery and there are workshops, 'retreats' and a biannual festival. There is also a bookshop. From all over the country people make their way to experience the harmony, the interest in the arts and the friendship offered in this remote spot, the erstwhile 'Lair' of the wolf.

The way onward from Bleddfa to Pen-y-bont and Abbey Cwmhir grows ever more lonely and wild. The slopes of great hills under a wide sky dipping and sweeping on all sides. About three miles from Penybont, high above the village of Dolau, is the church of St Michaels All Angels. In icy weather the almost perpendicular angle of the path up to the church gate must give rise to quite a bit of involuntary skating. It was in this little church in 1952 that the bell ringers achieved a world record in bell ringing and were for some time in the *Guinness Book of Records*. They rang five peels with twenty- five thousand two hundred changes, more than one team of bell ringers had ever managed before. How magnificent they must have sounded ringing out from such an eminence over the hills and valleys around.

Nearing Pen-y-Bont, the road crosses a wide stretch of moorland where sheep and ponies wander at will. Not a place on which to run out of petrol on a winter's night. Quite suddenly the moor is behind us and we have arrived at a T-junction and facing us across the road is a rambling, many-gabled old inn, The Severn Arms. It used to be a well known coaching inn and was then, appropriately for an inn in the heart of the sheep farming country, called The Fleece. Its change of nomenclature in the early eighteen hundreds had nothing to do with the River Severn but was a compliment to a local landowner by that name.

In those coaching days the light streaming from the windows of the inn must have been a welcome sight to the passengers and coachmen as they left the moor behind. About twenty-five years ago, when I first visited the place, the atmosphere of those old times still hung about it. Smoke from centuries of puffing churchwardens had turned the walls in the great flagged taproom a deep custard yellow, every conceivable object hung from the blackened beams overhead, ancient pewter mugs and copper jugs, strange farming implements, bunches of dried hops, bewhiskered with the cobwebs of ages, and over the bar, in pride of place, the very Hirlas of a hunting horn, draped with crumbling cords and tassels, a relic of a bygone age. No-one knew where it came from or who put it there. In those days, on a high backed settle by the fire, an old, old woman often sat nursing a bowl of gruel, or just dozing, her head nodding on her chest. Many times I tried to talk to her but she would just smile and close her eyes.

The place was always a hive of activity, sturdy farmers coming and going, border collies at their heels, a constant low rumble of talk punctuated by shouts of laughter and sometimes bursts of song in those wonderfully melodious Welsh voices. It was a wonderful place to visit then. Last year I called again with some American friends, having told them of it's attractions, but it was too much to expect things to be as they were a quarter of a century ago. Outside the place looks the same, but inside all is now tidied up and modernised with bright little chairs with red-plastic covered seats, and never a whiff of the old settles and dark wood, the yellowing prints and the Aladdin's cave of objects that hung from the beams of that bustling, rumbustious old hostelry of days long gone by.

When Bradley came trotting along he did not, for once, visit the local inn, for if he had he would surely have mentioned it. Instead he writes 'Pen-y-bont, that pleasant village on the banks of the Ithon, which here sparkles cheerily between its ruddy banks.' He paused long enough for his artist to make a drawing of the Ithon and very attractive it looks with tree girt banks and the shallow river, curling round the small boulders in its path, just the place to picnic. Perhaps that is what they did.

The road from the inn to Llandrindod Wells gathers a scattering of houses, as it winds along for the last mile or so to reach an island at Crossgates. Here a left hand turn leads straight into Llandrindod itself, but that is a pleasure to be deferred, for we are now on our way to Abbey Cwmhir and that means a right turn at the island. Very soon, after a left turn down a lane that meanders for about five miles, we reach this most sequestered of villages.

On the left, just before entering the village, a scramble over rough, tufty grass and down a short slope brings us to a long green glade surrounded by the jagged stone remains of the walls of what was once a great Cistercian Abbey, Abbey Cwmhir - the abbey in the long valley. Built on the banks of the Clywedog, with a nave two hundred and forty-two feet long, this abbey in this remote spot among the Welsh hills was of such splendour in its day that it was larger than any abbey in Britain save Durham, Winchester and York.

There is some confusion among historians about the date of the founding and building of the abbey, but most authorities agree that it was either founded or refounded in 1143 by Cadwallon ap Madog, the Lord of Maelienydd. Alas, the unfortunate Cadwallon crossed the path of the Mortimers and met a violent death. The abbey then enjoyed the doubtful privilege of Mortimer patronage. During the conflict between Llewellyn the Great and Henry III in the year 1231, an abbey friar purposely sent the English in the wrong direction, straight into the arms of the enemy, thus causing their defeat. This brought coals of fire on to the Abbot's head, for the King, on hearing of the matter, plundered and burned the monastery grange as an act of vengeance. He was about to give the abbey the full treatment too, but somehow the Abbot managed to scratch together three-hundred marks and the King accepted the money in lieu. Forty-five years later, along with other Cistercian abbeys, the Abbot of Abbey Cwmhir defended Llewellyn ap Gruffyd in his quarrel with the

Bishop of Saint Asaph, and when Llewellyn himself was finally defeated in 1282 his headless body was brought to Abbey Cwmhir for burial. An inscribed memorial stone lies on the soft green turf of the nave commemorating this great Welsh warrior, Llewellyn the Last. The abbey was attacked and burned by Owain Glyndwr in 1401 and suffered again at the dissolution of the monasteries. After the Dissolution only three monks were left in the abbey and they were pensioned off and went to live at Monaughty.

In the reign of Elizabeth I, the abbey came into the possession of Mr William Fowler of the Inner Temple in Shrewsbury and this made the Fowlers the richest family in Radnorshire. When the Civil War ended, commissioners were sent out by Parliament to collect fines from those who supported the Royalist cause. The commis sioner appointed to Radnorshire had a very thin time, everyone being so poor, the only bright spot in the gloom being Richard Fowler of Abbey Cwmhir. The commissioner put pen to paper and the following quotation is attributed to him. 'Radnorsheer, poor Radnorsheer, never a park and never a deer, Never a Squire of fivehundred a year, But Richard Fowler of Abbey Cwmhir'.

During the Civil War, Richard Fowler garrisoned it for the Royalists but it was besieged and captured by the Parliamentarians in 1644 and reduced to ruins. The old abbey then passed through many hands until, in 1837, it was bought by Francis Phillips and it remained with that family until well into this century.

After the destruction of the abbey, a church was built from the abbey stone by Sir William Fowler, but by 1824 it was necessary to install new pewing and flooring and to carry out extensive restoration work. In spite of this by the eighteen-sixties things were so bad that an entirely new church was built, thanks to the generosity of the squire's sister, Miss Mary Beatrice Phillips. It is rather a strange looking building said to be twelfth century gothic in style. There are a number of modern stained glass windows of which the less said the better. Even the tactful R.H. Howse in his book on Radnorshire, a modern classic, remarks 'They could hardly be worse', and the gentle Francis Kilvert is moved to write of one of them as being 'very peculiar'. However, the church is bright and warm and comfortable so, no doubt, considered very satisfactory.

In 1870 Francis Kilvert, when staying at Llwynharried Hall, Nantmel, with the squire, visited the Phillips at Abbey Cwmhir about five miles distant. He set off with Evans Cecil, the squire's son, and they arrived at a time when Mr Phillips was having the place virtually rebuilt. In his diary Kilvert records the occasion thus; 'At 11.30 Mr Evans Cecil and I started to walk over the hills to Abbey Cwmhir. We heard the musical 'dinner call' from the farmhouse, summoning the labourers, at work on the farm, to their noon day meal. And from the fields came the answering cry showing that the call was a welcome one. We rapidly descended the steep bank and got into the valley making for the great house, belonging to Mr Phillips, the squire, where we hoped to get some luncheon. The masons were at work all round the great new house, giving finishing touches to their work, and the place was full of joiners and painters.'

'Mr and Mrs Philips were at luncheon in the servants' hall which they are using now as a dining room until the house is finished. They both came to the door and welcomed us most kindly. They had us in and gave us some very good cold mutton, bread and butter and sherry and some splendid Burton beer. Mr Phillips, an Eton and CW. CH. man, and a great sportsman. He was very pleasant and hospitable; but seemed shy and reserved, very quiet in manner. Mrs Phillips young, lively, girlish and rather pretty.' Francis Kilvert and his friend were then shown over the house and church and Mrs Phillips walked a little way towards the abbey with them. He also remarks in his diary on the inn, the Happy Union, and the inn sign 'of a Welshman riding a goat, holding in one hand a tankard of ale, in the other hand, I think, some bread and cheese, and wearing a leek in the hat'.

The famous Puckhorn Goat, Happy Union Inn

The Happy Union, whitewashed and pristine, with pretty gothic style windows, still faces the church across the lane and the Welshman still rides his puckhorn goat on the swinging inn sign. It is certain that Francis Kilvert would recognise Abbey Cwmhir today, for very little has changed since he and his friend came over the hills nearly a century and a quarter ago to enjoy a 'Splendid Burton beer' with squire Phillips and his pretty girlish wife.

Mrs Jones is the innkeeper now and she also runs the Post Office Stores across the inn yard. Friendly and helpful, she settled me in her bar parlour with a succession of steaming cups of coffee and fascinating

13　*Front view of the Happy Union, Abbey Cwmhir*

unpublished record of the history of Abbey Cwmhir, garnered together over the years by a certain Mr Maddox. In it he recounts how, in the late nineteenth century, the then Mrs Phillips, surely not the one remembered by Parson Kilvert, was a very autocratic woman and 'deeply conscious that her tenantry belonged to the lower orders, and treated them as such'. She demanded their absolute adherence to a strict moral code, she also had the very unpleasant habit of, when visiting the tenantry, marching into their kitchens and 'without so much as a by your leave, lifting the lid of any saucepan that happened to be on the fire'. This was not in order to murmur compliments of the 'That smells delicious' variety, but to make sure that the pot did not contain any odd rabbit or game bird from the estate.

One old inhabitant remembered, when she was a child, meeting Mrs Phillips riding her bicycle in the lane. Anxious not to put a foot wrong with this rather alarming lady of the manor, she hastily dropped a curtsey and said a shy, 'Good morning, Ma'am'. The imperious woman, however, was not satisfied with this and she bade the child retrace her steps and curtsey more deeply than before. This was known as learning to respect one's betters. Mollified, the grande dame then rode on, only stopping to order the blacksmith and his assistant to leave their work and push her up the gradient leading to the Hall. The wonder is that there were no cries of 'To the barricades' during her reign.

A short distance from the village, behind a frontier of fields and muddy tracks, there stands an old farm, Troedrhiwfelen, parts of which date back to 1380. Mrs Jones had given me the name of the farmer and suggested I call on him. She assured me he would have 'Any amount of tales to tell'. Alas, a bout of 'flu intervened and when at last I drove up the long track to the farm it was to learn that Gilbert Lewis, the farmer, had recently died. This was sad and disappointing news. However, I spent some time with his wife and grandson, Bernard Pugh, and they were able to tell me quite a bit about grandfather Lewis and the farm.

Troedrhiwfelen, I was told, means 'The mill at the foot of the yellow hill'. The yellow being the broom and gorse which covered the hill in his grandfather's day but now is no more. The farm was once part of the Abbey Cwmhir estate and in later years, when the estate came into the hands of the Phillips, Bernard Pugh's great grandfather bought it from them. In 1988, when Bernard was investigating some particularly damp ground at the farm, his excavations brought to light several ancient querns and mill stones and he has since reinstated the mill pond. For over one hundred and thirty years the Lewis family have farmed sheep and cattle at Troedrhiwfelen. Bernard says that he and others have often unearthed musket and cannon balls when digging on the farm. These date from the days when the Abbey was besieged during the Civil War.

Grandfather Lewis belonged to a gang of salmon poachers. The week before poaching activities, he would be busy preparing beacon torches. These were made by soaking bundles of sacking in lamp oil and fixing them to long poles. Then he and his brothers and various neighbours would black their faces with corks, which they burned over candles, and at nightfall off they would go to fish for salmon in the River Ithon. If the water bailiffs were alerted they dared not challenge them, for they knew that the poachers would stand and fight. A row of cork blackened hostile faces in the light of the oil beacons would be enough to send quite a hardy bailiff speeding back to his perch.

In his last illness, grandfather Lewis remembered those nights out with his friends on the River Ithon, defying the bailiffs and keeping their catch. When the family were gathered round his deathbed he stirred and chuckled. Bending low to catch his words, they heard him say, 'We weren't afraid of they, but they were afraid of we'. Then turning over he died.

ii. *Learning to respect one's betters. (See page 71)*

Chapter 6

Llandrindod Wells, Rhayader and Wild Wales

From proud Plynlimmon's rugged flanks
Three streams rush forth with broadening banks;
To thousands at their mouths who tarry,
Honey and gold and mead they carry.

Lewis Glyn Cothi, 1425 - 1486
Translated by George Borrow

Leaving the cosy farm parlour, I said good-bye to Bernard Pugh and his grandmother and set off down the long, muddy drive to join the winding lane leading to the highway and the Cross Gate roundabout.

This time I followed the signs for Llandrindod Wells and very soon was passing the rows of unpretentious Victorian villas on the outskirts of the own. When Bradley came this way at the turn of the century he wrote, 'I am not going to criticise the architecture of the red-brick villas that have sprung up by the score on these heath lands, nor wax sentimental because I can remember the gorse blooming where many rows of them now stand.' He also conceded the fact that 'Many of them look extremely comfortable.' As it happens, he was considerably more restrained in his comments on the place than many subsequent writers have been and he also points out that a few years before, when Llandrindod was about to enter its heyday, 'there was no town to despoil.'

Llandrindod was built from scratch in the mid-Victorian era by Victorian architects and builders and it is, therefore, quite naturally a Victorian town, and very handsome and substantial many of the buildings are. One might pick out especially the numerous hotels and boarding houses that were necessary to accommodate the vast numbers of people, eighty-thousand a year at the height of the town's popularity, who came to drink the waters.

73

This century it has been the fashion to decry anything Victorian and Llandrindod came in for more than its share of odium. One writer, David Verey, in his guide to Brecon, Radnor and Montgomery, written in the nineteen sixties, seems to have been very disgruntled. He refers to some of the buildings as being of 'peculiar hideousness' and he adds gloomily, 'the place is pretty dead all the year round'. Still searching for adverse comments, he winds up with 'round every corner one expects to find the sea, but there is no sea, only rain.' Poor Llandrindod Wells, how dare it have the temerity to site itself in the heart of some of the most beautiful country in Wales and not on the coastline.

Happily, thanks in part to the late Sir John Betjeman's pioneering efforts, attitudes have changed. We can be thankful indeed that Llandrindod was not discovered in the more recent past and the architecture of the sixties and seventies let loose in this beautiful Welsh heartland. Instead of fine and sturdy buildings of red or yellow brick, with pretty white-painted iron balconies and railings lining the broad streets, whole battalions of high rise flats might have loomed up, shutting out the light and being an eyesore for miles around.

The medicinal value of the saline and sulphur springs was well known as early as the sixteenth century but people who then wished to try them had to find accommodation in the local farmhouses. However, in 1749 a Shropshire entrepreneur named Grosvenor saw the possibilities and he converted an enormous old mansion, Llandrindod Hall, into an hotel with enough rooms to receive several hundred guests. People came from far and wide, not only to drink the waters but also to sample other delights on offer. Shooting, racing and gaming were all provided by the hotel.

Buried in the heart of Wild Wales, surrounded by wooded hills, in the days before the telephone, it is hardly surprising that members of the criminal fraternity and professional gamblers, scenting rich pickings conveniently far from the arm of the law, soon arrived and briskly plied their trade. Huge fortunes were won and lost and inevitably the place got a very bad name. The licentious goings on were such that by 1787 the hotel had become so notorious that even the then proprietor had his misgivings and, having been converted to Methodism, he decided that such debauchery was not in keeping with his new life style. To end it all he chose a somewhat drastic but undoubtedly effective method (no pun intended) and demolished the building lock, stock and barrel. The less salubrious of his clients promptly disappeared but those people whose primary interest was to drink the waters still came, putting up, as in the past, at the local farmhouses.

Early in the nineteenth century, there was a little flurry of interest in the place and the first Pump House Hotel was built. This was the principal hotel for many years. There was a double tariff, one for first class visitors and the other for lesser lights. The two classes were known as the House of Lords and the House of Commons respectively. In 1865 everything changed, with the coming of the railway. The old Pump House Hotel was swept away and a new one built together with two other hotels, The Rock and The Lanerch. The Lanerch, in fact, replaced a former building of that name.

In 1867, two years after the railway arrived, some members of The Woolhope Naturalist Club paid a visit to Llandrindod Wells which was then on the eve of the great building operations. Recalling this visit in the club transactions, a member wrote that again and again he heard other members on arrival ask 'Where is Llandrindod Wells? 'Why here to be sure', was the reply. 'But where is the town?', they persisted. 'There is no town.' 'The village then?' 'There is no village.' He goes on to say that 'The Pump House Hotel is quite invisible, until you reach the grove of firs, alders and oaks which surround and conceal it.' 'But,' he adds, 'if Llandrindod Wells must be fixed by a single definitive spot, the Pump House Hotel unquestionably represents it. Here all the life and spirit of the place concentrates itself. The air is so pure that you find yourself involuntarily stretching your chest to fill it to the utmost, it makes breathing a positive enjoyment. Alas!' he adds, ' the spirit of change has invaded the common, the city of Llandrindod Wells that is to be, is on paper, with its villas, its new church, its grand hotels and its boarding house, and there, unmistakably in the turf, are the lines neatly cut for considerable portions of it.'

About twenty years after this visit by the Woolhope Club, Arthur Bradley also came upon the new Pump House Hotel with which the Woolhope member was so enraptured but Bradley laments the passing of the one it replaced which was, he wrote, 'A mixture of simplicity and comfort and social discrimination.' Here he must have been referring to the Lords and Commons situation, which, indeed,prevailed until the nineteen hundreds. 'There was a large kitchen too' he continues, 'where the guests smoked their pipes and mixed their punch, under oak rafters decorated with festoons of lordly hams.'

Rooting about in old family papers recently, I found some letters written from the Pump House Hotel in the year 1898. In common with many other hotels in those days, a drawing of the place headed the writing paper and what a splendid emporium it looked. Even the roof is busy; a flag flutters from a pole fixed to its highest point and that is flanked by rows of puffing chimneys and a weather vane atop an elegant cupola. The foreground is a positive hive of activity, guests stroll around or stand in little groups chatting, carriages fly back and forth from the hotel entrance, and a band is playing from a little circular bandstand with a gaily striped awning.

14   *Pump House Hotel, Llandrindod Wells*

It was obviously 'Boom time' when the letter was written, for one reads 'The hotel is full and there are a great many Birmingham people staying here.' These included a Mrs Frances who was, according to the writer 'Rather cross-grained, and certainly made up'. Obviously not the done thing a hundred years ago!

The Pump House Hotel, alas, was demolished in the nineteen eighties but it is still possible to take the waters in this town of wide streets and fine buildings, of green parks and, in the summertime, of multitudes of flowers spilling over balconies and out of hanging baskets like rainbow waterfalls. Llandrindod Wells is certainly a rather special town because it is very probably the only completely Victorian one in the whole of these islands.

Back at the Crossgates roundabout we take the last of the roads radiating from it and are on our way to Rhayader and the Elan Valley about eight miles distant. On our right, standing well back from the road a many gabled house, and on our left, one of the last of a dying breed, motel. Then almost at once we are driving through the hamlet of Gwstre and past a few sad looking houses strung out along the road but what a world of grandeur and wild beauty they lead us to.

The rounded slopes of the hills have given way to more craggy and robust heights and gone, for the most part, are the ubiquitous plantations of alien firs which so often stand out on distant skylines or march in serried ranks down the emerald and russet steeps.

A few miles along the road, in this lonely and sparsely populated countryside, there is a right-hand turn up a short hill to the village of Nantmel. The lane trails past the old stone village school and on up the hill to the church of Saint Cynlo. Flagged steps lead through an ancient beamed lych-gate with a stone tiled roof, then up another of Arthur Bradley's 'kill horse' paths and we are at the porch. From there the view, a wide panorama of old farmsteads and cottages, swooping hills and deep valleys, cannot fail to thrill.

Near to the porch, among the lichen covered gravestones, there is a sundial mounted on a cylinder of what appears to be polished pink granite. The sundial is dated 1775 but the inscription on the cylinder is in memory of a young pilot in the Royal Australian Airforce who was born in 1909 and died in 1950. His name was Pierson Jones and with a good Welsh name like that I suppose he came back to the land of his fathers for burial. Whenever I see a sundial I am reminded of Hilaire Belloc's amusing couplet,

'I am a sundial and I make a botch,
Of something done far better by a watch.'

Irreverent thoughts in a churchyard perhaps, but I think Pierson Jones would have chuckled. As is so often sadly the case these days, the church was locked. But to stand in the porch and look out over the many old yews below is reward enough for the climb.

It was while staying at nearby Llwynharried Hall in 1830 that Parson Kilvert and the squire's son set off to climb the hill looming up behind Nantmel to visit Mr Phillips of Abbey Cwmhir and enjoy the pot luck luncheon.

The entrance to Rhayader is rather depressing, the road being lined with terraces of uninspiring modern houses, but then the entrances to many towns belie the treats in store. Rhayader used to be known by the locals as Bwgy which was a contraction of Bach Gwy, the Little Wye. This was the name of a stream which once coursed down North Street. The town is the main gateway to the Elan Valley, which has become known, with justification, as 'The Welsh Lake District' for it is where a great necklace of reservoirs is strung along a valley of surpassing beauty. It is a mixture of brick and stone Victorian houses with, here and there, a sprinkling of Georgian elegance, such as the fine grey stone house in North Street with its pretty fanlight and many paned, white-painted windows. In this same street, a little further along on the opposite side, is a building which is most unprepossessing on the exterior being very reminiscent of a north country mill, a sign outside proudly proclaims, 'Workhouse Restaurant'. This needed investigation and indeed the place had been a workhouse and was built as such in the nineteenth century. However, anything less like a Dickensian establishment for the homeless it would be hard to find, for now it is a very comfortable hotel and restaurant.

Rhayader is a busy little market town with important sheep and cattle sales in the spring and autumn. Market day is Wednesday and the licence to hold the weekly market was granted nearly eight hundred years ago in the reign of Henry III. The town once had a castle which was built in 1177, not by a marauding Border Baron, but by the great Welshman, Lord Rhys. However, the Mortimers had their eyes on it, which usually meant the kiss of death one way or another. After they captured it, it was seized and burnt by another great Welshman, Llewellyn the Great. Only a grassy mound and some crumbling stones now remain.

The countryside around Rhayader is one of steep hills and rich pasture land and countless little streams that, bell-clear, scamper along over stony beds to join the Wye and Ithon. At the junction of the four main streets in the town, is one of those ornate stone clock towers so beloved of little Welsh towns. In the case of Rhayader the tower is combined with a war memorial, the names of the fallen being inscribed on the base. These clock towers do seem to have rather an unfortunate effect on various writers. I have several times read adverse remarks about them in books on Wales and the Border country. Some writers reveal an almost vitriolic dislike. David Verey, for instance, in his very interesting book on Mid-Wales refers, to Rhayader's clock tower as 'hideous'.

There must be something about towns set in mountainous country that triggers the desire for such a tower. In southern Germany and the Austrian and Swiss Alpine towns there is quite a profusion of them. Perhaps it is that they provide a focal point, other than a church, in parishes where many of the townsfolk live in remote farmsteads and houses tucked away in the folds of the hills.

I like them. They are friendly and dependable and often they sport amusing little bits and bobs, concession to some past stone mason's flight of fancy. Sometimes they are girdled with bright flower beds and sometimes, as at Knighton, a lively weekly market takes place around them. At all events they provide a heart for many little towns that would be the poorer without them.

15   *Rhayader Town Clock*

There are a number of inns in Rhayader and many of them looked most inviting but I much wanted to visit one in particular, The Lion Royal, because it was here that, on Tuesday June 23rd in 1896, those dear erudite gentlemen of The Woolhope Naturalist Club 'Fully aware' as their President, Cecil Moore, records in the club transactions, 'that they were travelling to a range of hills in Radnorshire where the yearly average (rainfall) is 68 inches the visitors took the precaution of providing themselves with such light waterproof coats as the heat of the summer permitted.' They were en route for the Elan Valley to 'Visit the works of the proposed Birmingham water supply.' Cecil Moore continues, 'Rhayader was reached, punctual to the programme, at 9.45am. Mr Hope Edwards, proprietor of the Royal Lion, was equal to the occasion and eighty-five seats were provided in his carriages in a manner creditable to the little town and to himself in particular.' For some reason this establishment is now known as the Lion Royal.

I drove under the stable arch at the Lion Royal and into the yard from which that happy band of Woolhopeans must have emerged, well raincoated and chattering with excitement and anticipation. The yard was empty save for a short line of washing blowing in the wind. I parked the car and walked round to the entrance. Standing in the deserted hall, I called out 'Hello! Hello! Anybody there?' Nothing. I tried again, nothing. I then opened various doors, nothing; and no one in sight. I pressed two old-fashioned bell pushes on the hall wall labelled 'Boots' and 'Chambermaid'; still nothing, not a sound. This seemed a far cry from that cheerful establishment presided over by the efficient Mr Hope Edwards with its stable yard full of horses and carriages all at the ready to transport those appreciative members of the Woolhope Club to the Elan Valley almost one hundred years ago.

The only other occupant of the hall was a stuffed fish in a glass case on the wall. His bleary regard was a little unnerving and even had a Boots or a chambermaid or, indeed, anyone else miraculously materialised, I had already decided to seek elsewhere for sustenance, hopefully in more welcoming surroundings.

The year after the Woolhope Club visited the Elan Valley the Birmingham City Council en bloc also visited it. A delightful old photograph shows some of them top-hatted and be-bowlered foregath-

16 *At 6.30 a.m. the City fathers gather at Birmingham for the visit to Elan Valley*

ering in Birmingham ready for the journey. Another taken on the site of the forthcoming dams, which by then was a hive of activity, shows them looking somewhat less dignified, seated in a long row of open cattle trucks which had transported them on the last stage of their journey from Rhayader to the Elan Valley. Another photograph depicts some of the

17 *For the City fathers it is now a case of shiver and long for home*

Council members seated on the ground, backs to a stone wall, and look
ing unutterably miserable. On the back of the photograph someone has
written 'The City fathers shiver and wish for home'. I know the feeling!

Foregoing the delights of the Lion Royal or Royal Lion, I decided to
have my 'ploughmans' in The Triangle at Cwmdauddwr. It had been
recommended to me by Lucy Burton who lives in the town and is a font
of wisdom about it and very helpful indeed. Cwmdauddwr (the valley of
the two waters) might almost be called a continuation of Rhayader on the
road to the Elan Valley and, although it has become technically part of
the town, it still retains its own identity and has its own church.

A turning left, opposite the Cwmdauddwr Arms, leads to the Triangle.
A pretty little fifteenth century weather-boarded building, so situated
that from the windows of the bar parlour can be seen the infant Wye
flowing past and so near to the inn that sitting at the back of the room,
with only water backed by hills visible from the windows, one has the
impression of being on a river boat. The ceilings of the inn are so low that
a hole has had to be cut in the floor to facilitate darts playing.

Blue and white plates and polished brass gleam on the walls of this old,
drover's inn and if the place cries out for an inglenook and blazing log
fire, as once there must have been, well, one can't have everything. The

81

bar parlour was warm and comfortable and the ploughman's lunch very good, and then, as an added bonus, there was Brian Hughes. Brian came over as I was talking to Jackie, the pleasant dark-haired barmaid. He had heard me discussing the dams and he said that, although he was now a local postman, in his youth he had worked on the Claerwen dam. The construction of this particular dam began in 1946 and, said Brian, 'It was opened by the Queen elect in 1952.' Brian was very anxious that I should get this correctly. 'She was the Queen elect then, not the Queen, because it was before her coronation.' Brian, who was fifteen years old and had just left school when he went to work on the dams, joined a team of electricians on the site. 'There were two ship's engines and three English Electric generators' he said, 'and there were thirty-two crushing motors on the crushing plant and many, many electric derricks and cranes.' I would like to have heard more but time was flying and I still had the dams to visit again so, regretfully, I left to continue my peregrinations. The Triangle is a pleasant place to pause a while and the 'ploughmans' is excellent and, who knows, you might meet Brian Hughes.

Ahead, on the road from Cwmdaudder to the dams, can be seen the huge bulk of two great craggy hills framing the flashing white waterfall of the Caban Coch Dam. Many times, when travelling this road, I have seen a buzzard lazily hovering before making his lightning swoop on some hapless victim in the field below, for this is buzzard country and these great hawks range high and wide in the Welsh skies.

In the late eighteen hundreds the City of Birmingham was very aware that it would need a greatly increased supply of water to deal with the rapidly growing population. A scheme was devised, following those of Glasgow and Liverpool, in which water would be taken from the distant hills instead of locally. A plan to do this was drawn up by the well-known engineer, James Mansergh, and received the approval of Parliament in 1892. In August, 1893 the great work began. Tributaries of the rivers Wye, Elan and Claerwen rise in the Welsh hills and, as they journey down to the valleys, hundreds of streams and rivulets run into them. The first of the great reservoirs to contain this water was built between 1892 and 1907 and nearly half-a-century later the great Claerwen reservoir joined them. Although the reservoirs in the first group were not finished until 1907, the work was sufficiently advanced by 1904 for the King, Edward VII, accompanied by Queen Alexandra, to open formally the new water works. The King was nearly half-an-hour late for the ceremony, the royal train having come to a halt on the way to Rhayader because it was unable to climb a steep incline. It was said at the time that the King was not best pleased and his irritation was apparent. The ladies on board were also a bit disgruntled, their frills and furbelows having received a liberal sprinkling of smuts in a tunnel. Smuts were obviously quite a problem for, in a printed leaflet of instructions issued on the day and given to each council member, there is a warning, 'Lady visitors are reminded that the Corporation train will pass through the Rhayader tunnel, two-hundred and thirty-yards long on both outward and return journeys. They are accordingly recommended to be provided with the means of protecting their garments against smoke.' On the same leaflet gentlemen were instructed to wear 'Black coats and silk hats.'

21   *Birmingham City Council at Elan Valley May 28, 1897*

However, it was a great occasion. The sun was shining, Rhayader was bedecked with flowers and flags and, from far and wide, people were travelling, in wagonnettes or traps, on foot or on bicycles, making their way to Rhayader town and the Elan Valley to take part in the day's jollifications. An enormous number of dignitaries, including the Lord-Lieutenant and the High-Sheriff of Radnorshire, The Earl and Countess of Powys, the Lord Bishop of Saint David's and the Lord Mayor of

Birmingham awaited the arrival of the King and Queen at Rhayader station. A guard of honour of the First Herefordshire Regiment was at the ready, indeed, several other regiments, including the Montgomery Imperial Yeomanry and the King's Shropshire Light Infantry, shared the various duties on that great day.

The Lord Mayor of Birmingham, Alderman Hallewell Rogers, welcomed the King at the station, whereupon His Majesty conferred a knighthood on him. This was most fortuitous for the Alderman who, as it happened, had only been made Lord Mayor for that particular year by stepping into the shoes of the Mayor elect, Councillor G.H. Johnson, who had stepped down because of ill-health. Having dealt with Alderman Hallewell Rogers, the King then turned a silver and gold wheel thus releasing the first water from those wild and beautiful rivers in the very heart of Wales to surge and dash along its seventy-five mile long journey to the great Midland city of Birmingham.

During luncheon, which was served in a large marquee, the Royal Party was serenaded by the famous choir of Mr W. Thomas of Llandrindod Wells and a band of harps. Smuts were forgotten and the King and his company, having enjoyed a splendid luncheon in matchless surroundings and received much adulation, appeared very gruntled and the day ended in smiles.

Just below the Caban Coch Dam a little slip road to the left leads to Elan village. Until fairly recently, the way to the village lay over a small suspension bridge spanning the river. However, latterly the bridge was found to be unsafe and a temporary one now crosses the river alongside it. I hope it really is temporary because the original bridge, in its coat of pristine white, seemed to skip joyously over the water and the present one just plods. Elan village was built to house the maintenance workers on the dams. The houses are in stone and most of them face the river across a green mead shaded by great trees. The river here is shallow and clear and frisks along, surging and eddying around smooth boulders. There is a church and a school and everything is stone built and, like all else to do with the dams, well built and very attractive.

There was a village on this site before the present one but it was of a very different kind. It was built to house over one thousand workmen engaged in the building of the dams and consisted mainly of wooden huts. There was also a chapel and next to it a prison and some stables. On the hill about one-hundred and fifty-feet up was the Fever and Infectious Diseases Hospital.

Another building, which was known as 'The Doss House', contained two dormitories with nineteen beds in each and a superintendent known as the 'Chucker out'. This was where candidates for employment on the dams were kept after application in order to be deloused and vetted. Each candidate had a bath while his clothes were being disinfected. He was then privileged to pay three-pence for his night's lodging and to pay for his food 'according to his appetite'. To be fair the delousing was probably a necessary precaution in most cases and would help to ensure a reduction in illness among the work force but, for those individuals who were clean, it must have been a very humiliating experience.

A visitor to the village in 1890 recalled, 'In this secluded valley, begirt with wooded hills, penetrated by the babbling River Elan, presenting an exquisite blending of woodland and river scenery, the city (Birmingham) which claims to be the best governed in the kingdom, has verified its claim. The inhabitants under its enviable regime have settled in pleasant places, even in Arcadia.'

Running along beside the reservoirs is a splendid road so that it is possible to drive around all of them. The section of road skirting the Caban Coch reservoir lies at the foot of rugged heights down which bright, leaping ribbons of water cascade over mossy rocks and under canopies of fern to cross beneath the road and empty their mountain freshness in the great man-made lake. Many trees have found footholds on the steep hillside so that the road runs through a virtual glade. On the far side of the reservoir the hills are less precipitous and their green slopes are chequered with patches of heather and bracken and little copses of

19   *Peny-garrog Dam*

85

trees. When the dams were built, a church, a chapel, many farmsteads, a hamlet and two great houses with their estates Cwm Elan, (the roe valley), and Nantgwyllt, (the wild brook) were submerged. The church lies ninety-feet beneath the waters of the Caban Coch Dam, and the estates of Cwm Elan and Nantgwyllt at forty- and sixty-feet respectively.

Cwm Elan belonged to a Wiltshire family named Grove, they were cousins of the poet, Percy Bysshe Shelley. In 1810 Shelley was sent down from Oxford for foolishly publishing, against the pleas of his doting father, a pamphlet *'The Necessity of Atheism'*. At the time he was half engaged to Harriet Grove, the daughter of these cousins and, presumably to escape parental reproaches as a result of his stupidity, he rushed off to stay in their house in this secluded and beautiful part of Wales.

The poet's mood while there was mainly one of depression, and he later wrote of the period,

> The moonlight was my dearer day
> Then would I wander far away
> And lingering on the wild brook shore
> To hear its unremitting roar
> Would lose in the ideal flow
> All sense of overwhelming woe
> Or at the noiseless noon of night
> Would climb some heathy mountain height
> And listen to the mystic sound
> That stole in fitful gusts around.

Arthur Bradley remembered Cwm Elan before the inundation as 'A plain four storied house with lofty wings nestling at the foot of an almost perpendicular hill, thickly clad to the summit with pines and hemlocks and oaks.' Bradley also recalls meeting an old, old woman who, reminiscing, remembered Shelley in some of his lighter moments. She told Bradley that he used to 'Amuse himself by descending the rushing torrent of the Elan on a plank and, on one occasion at any rate, sharing his narrow barque with a protesting cat.' It was while he was at Cwm Elan that Shelley received a letter from Harriet Westbrook, a school friend of his sister Elizabeth, as a result of which he promptly dropped Harriet Grove who, in the light of his subsequent behaviour, could congratulate herself on a lucky escape. He and Harriet Westbrook then eloped. This caused another furore especially as Harriet was only sixteen years old at the time. Once more away he sped to the romantic beauty of the Elan

Valley, this time dragging his child bride with him. They did not stay at Cwm Elan, instead Shelley rented Nantgwyllt, which was about a mile away from his cousin's place. The Woolhope Club members, when they visited the area in 1896, remembered Nantgwyllt as 'This plain massive charmingly situated mansion'. At about the time they saw it, it was the home of the resident engineer for the dam building operation, Mr E.N. Yourdi. Somewhere I read a delightful contemporary description of him but I cannot remember where. However, I made a note of it and here it is. 'This unusual little man, diminutive and moustachioed, who rushes here, there and everywhere over the Elan Valley was of Greek extraction, his father was Greek Consul at Cork and married an Irish woman.' The inhabitants of Nantgwyllt seem to have been anything but run of the mill.

At Nantgwyllt, the black cloud of Shelley's Oxford expulsion had lifted. For a while the two young lovers were idyllicly happy in those most romantic of surroundings. Shelley wrote that they were 'Embosomed in the solitude of mountains, woods, rivers, silent, solitary and old, among ghosts, witches, fairies and hobgoblins.' However, as the months passed and his mercurial temperament asserted itself, he eventually began his life of wandering. Harriet dutifully followed him from pillar to post, supporting him in all his wild schemes but, alas, she no longer captivated him. When he fell passionately in love with Mary Godwin and ran off with her, Harriet, whom he had magnanimously invited to be part of a menage à trois, refused to do so, particularly since he also added Claire Clairmont, Mary's half sister, to his harem. Most indignant that Harriet should decline this offer, Shelley behaved with monstrous selfishness and wrote Harriet a letter of such unpleasantness that the poor, bewildered and wretchedly unhappy girl, jumped into the Serpentine and drowned herself. The poet appeared quite unmoved by the tragedy, insisting that Harriet had behaved very badly and that he himself was a monument of propriety.

Six years after the despairing Harriet's sad death, in the summer of 1822, Shelley, too, was drowned, while sailing with a friend in Italy.

During the great drought of the late nineteen-seventies, a friend of mine, Paddy Salt and her daughter Judith, and I and my son Rupert, together with two of his school friends, took a picnic to high above the dams where the River Elan tumbles along its rocky bed. We cooled a bottle of wine in the shallows and spread our goodies under the shade of an oak tree on the grassy bank which, being so close to the water, unlike the poor, parched and arid fields of that burning summer, had remained a verdant green. As the afternoon wore on Judith, or 'Queen Jude' as the boys christened her, and the others, full of high spirits in those first days after the end of term, cavorted so much on the river bank that inevitably one after the other they fell into the water. This was little problem, soggy shorts were removed and with towels wrapped round their waists we set off for home.

When we were driving along the stretch of road by the Caban Coch Dam, we saw that the waters had completely disappeared, leaving the bed of the lake quite dry, and there, after having been submerged fathoms deep for nearly three-quarters of a century, were great stretches of stone wall, which had once surrounded part of the garden of the old mansion of Nantgwyllt, standing sturdily strong with even the coping stones in place.

We scrambled down the embankment and walked towards this extraordinary reminder of the past. The gateway in the wall was not important enough to have been the main entrance for such a sizeable house and it certainly would not have accommodated carriages. Was it just the tradesman's entrance? Or perhaps the wall once surrounded a kitchen garden? If so, were there peaches and espalier pears sunning themselves on it in those halcyon early days of marriage, when Harriet and Shelley lived at Nantgwyllt? And did Shelley chase Harriet laughing through rows of raspberry canes or share with her a bowl of fresh picked strawberries? Strange that this house, the scene of their early happiness, should sink beneath the waters, as both Harriet and her wandering poet had done long ago and far away.

In this romantic frame of mind, I decided to photograph 'Queen Jude' and one of the boys standing in the gateway. If not a latter day poet and his bride, they were at least the same age as Shelley and Harriet when they lived at Nantgwyllt. It was not to be. The boys girded in towel loin-cloths insisted on all being taken and 'Queen Jude' refused to be taken. However, I took my photograph, notwithstanding, reasoning that, when this drought was over, it would probably never again be possible to photograph any part of Nantgwyllt. Romantic the picture is not, but at least it shows the wall and the gateway.

Arthur Bradley, standing on the hills above Cwm Elan and Nantgwyllt before the deluge, reflected 'Not only Cwm Elan and Nantgwyllt, but the scanty homesteads with their protecting groves and the humble cottage with its mossy roof that here and there have taken firm root in the deep valley are all to be the abodes of slimy eels and the lair of monster trout.' He continues, 'May you and I, dear reader, be alive to come again and behold a spectacle upon whose possibilities I dare not venture to enlarge'.

Bradley did visit the Elan Valley again, it was thirty years later and he was an old man of seventy-eight years. He was writing what he called 'Almost certainly the last of my many books on Wales and the March'. I think I must let him finish this chapter in his own inimitable way. 'The old seat of Nantgwyllt', he wrote, 'nestling under the mountain foot where the deep vales of Elan and Claerwen meet, the mansion of Cwm Elan a mile up the former sream which harboured in turn the poet Shelley and his hapless Harriet, and then stood among the ancient groves as the young poet knew and sung of them, all are now this long time sunk beneath the dark waters, and the angler may cast his fly, as in truth I have often done myself, far above where their hearth fires once burned.'

20 *Nantgwyllt wall and gateway exposed by the drought of the 1970s (photograph by Veronica Thackeray)*

21   *Birmingham City Council at Elan Valley May 28, 1897*

Chapter 7

Cefn Einion & Bishop's Castle

The road from Clun to Bishop's Castle is a typical up hill and down dale border road running between green meadows and little copses which straggle down from the surrounding hills. Now and again a lane wanders off from the highway into the valleys or climbs the lower slopes. Tempted by one of these signposted Cefn Einion, I turned off to the left.

Cefn Einion was once famous for the quality of its smocks. This was in the days when every shepherd in this sheep-rearing border country wore one and aspired to have a special one for Sundays. Sunday ones were beautifully smocked and embroidered, always in self coloured cottons on heavy cream material, often linen. In Clun Museum there is an example of one of these Sunday smocks and Mrs Hudson, the curator of the museum, told me that Queen Alexandra actually purchased smocks from Cefn Einion. A smock seems a rather unlikely garment for a queen to buy and one wonders whether she was emulating Marie Antoinette and creating an idyllic farm, like the Petit Trianon at Versailles where the French Queen and her ladies and courtiers would play at being shepherds and dairymaids.

The lane to Cefn Einion resembles a switch back, so steep are the ups and downs. It is the sort of lane Arthur Bradley, in his pony and trap, would have referred to as 'Kill horse'. After a mile or two there is a small roadside chapel set sufficiently far from the hamlet to ensure that the congregation was far too winded on arrival to be anything but docile while trying to get their breath back for the homeward run.

Cefn Einion itself is a very small hamlet, just a grouping of a few cottages, in a hollow formed by two steep hills. Remarkable to think of a handful of women stitching away by the light of oil lamps, during the long winter evenings, or sitting in their little gardens in the summer, needles flying, producing work that would, unofficially at least, be by Royal Appointment. Leaving the hamlet behind, the road climbs high to join once again the Clun-Bishop's Castle highway where, almost immediately, it winds through the village of Colebatch. This village seems to consist of several old homesteads and farmhouses strung out along the road and once, when I asked a group of young people the way to the church, the reply was 'There isn't one and there isn't a pub either'. In Bradley's day this would have presented no problem for, at the turn of the century, nearby Bishop's Castle boasted twelve such temples of refreshment and a great many private houses had a licence to brew their own ale.

Very soon after Colebatch a left hand turn leads into the old market town. Bishop's Castle used to be called Lydbury Castle but that was some centuries ago, when Offa was King of Mercia. The story of the change of name is one of love, greed and ruthless intrigue. King Offa had a beautiful daughter named Elfrida and Ethelbert, the King of East Anglia, fell deeply in love with her. Offa himself was not against the two young people marrying but his wife was. She feared that, if the marriage took place, Ethelbert might supplant Offa thus considerably reducing her status. Brooding on this she conceived a plan to murder her daughter's suitor. She invited him to visit her and when he arrived graciously indicated that he be seated in a certain chair. She had arranged for this particular chair to be placed over a trap door covering a deep pit. When the unsuspecting King was nicely settled the trap door opened and he and chair together dropped in to the pit where the evil women's servants fell upon him and stabbed him to death.

Ethelbert was buried at Hereford and very soon after his death people began to experience miraculous cures, when visiting his grave. He was duly canonised and Hereford Cathedral was built over his tomb. It is thought that Offa himself was not party to the murder but, nevertheless, he is known to have done penance for it.

One of the cures resulting from a visit to Ethelbert's tomb was that of Egwin Shakehead who suffered from the palsy. So grateful was he for his recovery that he gave his entire manor of Lydbury, consisting of eighty-thousand acres, to the Bishop of Hereford and from then on Lydbury Castle became Bishop's Castle which, as the centuries passed, grew to a place of considerable importance. It was a municipal borough and returned two members of parliament until 1967. It still retains a Mayor and Council.

On the right hand side on entering the town, there is a fine sixteenth century black and white house and here lived in the fairly recent past the vicar of Mainstone. His church was about three miles from Bishop's Castle and every Sunday he would order a car from the local garage to take him to the services. Consequently, every Saturday various employees at the garage spent some time giving an available vehicle a good spit and polish. Not unnaturally this was not a popular chore on a Saturday afternoon but eventually the time spent was dramatically halved. One of their number pointed out that if the vicar boarded and alighted on the same side, he need only ever see one half of the car. With a little judicious manoeuvring this was achieved and the parson pranced in and out of church quite unaware of the schizophrenic nature of his conveyance.

Diagonally opposite the vicar of Mainstone's house is the Church of Saint John the Baptist. The original church was almost destroyed in the Civil War but was restored in 1666. Much later in the nineteenth century, it was, apart from the tower, entirely rebuilt. Bishop's Castle and neighbouring Clun grew so exasperated with both sides and their wanton destruction during the Civil War that about a thousand men from the two places banded together to defend their towns from the onslaughts of either side. They declared they were neither for the King nor for the Parliament but 'stood only upon their own guard for the preservation of their lives and fortunes.'

In the graveyard, near the tower, there is a very interesting old gravestone. The inscription in French reads 'To the memory of Louis Paces, Lieutenant-Colonel of the Light Horse, Chevalier of the military orders of the two Scillies and of Spain. Died at Bishop's Castle, May 1st 1814, aged forty years.' During the Napoleonic Wars many French prisoners were billeted at Bishop's Castle. Indeed, the first milestone on the road to Shrewsbury is known locally as Frenchman's mile, because it marks the limit of the parole walks allowed to the prisoners of war.

The lych-gate, at the entrance to the church, looks up Church Street, the main street in this little town, to where the eighteenth century Town Hall, with its pretty little white painted cupola, is built across the upper end. This old street climbs steadily, becoming steeper as it goes. Quaint timber-framed cottages, small, elegant Georgian houses, solid Victorian dwellings and the fascinating Tudor Porch House, home in its time for many of those French prisoners of war, are all here, cheek by jowl, while between them numerous little 'Shuts' or alleyways lead off, revealing intriguing glimpses of old courtyards redolent of bygone days.

22   *Bishop's Castle - looking down the main street*

Tucked away to the left of the Town Hall is the early seventeenth century 'house on crutches', so called because the projecting first floor is supported by wooden pillars. Sadly, it was neglected until recently but has now been restored and houses an admirable museum.

Behind the Town Hall is the market square and away to the left the Castle Hotel and the bowling green, each being built on part of the site of the castle. Various streets lead off from the market square, among them Bull Street. Here lives the artist, Mary Jones. Her tall many windowed house with its terracotta pink stucco has a whiff of Tuscany about it. The little garden behind, bounded by the walls of the middle bailey, with its old steps lined with pots and containers of flowers, adds to the Mediterranean feel. All this, however, belies the interior which, with its gleaming oak floors and refectory table, its old beams and jugs of country flowers, is as English as apple tart and cream.

It was Mary Jones who took me on a ramble around Bishop's Castle, showing me much I might have missed on my own, and introducing me to Mrs Jarvis and Mr Roberts, both of whom had fascinating stories to tell. Mr and Mrs Jarvis live in Salop Street, one of the streets leading off from the market square. Mr Jarvis was Mayor of Bishop's Castle six times. 'When we lost our borough status', Mrs Jarvis said, 'the Mayor of Much Wenlock was an inspiration to us all and rallied us in our successful fight to keep our Mayor.' Mrs Jarvis's grandfather was a wheelwright and coffin maker and he built his own house. It was a snatch house, she said, ' You could snatch a bit of ground and start building on it and, if you got a chimney up by the morning, it was yours'. Once the position was established, it was quite usual to demolish the wooden edifice and build a more permanent dwelling in brick or stone. Mrs Jarvis showed me an old photograph of her grandparents' snatch house. It was taken in 1843 and a great pile of bricks stands nearby ready for the metamorphosis.

'My father was the Bishop's Castle coal merchant', she continued, 'and he also kept a few cows. He was away all day on Sundays, tramping many miles to preach in Methodist churches. Most people didn't have cars in those days and no one in Bishop's Castle did. I can remember vividly when the first car came to Bishop's Castle. I was a small girl at the time and every morning, at eleven o'clock, my mother allowed me to go to the baker's shop in the market square to buy myself a hot ha'penny bun. One morning, there was a great deal of shouting and running hither and thither and a lot of strange explosive noises. My mother rushed out to find me and then we realised the uproar was caused by the first car to come through our town. When the new high school was built, I was one of the first pupils. Lady Clive came to perform the opening ceremony, it was all very exciting, but our new school uniforms hadn't arrived, so all we children had to wear our Sunday best. I was so proud of my dress, it was dark green and lavishly embroidered with gold beads.'

The mention of Lady Clive reminded me of a story told me a week or two before, by a friend living near Montgomery. I mentioned that I had always wanted to see Lymore, the house in Montgomery in which Lord Edward Herbert, famous for his bravery, his beauty and his writing, was born. He lived there for many years, after the family castle at Montgomery was dismantled at the close of the Civil War. Arthur Bradley, who saw the house in the latter part of the last century, writes of it as 'The beautiful timbered house of Lymore where the autobiography (Lord Herbert's) was mostly written and first deposited ... with its dark august wood-lands and twin pools glittering like jewels amid the surrounding greenery'. At that time the house belonged to Lord Clive and Bradley refers to it as 'Probably the largest timbered mansion on the Marches.' During his visit, he wanders from room to room, commenting that 'they are virtually stripped of furniture', but he adds, 'Most of the numerous square, low pitched chambers upstairs contain four-poster beds, hangings and wallpapers. Lymore as regards its upper stories, except for the fact of being kept clean and aired, suggests a house suddenly abandoned and locked up in the time of George II and recently opened. At any rate the galleries of silent half furnished long forgotten rooms are extremely realistic and as a matter of fact have not been inhabited since about 1750.'

I longed to see this old house, with its atmosphere of desolation and its sense of the past. Alas, I was told that it gradually fell into a ruinous state and was demolished many years ago. How could this be allowed to happen? How tragic that this wonderful old place, repository of so much history and home for so long of the Herberts, a family of whom Bradley remarks 'Surely no stock in Britain counts so many outstanding members of its name as the Herberts ', should be destroyed? Lymore was sold before being demolished and my Montgomery friend told me that on the day of the sale a platform was erected in the house on which the auctioneer sat, together with Lady Clive. When the final bid came the auctioneer raised his gavel and crying 'Going, going, gone' he brought it down with a bang, whereupon there was a loud cracking noise and a large hole appeared in the platform of rotten floor boards through which Lady Clive promptly disappeared. 'Eclipse of stout party' as *Punch* would say. As Mrs Jarvis had always lived in the area, I asked her if this really had happened. 'Oh yes indeed,' she replied, 'and my grandfather was on the platform at the time and he went down with her'. This gave the whole incident a nautical flavour. One envisaged an impressive liner and an attendant tug vanishing beneath the waves.

'There were quite a few characters in Bishop's Castle in the old days', said Mrs Jarvis, 'and like most places there was a great deal of drunkenness. I remember when the vicar we had then met a local man who was almost always drunk. "Well, well", he said reprovingly, "drunk again?" "Dear me", replied the inebriated one, "never mind vicar, I am too".'

I was sad to leave Mrs Jarvis and her little sitting room, so warm and inviting, but a few hundred yards along, in Salop Street is The Three Tuns, an old coaching hostelry I much wanted to visit, for when Arthur Bradley came to Bishop's Castle it was there that he spent a night and wrote about it afterwards in his book.

Arthur Bradley set off for Bishop's Castle on a hot summer's day in the 1880's and, as he trotted along in his trap, he was rather surprised to see a positive menagerie of animals coming towards him. A bull, a mare and foal, a Shropshire ram and a shire horse passed him, all with large notices hung round their necks proclaiming them first, second and third prize winners. It gradually dawned on him that he had picked the annual fair day to visit the town. His first impulse was to bypass the place and make for somewhere else, however, there was such an ominous lowering of clouds in the south-west that he felt he would have to chance his luck and hope that, in spite of the jollifications of the day, he would be able to find a bed for the night. He was fortunate. There was a room vacant at The Three Tuns. 'Mine inn', he writes, 'exhibited as cheerful a pandemonium as the occasion could possibly demand. Traps of all varieties stood waiting their turn in serried ranks, while distracted and perspiring ostlers and grooms struggled with the chaos.'

23   *Arthur Bradley in the photograph from the Three Tuns. He is sitting in the front complete with a long church warden pipe*

Sitting by the window of the heavily beamed bar with Mary Jones, looking across that same yard, I saw only a solitary Landrover drive in to keep my Morris Traveller company. Gone was the hustle and bustle and the hurly-burly of yesteryear.

Many ancient farm instruments have found a place in the bar at The Three Tuns and, while looking at some of these, I noticed a faded photograph pinned to the wall. It was taken in the 1880's and showed several men standing and sitting on the steps of the Three Tuns. Most of them were obviously farm or estate workers, but one of those sitting on the bottom step was wearing a deerstalker cap and Norfolk jacket and sporting a gaily striped cravat and in his hand was a long churchwarden pipe. He was a man who looked just the tiniest bit out of place in the rough and ready group. I glanced at the caption. I could not believe my eyes - what a cliché but so true. I read 'Seated on step with churchwarden pipe, Mr Arthur Bradley, behind him . . . ' Arthur Bradley probably never knew that his photograph graced the walls of The Three Tuns after his visit. A visit about which he spoke with such pleasure in his book, writng that, 'As I wended my way bedwards along the corridors of this typical old posting-inn, I felt as if I had lived in Bishop's Castle all my life and knew the idiosyncrasies of every man, woman and child within it and for ten miles around'.

A bow shot away from The Three Tuns, lives John Roberts and his wife. Their house is built on the middle bailey of the Norman castle and its long wide windows lead from the sitting room on to a semi-circular terrace, with a low stone balustrade overlooking the town. From this vantage point of 800 feet, the eye takes in the little streets, the old roof tops where Mary and Hugh Jones's attic-studio windows glint in the sun and the cupola on the Town Hall which, from 100 feet above it, looks like a pretty toy, while far below the church tower sets the boundary. The hills crowd all around and a little white farmhouse, away to the right, peers above the folds of the green slopes at one thousand feet. Those Marcher Lords of old knew well where to site a castle. With lookouts commanding such a view, there was no chance of them being taken unawares. John Robert's great- grandparents farmed at Llanwnog above Montgomery. As a young man, his grandfather lived at home and helped his parents and his six brothers run the farm. Times were hard and it was difficult to make a living. One day, after spending many hours with his brothers digging by hand a field of potatoes, they found that the crop was very poor and would fetch next to nothing. Grandfather decided once and for al that there was no money to be had in farming. Without more ado, he upped sticks and set off for London, where one of his uncles was a tea importer. Fortunately, this uncle was able to give his nephew work. The young man did well and eventually became a tea taster. He stayed in London for some years, but his health was not good and he found the dreadful smogs of London in those days very bad for his lungs. Eventually, he decided to return to the clean air of Wales and the border country. Having made a little money, he bought The Three Tuns in Bishop's Castle and, soon after, built the brewery which still stands. John Roberts told me there are only four public houses in England that brew their own beer. He showed me an old poster proclaiming ' Roberts home brewed ales sixpence, ninepence and a shilling a gallon. Harvesters threepence a gallon.'

24   *The Old Brewery, Bishop's Castle*

Grandfather Roberts bought his whiskey in bulk and broke it down to different strengths with distilled water. Soon after grandfather began brewing, the owner of Walcot Hall an estate two or three miles from Bishop's Castle, got him to put down a hogshead of the brew, on the birth of his son, so that he could give a party to all his tenant farmers and estate workers and the local mayor, on the child's coming of age. 'Great lumps of meat and plenty of hops were shovelled in', John Roberts told me, and he continued, 'when it was opened for the twenty-first birthday party only eighteen gallons were left of the fifty-four in the hogshead.' Grandfather Roberts bottled it up in half pint bottles so that the two-hundred odd guests all had a bottle. 'And', said John Roberts, 'if any man was so foolish as to drink his wife's share as well as his own, he promptly collapsed and was laid out in the park. Rows of them finished up like that, side by side.'

'In my grandfather's day', John Roberts continued, 'the post came on Sundays, as well as weekdays, but as there was no delivery on Sunday all the big houses around would send a coachman to pick up the mail. They usually came in a trap or a dog cart, but one very rich American, who came to live in the area, he was called Quinton Dick, I remember, would send a coach-and-four for his mail. His coachman would thunder up to join the queue of patiently waiting little vehicles at the post and, having collected the mail, he would wheel round and head for The Three Tuns and a glass of grandfather's home brew. That coachman was so skilful he could drive up the hill at a spanking pace and then, doing almost a u-turn, charge through the gates of The Three Tuns yard without slackening. He did this without doing a speck of damage to the coach nor the gate posts, never mind the horses.'

A splendid testimony to the quality of Grandfather Robert's brew came in the form of a letter to him from the Rector of Wentnor, near Bishop's Castle. Dated March 27th 1899, it reads as follows:

My Dear Roberts,

I hope you will not forget to send me some beer tomorrow, Tuesday as I have not had a glass since I last saw you. Please send it good as I shall have the Bishop and some clergy here on Monday week and you know there are no people in the world better judges of drink than they are. I want them to be able to exclaim as with one voice, after they have tasted your brew, 'Roberts deserves well of his country as he is the only man who has discovered a cure for agricultural depression.

W. Glenn

When John Robert's father took over The Three Tuns from Grandfather Roberts, among other improvements, he set about exposing the beams. Roberts senior did not approve and could be heard grumbling without ceasing, 'He's knocking the bloody house down about my ears.' However, he continued to live at the inn after the changeover and must have been not a little trying at times. He would always go to bed in the afternoon rising at four o'clock to sit by the parlour fire. Looking down the years, John Roberts told me 'I was a small boy at the time but I can see him now as clearly as if it was yesterday. He'd sit there by the huge range - took three or four buckets of coal at a time to keep that going - he'd be on a three-legged stool, with a curved back with spindles, rather like a hay manger. He'd be smoking and occasionally spitting into the fire. I remember,' he added ruefully, 'thinking this was the proper grown-up thing to do and having a go myself, but my mother caught me and I didn't do it again I can tell you. At four-thirty grandfather would go into the bar and call for a glass of beer. He would take a sip, swill it round his mouth and if it was not to his liking spit it into the spittoon and tell my father to get another barrel up.'

'In the 1930's when my father felt that a war was imminent, he ordered a lorry load of whiskey. He had it stored in the cellars of the Midland Bank and we used the last drop in the 1950's.'

On the subject of whiskey John Roberts recalled that about twenty-five years ago the Six Bells in Clun caught fire. 'My friend, Bob Davies,' he said, ' was on his way to church with his wife and saw the conflagration. Wife went on to church but Bob went to help the firemen man the pumps and pump the water up from the river. There was a rate for doing this you know, I think it was half a crown an hour. Well, as the flames roared up, a ham fell from where it was hanging on the rafters straight through the floor onto a barrel of whiskey below. The heat was tremendous and the whiskey began to boil. When at last the fire was out, they found the ham still in the barrel, done to a turn in the whiskey. They carved it up and they all took a share home, my word, it tasted ridiculously good I can tell you.'

The Three Tuns still has the hand bell that used to be rung to alert would-be passengers that they must drink up, for the departure of their train on the Bishop's Castle-Craven Arms line was imminent. This little railway, alas, now defunct, was opened in 1865 to run from Craven Arms to Lydham Heath. The engine would then reverse back the two miles to Bishop's Castle.

Various landowners in the area, such as the Mores of Linley, raised the finances for the railway and provided the land for the track. However, very soon the company ran into difficulties and was unable to pay either interest or repay capital. Eventually in 1887, one of the landowners, a certain Dr Eddoes, died. His widow decided on strong arm tactics. She called in the bailiffs. Rails were removed and a barricade erected where the track ran over Eddoes' land. For two weeks no supplies reached Bishop's Castle and food for humans and animals was running very low. At last the railway company decided something must be done to break the deadlock. They employed a number of men to entice the bailiffs into a nearby public house and regale them with drink. While they were getting ever merrier, another group of men cleared the obstructions and repaired the track, after which an enormously long train left Craven Arms. Hauled by several locomotives, it carried vast stocks of food, fodder and other provisions. As it puffed into Bishop's Castle, the inhabitants of the beleaguered town cheered until they were hoarse.

Eventually, a Bishop's Castle Railway Defence Trust was set up and the landowners were bought out. There is a delicious account of the nine-mile journey between Craven Arms and Lydham Heath, in the book *A Tale of Two Houses* by Jasper More, M.P., whose father and grandfather were landowners involved in the project. Describing a part of a particular journey he made, between Craven Arms and Lydham when a small boy, he writes, 'At Plowden was a bridge built of transverse timbers with gaps in between, it was here, on one of our journeys that we sighted a cow with all four legs fallen through the gaps and its horns waving over the line Cadwallader (the guard) had to pull it by the horns with main force while the station master sat on its head and Whitaker slowly drew the coaches past.' Eaton, a halt on the route, we learn from the book had no station master but was looked after by the redoubtable Mrs Bason 'A station mistress of Character, who, if there were no waiting passengers, would signal the train through at walking pace. Newspapers and packets would be thrown out by Cadwallader on to the platform while any more fragile parcels would be lobbed into Mrs Bason's outstretched skirt.' Cattle and goods as well as passengers travelled on the train and Jasper More continues, 'Sometimes it would be cattle rather than passengers who finished up opposite Lydham Heath platform. In my grandmother's day Cadwallader had had an occasion to shout in broadest Shropshire to the driver 'Hitch up the train a bit Harry, so Mrs More can get in'.

CEFN EINION AND BISHOP'S CASTLE

Long ago when I was small girl, I was given a book called *Eyes and No Eyes*. In the book two children are taken on a series of walks, one of them, No Eyes, sees virtually nothing in the countryside around her but her sister, Eyes, is filled with wonder and fascination at the myriad things to be seen. I must admit that at the time I did have rather a sneaking feeling that sister Eyes was much too prissy for her own good. However, I was recently given another book, this time on the Welsh March by John C. Moore. As I had just written the above chapter, I eagerly turned the pages to see what he had to say about Bishop's castle. I soon realised that John C. Moore was the archetypal model for No Eyes. 'Bishop's Castle', he writes, 'is the sort of place about which there is absolutely nothing to say. It possesses houses and a street but no character at all. It is neither old nor new. Pleasant or unpleasant. It is merely houses and a street. I passed through it quickly and took the road to Montgomery'.

Poor Montgomery fares even worse. He begins by denigrating the road between Bishop's Castle and Montgomery. 'If there is hell for hikers', he writes, 'such roads will surely exist there'. When he reaches Montgomery he declares 'I discovered that Montgomery had been dead for a very long time, ruin and decay had come to it, I was so bored that I do not remember what the place looked like, I remember only that it was a miserable little town set on the slope of a wooded hill. As soon as I could I left it.'

Absolutely hopping with indignation, I turned to the front of the book to find the publisher's name, already rehearsing in my mind the stinging letter I was about to write. Alas it was far too late. The book was published in 1933, over sixty years ago. Mr 'no eyes' Moore must either be dead or far too old to cross swords. Slowly my indignation has turned to pity for a man who was fortunate enough to visit two delightful towns, set in the beautiful Borderland and Wales, and be blind to their quaint little streets, fascinating buildings and all pervading sense of history. If only someone had given him *Eyes and No Eyes* when he was a child, life might have been much richer for him.

25   *The Old House, Bishop's Castle*

Chapter 8

Montgomery, Berriew & Chirbury

Underneath the frowning scaur
Still the daisy lights her star
But the sun and moon behold
Other shepheards than of old.
Ceiriog, 1832 - 1887
Translated by Alfred Perceval Graves

The nine-mile drive from Bishop's Castle to Montgomery, contrary to he opinion of Mr 'No Eyes' in a previous chapter, is, in fact, a beautiful and tranquil journey. The road follows all the vagaries of the Borderland, at one moment we are being welcomed to Wales, and the next Shropshire is hailing us back, then, presto! another sign tells us we are again in the Principality.

On our Eastern side, range upon range of hills follow the road, many of them reaching heights of 1,700 feet. Tantalising glimpses of white-painted farmsteads peep from their skirts and the russet brown, ploughed fields and emerald meads drape the lower slopes like a huge patchwork quilt. To the west, the hills are fewer and dark woods run down their backs to spread themselves along the roadside and, nearing the hamlet of Mellington, fine oaks patrol the hedgerows. All is so rural and peaceful that it is not at all surprising to remark a very early, hand-operated petrol pump outside the Blue Bell Inn. Soon after Mellington, about three quarters of a mile from Montgomery, the jagged ruins of Montgomery Castle can be seen ahead, crowning the great rocky ridge which towers three-hundred and fifty-feet above the town. Montgomery, Trefaldwyn to give it its Welsh name - was once a town of great strategic importance

105

being the virtual portway to the very heart of Wales, via the great corridor running along by the River Severn and thence to the coast. The town took its name from the mighty border baron, Roger de Montgomery, the first Earl of Shrewsbury. In the year 1070, he erected a motte and bailey castle at Hen Domen, about a mile to the north-west. Eventually the castle came into the hands of another border baron, Baldwin de Boulers, and it was he who gave the town its Welsh name Trefaldwyn, Baldwin's town.

Some years later in 1223, Henry III built a great stone castle on the rocky ridge, which dominates the town and in 1227 he granted the town its charter to hold a weekly market. He also gave permission for the Montgomery town walls to be built; these, alas, are no longer standing. A year after this, another great border baron, Hubert de Burgh, was granted the wardenship of the castle. Hubert de Burgh was rich and powerful; he was the Chief Justice of England for fifteen years, from 1219 to 1234; and he owned much property in England and on the continent. However, he was a greedy and grasping man and, not content with what he already had, set about trying to acquire yet more by penetrating into Wales. To facilitate this warlike enterprise, he ordered the destruction of a great wooded area in Wales which extended to more than five miles. This was a fatal mistake for he was moving into the territory of Prince Llewellyn ap Iorwerth, Llewellyn the Great. At the time Llewellyn's relationship with the King which had been, to say the least, turbulent, was relatively peaceful, possibly helped by the fact that his wife, Joan, was the King's natural daughter, and many of his children had married into the families of Norman barons.

For a while he sat on the sidelines, waiting and watching, but then Hubert, with the King's consent, began the building of yet another castle at nearby Sarn, which was to be an outpost for Montgomery. He tried to stop the work by peaceful persuasion, but to no avail, the building continued apace. Llewellyn, his patience exhausted, pounced; he attacked and besieged Hubert at Montgomery Castle. Montgomery was such an important bastion that the King himself had to dash to the rescue and having, with difficulty ousted Llewellyn, he then chanced his luck by foolishly venturing further into Wales, destroying and pillaging as he advanced. Soon, however, things began to go very wrong. The sympathies of many of the King's knights and soldiers were with the Welsh and provisions were running dangerously low. At last, the King decided he must end this ignominious expedition and call for a treaty with Llewellyn. Part of the price Llewellyn demanded was the destruction of the castle

Hubert de Burgh was building at Sarn Matthew of Paris recounting the beseigement and aftermath tells us that when Hubert began the building of this castle, he himself referred to it, jokingly no doubt, as Hubert's folly. Matthew adds that its destruction 'Did now move many to laugh at the thing, who seeing that castle and sumptuous building to be made equal with the ground, said that Hubert was a prophet.'

Over the centuries, Montgomery Castle did not escape the attentions of the acquisitive Mortimers who reigned there for many years but, eventually, it became the property of a less warlike family, the Herberts. However, the days of its glory were ended when in the Civil War Sir Thomas Middleton, the Parliamentarian, defeated the Royalist garrison there and, having taken the castle, he at once set about dismantling it so that it fell into ruin.

On the left, as one enters the town, are some pretty Georgian cottages leading along to the old Crown Inn. Montgomery is a truly delightful Georgian town. When Bradley in his trap, clattered over the cobbles, after spending the night at The Three Tuns Inn in Bishop's Castle, he wrote 'It is a quaint and quite alluring place.' It is still one of the most attractive of all the Welsh Border towns. For lovers of Georgiana, here is a veritable feast of Georgian buildings, What a variety of charming fanlights can be seen, all in the right place over the door, never a whisker of those dreadful modern travesties, where the imitation Georgian fanlight is inserted into the top panels of the door itself. Neither are there any unfortunate rashes of twentieth century so called 'bulls-eyes' in the window panes.

Broad Street is the heart of the little town. The name is very apposite, for it is almost as broad as it is long, and with its cupola topped late-Georgian town hall across the bottom end, rendering it a virtual cul de sac, it surely merits the title of square. Small, unpretentious but charming Georgian houses run down either side of the street, cheek by jowl with the old Chequers Inn, where tables and chairs are invitingly placed on the pavement, and branches of the National Westminster Bank and the Midland Bank which, in their Georgian cloaks, seem far too attractively housed to have anything to do with such vulgarities as finance.

Just past the many-paned, double bow-windowed shop, a perfect place and most suitably genteel for Cranford's Miss Matty to dispense her packets of tea, there is a narrow road to the left of the Town Hall, which wanders past the half-timbered Dragon Hotel and then rears up to become one of dear Mr Bradley's 'kill horse lanes' until it reaches the

107

crumbling, windswept walls of the once mighty castle Directly behind the Town Hall, there is a quite important looking town house, with a pillared porch, the Rock House, aptly named since it backs onto the rocky heights on which the remains of the castle stand. Walking past Rock House and down the other side of the Town Hall and into Arthur Street a further treat awaits, for here is such a feast of delicious domestic architecture as to be almost indigestible.

26   *The corner of Arthur Street, Montgomery*

Red brick Georgian houses crowd together on either side, flights o steps with white painted railings leading up to their doors, elegan fanlights and sash windows adding to their charm. Towards the end of th street, is a dear little higgeldy-piggeldy house, which judging by its outsid ramifications must have a maze of little passages and steps up and dow inside. One of its latter day Georgian embellishments is what must be th smallest venetian window ever. It is most exactly positioned in the centre of the gable facing the street. Just past this so intriguing place is a little clutch of black and white Tudor houses, looking not a wit out of place beside their elegant Georgian sisters.

In front of the houses, on each side, a wide kidney-stone walkway runs the length of the street. On the left is a small paved public gardens, a perfect place to collapse with shopping basket after a foray into the town or just to sit and gossip, as two venerable gentlemen were doing when I passed. At the end of this enchanting and sequestered road is a gentle view of wooded slopes, green undulations and fertile meadows.

Opposite the square a road climbs high to the Parish Church of Saint Nicholas. The path to the church porch runs through a mini-gorge with steep banks on either side. Someone has had the happy thought of planting these banks with a variety of spring flowers, so that primroses and violets and those little wild daffodils, so much more attractive than their more strident garden sisters, nod at the passing pilgrim.

This beautiful church was built in 1225, apart from the tower which was built in 1816. The rood loft and miserichords are thought to have come from Chirbury Abbey at the time of the dissolution of the monasteries. The very handsome canopied tomb is that of Sir Richard Herbert and his wife Magdelen. Effigies of their eight children dutifully kneel behind. Among them is George Herbert who became one of our great metaphysical poets. Another metaphysical poet John Donne, who was a friend of George Herbert and sometimes stayed at Montgomery Castle, wrote a delightful poem entitled *The Primrose at Montgomery Castle upon the hill on which it is situate.* George Herbert's mother, Magdalen, is said to have been a kind and beautiful woman and it was she who inspired John Donne's graceful tribute to the not so young

No Spring nor Summer beauty has such grace,
As I have seen in one Autumnal face.

After much questioning and mental anguish, George Herbert entered the church. His brother, Lord Herbert of Cherbury, was also a meta-physical poet, but there the resemblance ends, for while George was spending his days as a quiet country cleric in Wiltshire, Edward, who had inherited Montgomery Castle at the age of sixteen, led a life of high adventure. His autobiography, which he wrote at Lymore, that magnifi-cent timber-framed house in the lee of the castle and which was so regrettably destroyed in the nineteen sixties, and where dear Lady Clive did her vanishing act (see page 96), is a highly entertaining and rip-roaring read. Some critics have called it egotistical, but then I suppose all autobiographies by their very nature must, to a degree, be so. He was ever ready to draw his sword in an honourable cause but he was also a most learned and enlightened man and became the English ambassador at the court of France. In later years, however, he quietened down considerably, returned to Montgomery and,surrounded by his books, led a quiet and secluded life.

The churchyard of Saint Nicholas Church is remarkably large and being so high is also, when there is a brisk wind, remarkably chilly, as on the day I visited it. I was buffeted from gravestone to gravestone by a very searching wind, but I persevered because I particularly wished to find the grave of John Newton, who was hanged for a crime it is generally accepted he did not commit. I finally alighted at his resting place, which is at the side of the path leading out from the rear of the church, about three quarters of the way down.

John Newton's story is sad indeed. It began when he came to work in Montgomery in the early eighteen-hundreds. Not far from the town there lived, in a beautiful old manor house, a widow and her pretty daughter, Jane. The widow's husband had died recently and she was struggling to manage the house and farm on her own. Fairly near to the widow lived another farmer named Thomas Pearce. His ancestors had once owned Oakfield, the widow's manor house, and were respected landowners, until one of their number squandered his inheritance with riotous living and eventually sold the property for a song. Thomas had long nursed the ambition to regain Oakfield and live in it himself and, when James Morris was dying, he visited him and struck a bargain with him that, in the event of Mrs Morris being unable to keep the place going, he, Thomas Pearce, should have it.

James Morris, like Thomas Pearce's forebear, had been indolent and dissolute. When he died Oakfield was in a grievous state. The poor widow and her daughter struggled on for a while but it was obvious to Thomas Pearce that the plum was ripe and about to fall into his hands. However, he had reckoned without the widow's brother who visited her some time after her husband's death. He sized up the situation and brought into Oakfield a young man to help her get the place in order. John Newton, for that was his name, came from far away but he had brought most excellent references and soon, thanks to his hard work, the farm began to prosper. He was upright, sober, hard working and likeable and after he had been with them for two years, with everything going along as merry as a marriage bell, it was obvious to the widow that her daughter was becoming increasingly attracted to John and that her feelings were reciprocated. As she was much in favour of a marriage between the two young people, the future looked rosy indeed.

Alas, there were two very large flies in the ointment in the form of Thomas Pearce and a farmer friend of his named Robert Parker, to whom he had confided his hopes of regaining Oakfield. Robert Parker was also feeling very aggrieved because he had had his eye on the fair Jane Morris for some time and could see that he was likely to be pipped at the post. The two farmers put their heads together and formulated an evil plan which they felt would discredit John Newton so much that he would have to leave the district. Accordingly, one dark November night the two villainous creatures waylaid him as he was walking back to Oakfield from a local agricultural fair. Between them they dragged him into Montgomery accusing him of having attacked and robbed them. He was brought before the magistrate and charged with highway robbery with violence and committed for trial.

Parker and Pearce were both respected and established farmers and the jury believed their story. John Newton was found guilty of the crime and duly hanged. When asked by the judge if he had anything to say as to why sentence of death should not be passed on him, he made quite a long speech in which he pardoned his accusers, and while acknowledging that his life had not been without sin, he insisted that he was innocent of the crime for which he had been tried. In a trembling voice and with tears in his eyes, he said, 'I devoutly hope that my good mistress and her kind and excellent daughter may yet be convinced that they have not cherished and befriended a highway robber, for if', he added, 'I am innocent of the crime for which I suffer, the grass, for one generation at least, will not cover my grave.' Recounting his story thirty years after his death a contemporary wrote, 'Thirty years have passed away and the grass has not covered his grave'. This same man also recalls meeting the man who was Parish Clerk at the time of the hanging and hearing from him a most interesting story about the execution. 'That day', the clerk said, 'was serene and beautiful', until the prison bell tolled to announce the hour of the execution. Then the weather changed abruptly to bleak and stormy skies and, as John Newton placed his foot on the scaffold, 'A fearful darkness spread around', As the bolt was withdrawn vivid streaks of lightening flashed across the black skies and great peels of thunder rolled 'until the town hill seemed shaken to its base'. The heavens opened and torrential rains lashed down on the onlookers, so that they ran for shelter, many of them crying 'It is the end of the world'. This terrible storm continued in all its fury until John Newton's body was taken away for burial, 'When all became calm and clear again.'

As to those two unprincipled farmers, Robert Parker left the neighbourhood and took to drink. He was killed soon after in a blasting accident at the place where he had found work. Thomas Pearce changed from the genial, friendly farmer of former days and became a depressed and reclusive man until, in the words of the Parish Clerk, he 'just wasted away from the earth'. Widow Morris and her daughter left Oakfield and went to live with her brother but what happened to the old manor house none can say.

Finishing his account of the tragedy the same contemporary wrote, 'Numerous attempts have from time to time been made by some who are still alive, and others who have passed away, to bring grass upon that spot. Fresh soil has been frequently spread on it and seeds of various kinds have been sown; but not a blade has ever been known to spring from them, and the soil has soon become smooth and cold and barren clay.'

There are a few overgrown, scrubby shrubs around the grave now and on it a small bare patch in the shape of an almost obliterated cross. I remarked on this to the rector, the Reverend Barry Letson, and he said he had wondered if a little judicious weeding was carried out from time to time to preserve the cross. Well, as John Newton only promised that no grass would grow on his grave for 'at least a generation' and as we know that thirty years later, in spite of various efforts to induce the grass to grow, nothing had prevailed, his rather mild and harmless curse, which I suppose is what it was, has certainly proved itself and if some kindly souls are weeding the grave in his memory, full marks to them.

I asked the Rector why a convicted and executed felon had been buried in consecrated ground and he replied, 'I suppose nobody ever really thought him guilty.'

Like Arthur Bradley, I had 'set Montgomery as my northern limit' but, also like him, I could not resist a quick sprint to Chirbury, just three miles to the north-east. So, still in his footsteps, I wandered on up the border for a brief visit to Welshpool. I also made a detour to the little township of Berriew, a place I much regret Bradley did not visit. I have no doubt that this was because it is so successfully tucked away down a very discreet lane leading off the A483 Welshpool road. Had he discovered its hiding place I am sure he would have agreed that it is the very crême de la crême of all the townlets along the northern border.

First, I must set off to Chirbury just three miles away. This drowsy and charming village is the one from which Lord Herbert took his title, although for some reason he spelt it differently using an 'e' Cherbury, where the village uses an 'i' Chirbury. Chirbury was in fact named after a camp, Caer Bre, overlooking nearby Marrington Dingle, so I suppose when it comes to deciding on a later interpretation 'you pays yer money and takes yer choice.'

The twelfth century church of Saint Michael and an old Inn, the Herbert Arms, dominate the centre of the village. The inn being but a pace or two from the lych gate is, as is so often the case, most strategically placed to receive any members of the congregation who, having been suitably uplifted by parson's sermon feel the need of an uplift of a different kind before trundling or rolling home to Sunday luncheon. Sprinkled around the village are several very attractive houses and cottages, many of them timber-framed, stone or old mellow brick

Tradition has it that in the year 917 King Arthur's daughter, Aethelflaeda, built a castle in Chirbury, it was called Cyriobynig. She chose a site west of the church which is now known as the King's orchard.

Two and a half centuries later, in the reign of Henry III, a priory of Augustinians or black canons, so called because of the colour of their robes, which was founded by Robert de Boulers at nearby Snead, was removed to Chirbury where it remained until the dissolution of the monasteries. In 1285 it came to the ears of Bishop Swinfield that the Prior and canons were behaving with great impropriety, indeed the stories of the irregularities at Chirbury were such that the good Bishop made all haste to visit the place. He found the canons a most undisciplined lot, allowed to do just as they pleased. They and the Prior were severely reprimanded and the Bishop swept off vowing to return within the year. As good as his word, he appeared again before the year was out. He found that his castigations had had the desired effect and that there had been a remarkable turn around. The canons were all very subdued and as good as gold. The much mollified Bishop actually commended them on their 'piety and almsgiving'.

The church of Saint Michael is a beautiful stone building said to have been erected on the site of the old priory and, indeed, to contain within it some of the earlier priory building. Sadly, the fine rood screen was removed in the last century and taken to Montgomery Parish Church but the font, which was found some years ago doing time as a water trough, was rescued and restored to its rightful place When Lord Herbert died, he left to Chirbury a magnificent chained-library. This was kept in the vicarage for many years but is now in the County Archives. There are said to be about two hundred volumes.

There is so much to delight and interest in and around this sequestered village but as I only came, as did Arthur Bradley, for the briefest of scampers round, before setting off for Welshpool, I must not linger. All the same, I cannot leave without recounting one local legend. It concerns a circle of stones on Stapeley Hill at Middleton about a mile from Chirbury. There are about three different versions of this legend but they only vary in small particulars.

It seems that many years ago the village and the surrounding country-side was devastated by a dreadful famine. The rivers ran dry, the crops failed and the people were dying of starvation. When the troubles were at their height help came from an unexpected quarter. Living in the hills around was a giant and, unlike the usual run of giants, he was a very friendly sort of chap, rejoicing in the nice, comfortable, down to earth name of Mitchell. He owned a remarkable, one might say magical cow, and, like her master, she was a most obliging creature. Because of the famine, she agreed to give a bucketful of milk to anyone who milked her but on one condition, which was that no one should try to have more than one bucketful.

All went well for some time and the people began to recover thanks to this bovine benevolence. However, another denizen of the surrounding hills was not so well disposed. This was a most unpleasant witch, unpleasant by name, the Ugg of Hell, as well as by nature. Instead of taking a bucket to get her share of the milk she took a colander to fool the cow and milk her dry, thus depriving the people of their life saving elixir. However, the malevolent creature met her match in the giant Mitchell who, spotting her little deception, not all that difficult one would suppose with ground awash with milk, acted with commendable speed and turned her into a pillar of stone. The people, rejoicing at her come uppance, built a wall of stone pillars around her, in case she should ever try to burst forth. Some of the stones from that great circle still stand on Stapeley Hill and are known as Mitchell's Fold.

But now it really is high time we wended our way back to Montgomery to join the B4385 for Welshpool. It is well worth pausing a few hundred yards along this road to look back and see what must be surely the most dramatic view of the castle. Strung along the rocky heights the windswept walls stand proud and defiant three-hundred and fifty-feet above the little town.

The chilling wind which had hurried me up in Saint Nicholas churchyard was still unpleasantly active. Sombre rain clouds were piling up behind the desolate stone remains. Perhaps it was a trick of the light but I had the distinct if fleeting impression that a section of those jagged ruins resembled a giant bird with hunched wings. Into my mind came the poet Tennyson's words from his poem *The Eagle,*

> He clasps the rock with crooked hands,
> Close to the sun in lonely lands,
> Ringed with the azure world he stands,
> The wrinkled sea beneath him crawls,
> He watches from the mountain walls,
> And like a thunderbolt he falls.

True there is no 'wrinkled sea' beneath those 'crooked hands', just the houses huddled in the town below and to the east the hills of Shropshire, while away to the west are the mountains and valleys of Wales; but what dread that castle must have inspired in the hearts of any preparing to attack it on its seemingly impregnable perch and how like a falling thunderbolt would seem the retaliation.

Two or three miles along the B4385 at Garthmyl there is a junction and, turning right here we are on the A483 Welshpool road. Barely a mile along it is the easily missed left-hand turn which runs straight into Berriew, passing the Vaynor parklands on the left. Berriew-Aberriw lies near the mouth of the river Rhiw. The history of this fascinating place goes back to Roman times and there is much evidence to show that there was a settlement here in the Neolithic and the Bronze ages. In Tudor and Stuart times, like much of England, Berriew 'Rode the back of the sheep', and became a rich and thriving place thereby. This was the very heart of the sheep rearing country and the Berriew market hall which until 1875 stood near the main entrance of the church, was the perfect place to store and bale the huge quantities of wool from the surrounding countryside. It was during this period of affluence that many of the handsome half-timbered houses in the town were built.

While wandering in the area, I was lent a very interesting and erudite booklet entitled *Aberriew t Berriew,* written by D.W. Smith and published in 1992. It is a most comprehensive and intriguing story of this small township down the years. From it I learned that in the seventeenth century Berriew acquired the name of 'Village of many squires'. This was because of the number of rich landowners in the area.

Since those halcyon days a great many of the fine houses in the countryside around have gone, but Berriew itself has retained many charming half-timbered properties including the seventeenth century Lion Inn and the handsome vicarage with its jetted flooring. The elaborate pseudo-Tudor chimneys on many of the houses were part of a nineteenth century beautification and face lift endured by the town, but the kindly years have softened their impact and they now blend in well and, in some cases, even add to the charm of this little Welsh town which can rank with any of those places on the famous 'Black and White Trail' in Herefordshire..

The present church was built in the nineteenth century on the site of three former religious houses. The last of the earlier churches was in such a bad state at the end of the eighteenth century that the vicar, the Reverend William Browne, made a national appeal for funds to restore it. Alas, the response was very feeble being a little over one hundred pounds. A new vicar, the Reverend Edward Jones, with his church falling about his ears, also launched a national appeal. By then the position was desperate indeed and this no doubt added grist to his supplications, at all events the national conscience was stirred and the funds were forthcoming. On June 1st, 1800 the Reverend Edward Jones conducted the last wedding in his old church, which was then demolished and work on the new building began. The first wedding to take place in the new church was on October 14th, 1802, just over two-years and four-months after the destruction of the old building. One way and another, one is left with the impression that Parson Jones was something of a live wire. In 1875 there were extensive alterations to the church when the tower was replaced by a spire a little out of the true. It has become known as 'haycocks folly' after the architect who designed it.

One of the graves in the churchyard is that of Mary Morris who died in 1741. Mary's father was a Berriew farmer, and when a rich widower, Sir John Pryce, the 5th baronet with a seat at nearby Newtown, came to pay court to his daughter, it must have seemed a most desirable match. In 1737 Mary Morris duly became Lady Pryce, the châtelaine of Newtown Hall a magnificent sixteenth century mansion. Sir John's first wife was his cousin, Elizabeth Powell, and, when she died in childbirth in 1731, her devoted widower hit on the novel idea of having her embalmed;

furthermore, he had her placed alongside his bed. Presumably Mary tolerated her beloved's little foibles, for the first Lady Pryce remained in situ, and indeed when Mary became pregnant and died in childbirth she too was embalmed, so that the first and second wives lay on either side of Sir John's bed.

In December of the same year in which Mary died, Sir John married again, this time to Elizabeth Jones a rich widow. There was a slight hiccup during the courtship for when Elizabeth learned of her embalmed predecessors guarding the nuptial couch she refused to marry him until they were removed. Elizabeth died in 1748 and a few years later the much married Sir John was busily courting yet again. His intended fourth wife was a Margaret Harries of Haverfordwest. However, he died before he could marry her, which, in view of his fast turnover in wives, was perhaps just as well.

One of the great estates still remaining in the area is Vaynor. An old, old Welsh family owned Vaynor or Faenor as it then was, from 1200 - 1500. They were descendants of Brochwel, a prince of Powys. Richard ap Edward, the last member of this ancient family, had no sons to inherit and eventually Faenor was bought by a Mr Pryce of Newtown whose great granddaughter, Bridget, married George Devereux in 1636 and brought with her to the marriage the great Faenor estates. Four years after this, the old Faenor Hall was demolished and a new hall erected in the then fashionable brick. Vaynor was in fact the first brick built house in the area and must have been quite a wonder in its day. There have been alterations over the years, of course, but it still stands in its lovely parkland, a fine and elegant Carolean mansion much as George and his wife Bridget left it.

Over the years, the estate passed to the Herefords. When the tenth viscount died in 1748, a lawyer named Robert Moxon was the next owner. Robert's niece, Anne, and her husband, John Winder, inherited it from him, thus, as Mr Smith tells us in his interesting booklet, 'Establishing a new family at Vaynor'.

The very long drive up to Vaynor Hall is, at first, surrounded by undulating hills, fat sheep contentedly grazing on their slopes but after a while it runs past steep sided banks , tree clad, until ahead is seen the elegant outline of the Hall. In front of the Hall, the drive opens into a great circle bordered on one side by a high, brick wall. A delightful conservatory, much resembling a small orangery, has been built into part of this wall. It was designed by Ailsa Corbett-Winder who now lives in the dower house, and it is known by her children as 'Mum's folly' The gardens at Vaynor are very reminiscent, on a smaller scale, of those at Powis Castle. First, we come upon a long, wide stretch of greensward known as 'The Archer's Terrace'. Presumably this was used in former times, long before the days of George Devereux, for the young men to practice that most essential of skills in those days archery. This terrace falls away in further terraces to where, far below, a sundial stands in the middle of a huge circle marked out in hours by grass paths.

Old stone steps, flower-flanked, lead down through a variety of exotic rhododendrons to the lower levels. Clumps of bright flowers splash their colour on the dark foliage around and the only sound, in this age old haven of peace, was that of a bird tapping a snail shell on the steps and the distant shouts of the Corbett-Winder children playing on the circular drive on their bicycles.

Ailsa Corbett-Winder and her late husband loved the gardens and spent countless hours gardening, a joy they shared with the late Lord Clive of Powis Castle and many a rare cutting they exchanged with him, especially from the rhododendron tribe. Aisla Corbett-Winder's son and his wife now live at the hall, so perhaps this most delightful of gardens will still be cherished to enrich future generations.

I lingered longer than intended in beautiful Berriew. As I left the sun was dipping behind the hills. Welshpool would have to wait for another day but, as it is right on the route which I have chosen for a visit to Llangollen, it will fit very well into the next chapter.

Chapter 9

Shrewsbury Cakes & Salop, Welshpool & Bala

The weather changed very much for the worse after my Montgomery and Berriew trundles and it was some days before I could set out for Welshpool. In the interim, however, I saw in the local paper notice of a book sale in Ludlow. Books have always held a fatal fascination for me but, alas, the sale was on that very day and, indeed, had already begun. However, always hopeful of getting a few last minute bargains I rushed off at once. When I got there, after spending some time finding a place to park, the sale was almost over. As I was about to leave, the auctioneer called out, 'Lot 143a, not in your catalogue ladies and gentlemen. A box of assorted books. What am I bid?'

Nobody took the slightest notice, a queue had already formed at the office in order to pay for and collect their purchases, while others were gathering their bits and bobs together and making for the exit. 'Come along Ladies', the auctioneer called, addressing himself to the more domestic looking half of those remaining, 'A nice little lot of cookery books here, plenty of time to make those Christmas puddings.' Not a flicker of interest. 'Come along', he went on, a note of impatience in his voice. 'Come along, who'll start me off? How about twenty five p.!'

Well, I thought, anything was better than going home empty handed and perhaps there were a few useful recipes among them. I waved my catalogue and called '10p'. '10p!!', the auctioneer's scandalised voice had me cowering in my seat; but there was no advance on my modest bid. 'All right ladies', he boomed, 'I am giving them away, but if that's how you want it, they're sold at 10p.' and down came his gavel.

119

When I got home, I dumped the box on the table and began to look through it. Lot 143a was singularly unimpressive. Various assorted modern cookery books, all for electric cookers; I use calor gas. The ubiquitous Mrs Beeton, modern, much abridged and very shabby and a collection of recipes torn from old magazines. I picked the box up but dropped it hastily when I saw an enormous spider scrambling over the crumpled newspapers in the bottom. As the box dropped on the floor the bottom fell out, so did the newspapers and another book which had been hidden beneath them. It was a very battered old warrior and, as I bent to pick it up, I saw that it had fallen open at a recipe headed 'To fry foals'. Good Heavens! I looked at the next one and read 'To marinate foals'. Indignation was rising. I must get on to the R.S.P.C.A. Who were the publishers? I flipped the pages back and read *The ladies complete guide on cookery in all its branches. Also the complete brewer, like-wise the family physician.* By Mrs Mary Cole, printed by G Kearsley, No.46 Fleet Street.1791.

Vastly relieved and rather excited to find this unexpected swan among the geese, I realised that 'To fry foals' was a combination of the old English long S and the vagaries of Georgian spelling. In her preface Mary Cole writes, 'I flatter myself that my instructions will entitle me to the approbation of my readers.' Modest she was not, but intrepid she most certainly was. Witness her recipe for roast pig. Anyone feeling rather fragile had better skip the next bit.

'Stick your pig', she writes, 'just above the breast bone and run your knife to the heart. When it is dead, put it in cold water for a few minutes, then rub it over with a little rosin beat exceedingly fine in its own blood. Lay it on a table, pull off the hairs as quick as possible. Take off the fore feet at first joint. Make a slit down its belly and take out all the entrails. When you roast it put it with a little sage and one teaspoonful of black pepper, two of salt and a crust of brown bread. Spit your pig and sew it up. Lay it down to a brisk fire'.

If you have stayed the course, you now know how to deal with your Christmas pork. While on the subject of Christmas, why not go the whole hog (sorry!) and plan your Christmas menu. There are several months left in which you can rehearse it. So now for the bird. How about a goose? On page 131 we find Goose à la Mode. 'Pick a large fine goose clean, skin and bone it nicely, then take a large tongue and boil it and peel it. Take a fowl and treat in the same manner as the goose, put both tongue and fowl into the goose.' A great many goodies go into the goose including ham, sweetbreads, truffles and mushrooms, which must be morels.

However, if you would rather stick to turkey, how about the recipe entitled 'To roast turkey in the genteel way'? On closer inspection this involves a great many oysters, a large fowl and a pound of veal as well as the basic bird, so perhaps it would be wiser to stick to the non-genteel goose. Or if you are feeling really poor you could turn to page 144 for 'A fowl servant fashion'

As to whether you start your Christmas dinner with Mrs Cole's special soup or not, depends on your stamina and the amount of room in your kitchen. Obviously, a particularly good soup is required on such an occasion and on page 185 we find the very thing, turtle soup, just the right touch of luxury. Before embarking on this, however, do bear in mind that a quite small, green turtle would weigh at least thirty pounds. The indefatigable Mary Cole is quite undeterred. Briskly, she instructs us to 'Take the turtle out of the water the night before you dress it. Lay it on its back. In the morning cut its head off and hang it up by its hind fins for it to bleed till the blood is all out. Then cut the callapee, which is the belly, round and raise it up. Cut the fins off and scald them, with the head. Take off all the scales. Take all the white meat out. Wash the lungs very clean from the blood, then take the guts and maw and slit them open.'

Strenuous this may seem but you are only half way there. There is a great deal more to be done involving an enormous number of spices, eggs and herbs and three pints of Madeira wine. If by this time the turtle is not the only green thing in the kitchen, it might be politic to employ some of the last named on the cook. Of course, it is conceivable that you are not able to lay your hands on a live, green turtle; in this case you could try Mrs Cole's mock turtle soup, but perhaps not, for apart from the 'Largest calves head you can find', and the requisite three pints of Madeira plus artichokes, mushrooms, eggs, lemons galore, another half of a calves head, some sweetbreads and anchovies, you will be expected to do such choice little chores as 'Taking out the eyes'.

The Georgian cook must have turned with some relief to the Christmas pudding, which at least did not require slaughter-house techniques. Mary Cole gives us her recipe for a 'Plum Porridge for Christmas'. This starts off with a shin of beef boiled in eight gallons of water to which you add six penny-loaves, two pounds of prunes, five pounds of 'Raisings of the sun', five pounds of currants, lemons and spices, a quart of sack and a quart of claret.

The pages, at the end of Mrs Coles's book, devoted to 'Pains in the stomach' and 'The heartburn', among other ailments, were obviously very necessary but the cures given consist mainly of inducing vomiting, applying leeches or taking large doses of rhubarb and senna and in really extreme cases 'going for a long ride on horseback'. Beware of hiccups. In certain cases, this is considered the forerunner of death and the hapless victim must be bled and have his stomach fomented with bladders filled with warn milk.

Among her many other remedies, Mary Cole gives one for the 'Bite of a viper' 'The grease', she writes, 'of this animal rubbed into the wound, is said to cure the viper bite', though she prudently adds, 'I should not think it is sufficient for the bite of an enraged viper'.

Her recipe for 'Syllabubs under the cow', eaten with a nice home baked Shrewsbury Cake sounds quite pleasant. To make the syllabub, 'Put into a punchbowl a pint of cider and a bottle of strong beer, grate in a small nutmeg and sweeten it to your taste. Then milk into it from the cow as much milk as will make a strong froth. Then let it stand an hour. Strew over it a few currants, well washed and plumped before the fire and it will be fit for service'.

Her recipe for Shrewsbury cakes is to 'Take Half a pound of butter, beat it to a cream, then put in half a pound of flour, one egg, six ounces of loaf sugar, beaten and sifted, half an ounce of caraway seed. Mix into a paste and roll thin, and cut them round with a small glass or little tins. Prick them and lay them on sheets of tin and bake them in a slow oven.'

If you have any wine left to drink with your meal after your cooking exploits, you'll be lucky, but in any case under 'Possets and Gruels', on page 346, there is a recipe for Salop - a very appropriate drink for the Border Country. 'Salop', writes Mary Cole, 'is sold at chemists. Take a large teaspoonful of the powder and put it into a pint of boiling water stirring it until a fine jelly, and add wine and sugar to your taste'. I looked up the main ingredient, Salop, and found it is made of the dried tuber of Orchis Mascula, which leaves me not much wiser. However, there is one thing we must remember, and that is to avoid hiccups and vipers especially enraged ones.

A few days after the book sale, the weather began to brighten up and my thoughts turned to Welshpool once again. I remember a visit I made to an old house there about fifteen years ago.

I had been turning over some old papers when I came across the account of some wonderful oak panelling which had been removed from London to a house in Wales in the middle of the last century. The house in question, Gungrog Hall on the outskirts of Welshpool, was a Georgian mansion which, in the eighteen sixties, when the account was written, stood high on a hill, surrounded by green meadows, ancient trees and purling streams. The simplicity of its Georgian facade giving no hint of the splendour of the rooms within.

These rooms were filled with magnificent old oak furniture, gleaming black with age, and the walls were covered with fine oak panelling surmounted by richly carved swags and mouldings. Panelling that had, in its time, sheltered no less than six reigning monarchs, together with numerous princes and princesses of the blood and their high born attendants.

It was in the year 1861 that the owner of Gungrog Hall heard of the proposed demolition of a very old house in London. He was a connoisseur and collector of fine oak furniture and carvings and he knew that the house in question, which was in Cheapside, had many superb examples of the woodcarver's art. Accordingly, he travelled up to London and attended the sale of the materials from the building. He bought the panelling and wood carving from what was known as the 'Great Room' and had them sent to beautify his house in the heart of Wales.

The old house in Cheapside was built by a rich haberdasher named Edward Waldo. The whole of the ground floor of his fine new house was given over to business, and the living quarters of the Waldo family were reached by a splendid oak staircase at the back of the shop. These quarters were very spacious and one particularly large room occupied the whole of the first floor. Here Edward Waldo spared no expense; the room was magnificently panelled in oak and richly decorated with carved fruit, flowers and foliage, and elegant swags and mouldings.

For centuries it had been the custom in England for each sovereign, early in the reign, to visit the City on Lord Mayor's Day and, after spending some time among his people, to watch the Lord Mayor's Show before going on to a banquet at the Guildhall. In former times, there was a balcony in front of the church in Cheapside from which the Sovereign and his suite could see the show. However, in the reign of Edward III the royal party had just settled nicely into their seats on the balcony when the whole edifice gave way and deposited them unceremoniously upon the heads of their loyal subjects. After this mishap, a stone gallery was built onto the side of the church, but this too fell down during the Great Fire of London.

When, therefore, Charles II expressed a wish to continue the old custom and visit the show, watching it from Cheapside, there was much consternation until someone thought of the rich haberdasher, Waldo, and his house near the church and realised that it would serve the purpose even better than the late lamented gallery had done. Accordingly, on October 29th, 1685, Edward Waldo and his excited family prepared for their beautiful 'Great Room' to be given the Royal baptism.

The London Gazette of the period says that 'Their Majesties accompanied by His Royal Highness, and their Highnesses the Lady Mary and the Lady Anne, and His Highness, the Prince of Orange, attended by a great many of the principal nobility and other persons of quality, having been pleased upon the humble petition of the City to honour them with their presence, first at a show in Cheapside being placed in a balcony under a canopy of state at the house of Sir Edward Waldo (Upon whom his Majesty was then pleased to confer the honour of knighthood), and afterwards at the Guildhall at dinner when the entertainment was very noble and magnificent in all kinds.'

James II, being afraid of assassination, stayed at home on Lord Mayor's Day. Queen Anne, however, desired to see the show from Cheapside. Fortunately, it was still the tradition that the sovereign should visit the show as early in the reign as possible. This must have spared Sir Edward Waldo some very nervous moments regarding his balcony, for a few years after she had visited his house, Queen Anne had grown so enormously fat that a machine had been especially contrived to winch the Royal Presence up and down through the ceilings at Windsor Castle because she could no longer climb stairs.

On October 29th 1715, Sir Edward Waldo, who was then an old man, entertained his King for the last time. George I, together with the Prince and Princess of Wales, walked through the haberdasher's shop and mounting the stairs at the back, sat with him on the balcony leading from his 'Great Room' in order to see the cavalcade. In 1727, when George I came to the house in Cheapside, Sir Edward had died and it was his daughter, Lady Hunsden, who did the honours.

Sometime during the reign of George II, the house became the property of David Barclay, a member of the famous Quaker banking family. Neither George IV, nor William IV, followed the age old custom of visiting the City to watch the Lord Mayor's Show, both of them feared demonstrations and riots against themselves or the policies of their governments. Queen Victoria, although visiting the City, refrained from watching the show and it was during her reign that the old house in Cheapside was pulled down.

When I visited Welshpool that long ago summer and climbed the hill to Gungrog Hall, it was sad to see that the park with its green meadows and great trees had disappeared entirely. In its place was a large council estate which had mushroomed up to within a few feet of the Hall. Gungrog Hall itself was scarcely recognisable as being of Georgian origin, so completely was it disguised by the many Victorian embellishments which had been added over the years.

I called at the house and asked the then owner if I might be permitted to see the panelling. I was told that it was no longer there, my rush of disappointment was, however, stemmed when she added, 'Yes, it was bought by Barclays some years ago for their bank in Cheapside'. Surely, I thought Sir Edward Waldo must have been watching from the shades as his 'Great Room' came home.

Gungrog Hall has changed hands again since my visit and is now owned by Edward Manton. The council estate is even larger and has climbed the hill above the Hall, so that, as well as being surrounded by houses, it is also overlooked by them.

But now the sun is really shining and the Welshpool of today is calling. Welshpool-y Trallwng was originally called Pool, but was later prefixed by Welsh to distinguish it from Poole in Dorset. Of course, the great glory of the place is Powis Castle. This proud fortress, known for centuries as Castell Coch - the red castle- because of the red sand-stone of which it is built. Once the home of the great princes of Upper Powis, it now towers over superbly terraced gardens. These terraces are nearly two-hundred yards long . There are four of them, cascading with flowers and flowering shrubs they drop down to the Severn Valley far below.

In 1587 Sir Edward Herbert purchased the castle and it remained with the Herbert family until the second Earl died and his sister inherited the estates. She married in 1784 Clive of India's son, Edward, who was created Earl of Powis in 1804 and he brought to Powis his father's great collection of Indian memorabilia. His father lived at beautiful Walcot Hall near Bishop's Castle, so he did not have far to take it.

In 1263 Gwynwynwyn, Prince of Powis, granted the town a charter to market and, lying in the fertile valley of the Severn, it grew into a flourishing market town. It is said that it has the largest one-day livestock market in Europe. Welshpool is a hotchpotch of houses of various periods: Georgian, Victorian and timber-framed. It is the sort of place which, if a Civic Society were to be let loose on it, would undoubtedly reveal many pleasing surprises.

Weaving my way along between the cars, lorries, vans and every other mode of transport towards Saint Mary's Church, I remembered with a pang, the words of S.P.B.Mais in his book on Wales and the March. Visiting in 1939 he wrote, 'Realising how rare a thing transport is in Welshpool, I boarded the first bus I saw'.

The church of Saint Mary stands high above the street, a great stone wall, heavily buttressed, holding back the bank on which it is built. Wide steps lead up to the churchyard and beside them on the right is, spick and span, windows gleaming, a minuscule black and white cottage. This is known as Grace Evans Cottage.

Early in the eighteenth century, Lord Nithsdale, the husband of the Earl of Powis's daughter, was arrested for his part in the rebellion of 1715 and was condemned to death. While he was languishing in the Tower of London awaiting his execution, his resourceful wife far away in Wales was not wringing her hands in despair, instead she briskly set about devising a plan to help him to escape.

Together with some women friends and her maid, the faithful Grace Evans, she set off for London. The plan was a bold one. All of the women were to visit him in the tower, smuggling under their voluminous garments some women's clothes. Her husband was to put these on and then, disguised as a woman, leave the prison in the midst of a chattering laughing group of women. It is stretching credulity to imagine the guards could not count, so either they must have left one of their number behind dressed in his clothes, in order to fool the guards, not a rush of volunteers for this part of the proceedings one would think, or they must have rigged up a dummy in his clothes, or, more likely, they bribed the guards. At all events Lady Nithsdale must have had very persuasive ways to get her friends to help her in such a hazardous project.

The plan succeeded and Lord Nithsdale was brought safely back to Wales, where Grace Evans hid him until the hue and cry had died down. To show her gratitude, Lady Nithsdale gave Grace Evans the little cottage by the church steps and always referred to her as 'My dear Evans'.

Tucked away behind the National Westminster bank in New Street is an eighteenth century cockpit. Thanks to grants from various bodies, it was restored in 1978 and is the only brick built cock fighting pit in Wales.

Cock fighting was common in ancient Greece and Rome but the first we hear of it in Britain is in the twelfth century, although, if it was so common with the Romans, they surely arranged fights here during their long occupation. In the reign of Edward III, it had become quite fashionable but by 1366 so much gambling was taking place at the fights that the sport was banned. However, there was a revival in later centuries and Henry VIII had a cockpit built at Whitehall. James I was very keen and is known to have attended fights twice a week.

In the reign of James II, a very popular type of cock fighting was known as the Welsh Main. This consisted of pitting ten to sixteen birds against each other and letting them fight until only one survived. From the time of George II long curved silver or steel blades were fitted over the cock's spurs. Some say this was to give cleaner wounds, which they may well have done, but an academic point surely, since in most cases, certainly the Welsh Main, the wounds were fatal. Cock fighting continued in London and the larger towns and cities until it was banned in 1849. It survived in remote country areas for almost another half century.

Some time ago I read a poem which is a marvellous evocation of the atmosphere at a cockfight. One has to remember that in the heyday of cockfighting, many great houses and estates were won or lost so that passions ran high.

'Nice piece, Sir.' I turned my head.
The dealer's hand caressed the chair.
'For watching cockfighting,' he said,
'Queen Anne, of course, its very rare.'

A long back for a hunting squire
to stretch his legs before the fire,
Upholstered in brass studded leather,
A little faded by the weather . . .
Carved walnut legs, the shade of honey,
Shelves for glasses, drawers for money.

The phone bell rang, 'Excuse me sir.'
Alone — I sank into the chair,
And, as I gripped its arms, began
To feel myself another man —
Clad in skirted velvet coat,
With ruffles at the wrists and throat,
A long peruke of powdered hair,
Pockets of guineas everywhere!
Then, vividly I saw again

The blood and sawdust of the main,
And, in the swaying lantern light,
The flying spurs, and feathers flight,
And heard, above the smoke filled air,
The battle cry of Chanticleer!

The wind blew through an open door,
Scattering cards across the floor,
Tankards hammered oaken tables,
The air smelt thick of sweat and stables;
With oaths and bets the rafters rang,
Some men sat sleeping, others sang
Strange songs and staves of other days
Churchwardens filled the room with haze.

Suddenly a hand, deep cuffed in lace,
Flung a full wine glass in my face!
I rose and lurched into the night,
Swords flickered in the cold moonlight,
Others were gambling on the fight . . .

Somehow I knew he died that night.

The dealer smiled, 'You wish to buy?'
Shuddering, I said, 'The price is high.'
Thinking of men who'd paid it there,
Sprawled in the old cock-fighting chair.

M H Hunt

New Street is a turning off Broad Street which is, as its name implies, a very wide street lined with various attractive properties. Gradually it merges into High Street, Mount Street and Raven Street and then we are on the open road again this time en route for the mountainous interior and Bala.

At first the countryside is undulating with no sudden eminencies thrusting themselves up from the plain until, nearing Llanfyllin, the hills increase in number and character and now they are great rugged steeps and tors. Some of the slopes are gilded with yellow gorse but many are a sombre brown where last years heather and ling have died. Two rivers, the Cain and the Abel, meet at Llanfyllin which is an attractive little town with many brick built Georgian houses. The Parish church is also brick built and was erected in 1706.

At Llanfyllin we take the B4391 going north and enter the Tanad Valley. About four or five miles along this road a branch right follows the river down to Llangynog. This townlet, with its whitewashed stone houses, two inns and a church was once a thriving and bustling lead mining and slate quarrying place. Great grey streaks on the flanks of the two gigantic hills that overhang the houses are the scars left from those activities. Arthur Bradley reminds us that in the eighteenth century one of the four lead mines at Llangynog is said to have brought an annual income of twenty-thousand pounds to the house of Powis for forty years.

The Tanad Valley Arms, a little whitewashed inn with diamond-paned windows, looked very inviting and just the place to pause awhile. Here were old settles and round tripod tables, a crackling fire, beams hung with numerous mugs and a cosy coterie at the bar. I gathered one of this group was a farmer, his name was Graham Lewis and, together with his mother and uncle, he farmed three hill farms. I asked him if he had lost any sheep in the appalling early spring weather. He certainly had, he said and when I asked him how many he replied, 'If I started counting them, I'd go bloody loopy'. Graham and Stan, his friend the wood turner, told me that when slate and lead were quarried and mined at Llanynog the population was two thousand and there were five inns. Now, the population is about three hundred and there are two inns.

High above the inn yard, which is the size of a postage stamp, stands the church. This is another church where a great strong wall holds back the bank on which it is built. With the church high above the village on the one side and the two great hills towering over it on the other, there would seem to be all the ingredients for a bad dose of claustrophobia. However, the white-painted stone houses, clustering round the church and the inns, only need a spillage of bouganvillia over their walls and a few sentinel cypresses in the gardens and Llangynog would resemble a little Mediterranean village with a bay just around the corner.

At first, on the road from Llangynog to Bala, the hills are of quite a modest size with remarkably fluffy sheep looking like huge balls of cotton wool grazing their lower slopes, or wandering at will in the road to sit contentedly munching the verge. One of their more dramatic little diversions in the long green days of this remote area would seem to be giving the occasional motorist on this lonely road a heart attack. There they are, comfortably seated in cosy groups, so that one is filled with a warm benevolence towards them, such gentle fluffy creatures, so useful to man, and so harmless, and then, suddenly as you approach, one of their number leaps up, separates himself from the group, and without warning, indulges in a death defying frisk across the road. Result - a mad screech of brakes as the car rackets from side to side and all benevolence flown out of the window.

This route from Llangynog to Bala is not for the faint hearted for, apart from kamikaze sheep, the hills grow ever more rugged with, here and there, bright rushing streams hurtling down their steep sides. The road winds tortuously along a virtual ledge, the land falling steeply away on one side to the valley far below. After one horrified look to the left, taking in the precipitous drop and the rocky terrain, I fixed my eyes firmly ahead and hugged the mountain side as I drove along. Geoffrey tells me that I missed some truly magnificent views.

There are no houses to be seen in these parts, save for a few broad-shouldered whitewashed cottages crouching on the lower slopes, their grey slate roofs peering cautiously from the craggy folds. This great range of hills and mountains is covered with wild moorland. Writing of the area Bradley says, 'The little town (Bala) is surrounded by the finest grouse moors in Wales'.

Gradually, on the long descent to the valley, the moors recede and a few grey stone houses skirt the way, until, far below, there is a glimpse of the glittering waters of Llyn Tegid, Bala Lake or Pimblemere as Geraldus Cambrensis called it, and indeed as it still is called by some of the locals. Dotted with the bright sails of little craft, it glimmers through the trees. Llyn Tegid is the largest natural lake in Wales, being nearly four miles long and about a mile wide at its broadest point and very deep, one-hundred feet or more in places. Right through it runs the River Dee, the Afon Dyfwdwg, the divine stream. Tradition has it that the waters of this holy river do not deign to mingle with the less exalted contents of the lake.

At the far end of Llyn Tegid are the slopes of the Aran mountains, Aran Benllyn and Aran Fawddwy. Away in the distance looms the outline of Cader Idris. Arthur Bradley recounts a little adventure he had in the late eighteenth century while fishing what he calls, 'A grim little tarn, tucked away under the eastern precipices of Aran Benllyn'. He had hired a boy from the village of Llanwywchllyn, which is situated at one end of Llyn Tegid, to help him carry his waders and tackle. The boy was about nine-years old and could only speak Welsh. At first, all went well and the lad skipped gaily back and forth with the landing net, as Bradley caught trout after trout. As the day wore on, however, the skies grew black with dark clouds. The fish, naturally, ceased to rise but, ever hopeful, as all true anglers are, Bradley fished on. Presently, realising how long it was since he had called for the landing net, he looked round but the boy was nowhere to be seen and there was no answer to his increasingly frantic calls. 'Filled with horrible forebodings', he hunted everywhere for the child but to no avail. Eventually, he found the landing net, lying on the bank in, he recalls, 'An ominous looking place, where some rocky ledge dropped sheer down into the dark depths.' In a state of great anxiety, he made his way back to the village. He was so distraught that he marched straight through a field with a bull in it without turning a hair. In fact, he writes, 'With meretricious courage I traversed the very centre of his beat'. His mind was full of dread at the thought of breaking the news to the boy's mother, for he felt sure the tarn had claimed a victim. However, when he arrived at the cottage where the boy lived, there he was, safe and sound and fit and flourishing. It appeared the child had been frightened by the gloomy aspect of the tarn when the skies darkened and, as there were no more calls for the landing net, he fled home.

Arthur Bradley was understandably very angry but in the end his sympathies were with the boy, for when the schoolmaster, who had recommended the lad, arrived on the scene, Arthur writes, 'He was rather severe with him and begged me not to give him his shilling. But I thought in this particular instance, perhaps, I understood the situation better than the pedagogue who provided me on the next occasion with a stouter hearted gillie, proof against hob-goblins and supernatural influences.'

Bala lake - Llyn Tegid - has a monster. It is locally known as Teggy and it has been seen regularly over the years until comparatively recently. There have been many descriptions of the creature and they all seem to tally. In 1983 at ten o'clock in the morning, a man out for a walk happened to look across the lake and saw an object about ten feet long coming towards the bank. He rushed down to the foreshore but by the time he got there the 'thing' had disappeared. Another local man was fishing the lake one day when the water was disturbed and a similar creature reared up and began swimming towards him. 'It had a large body', he reported, 'about eight feet long, and a huge head with glaring eyes, its skin was dark and shiny'. The creature continued swimming for about thirty seconds and then slipped beneath the waters.

Fish are plentiful in Bala lake - Glyn Tegid - though the number of pike has meant a reduction in trout but the Gwyniad, a fish resembling the salmon, is only found in the waters of this lake. This fish takes its name from the remarkable whiteness of its scales. Lord Littleton, writing in the eighteenth century, found its taste 'So beautifully delicate as to more than rival in flavour the lips of the fair maids of Bala.' However, we must not linger to ponder the delights of fishy and other embraces, but move on into Bala, the little town on the shores of the lake.

Past a few scattered grey stone houses and a patch of angry looking red brick dwellings, we arrive at a wide and handsome tree lined street bordered with pleasing stone houses and only a smidgen here and there of that vitriolic red brick. About half way down the main street, opposite the Ship Inn, is a statue of Thomas Edwards Ellis, born in 1859. Thomas Ellis was a farmer's son who became very active on the question of Land Reform, Home Rule and the disestablishment of the Church in Wales. He was a Liberal M.P. and was eventually made Chief Whip. He died in 1899 and is remembered with pride by his countrymen.

Another of Bala's notable men, the Reverend Thomas Charles, is also commemorated by a statue, subscribed for by Welshmen all over the world. Thomas Charles is certainly, as Arthur Bradley puts it, 'The patron saint of Bala', and there can be few of his countrymen who have not heard of Charles y Bala, as he is known, for his fame spread far beyond his native land. Bala was not his birthplace, however, for he was born in Caermarthanshire in the year 1755. As a young man, he took holy orders and was for some time a curate in Somerset. When he was twenty-nine years old, in 1784, he left Somerset to become a curate in Bala and he remained there for the rest of his life. His admiration for the Methodists and sympathy with their beliefs and practices was much frowned on in higher places and eventually cost him his curacy. He remained in Bala and spent much of his time teaching adults to read and write. He was also responsible for the opening of many Sunday schools in Wales.

In the year eighteen hundred, a very tired, travel-stained young girl from the village of Llanfihangel y Pennant arrived in Bala and called on Charles y Bala. She was the sixteen-year old daughter of a very poor weaver and her name was Mary Jones. Her feet were sore and bleeding, because she had travelled the whole twenty-five miles over the mountains barefoot. Her family were so impoverished there was no money to buy shoes. In spite of this, she had set off on the nightmare journey, because she had been told that she would be able to buy a Bible in Bala from the great revivalist preacher Thomas y Bala. Mary had saved hard for many,

many years and at last she thought her dream of owning a Bible of her own was about to be realised. Alas, when she called on the preacher it was to be told that he had sold all his Bibles. However, when he looked at the worn out girl who stood before him on the verge of tears and realised how far she had come and how much longer would seem the twenty-five mile trudge back, without her heart's desire, he was so distressed that he gave her his own Bible.

Some time later Charles y Bala was involved in a similar incident when he came upon a small girl whom he had seen in Sunday school the previous week. Bending down, he asked her to repeat a verse from the Bible which he had told the children to learn. He was surprised to find the child confused and embarrassed. Hanging her head, she confessed she could not repeat it for the only Welsh Bible she was able to use belonged to someone who lived in a house seven miles over the mountains and the weather had been too bad for her to attempt the long walk.

This child's story of her difficulty in obtaining a Bible in Welsh, coupled with the memory of Mary Jones's visit, made such an impression on Charles y Bala that he resolved to do something about it. First, he approached the Christian Knowledge Society, for they had published a number of Bibles in Welsh. They could not help him for they had none left and did not intend to publish more. Determined to remedy the situation, his mind teeming with ideas for producing Bibles in Welsh for the Welsh, he made the long journey to London to discuss the position with the Religious Tract Society. The visit was a success, the seeds were sewn, and from them grew The British and Foreign Bible Society.

In 1783, Charles y Bala married Sally Jones, whose father kept a shop in Bala. It was such a happy marriage that after ten years he was able to write 'He (The Lord) gave me ye only person I desired. No person in the world is happier in this respect than myself, I would not change my situation for an imperial crown.' Charles y Bala and his beloved Sally died in 1814 within three weeks of each other. They are buried in the graveyard of the mother church of Bala, which is about a mile along the Dolgelly road out of the town. From all over the world, people subscribed for a statue to be erected to him in the town he loved so well.

There is a tradition that early in the eighteenth century the parson of the church, in the graveyard of which lie Charles and his wife, decided to spruce the place up. As part of the great clean up, he ordered the rushes on the church floor to be cleared away, these had accumulated over the many years to form nice thick pads which eased rheumaticy knees lowered gingerly in prayer. There was, therefore, quite a furore at the idea of removing them. However, ignoring the outraged congregation, the parson and his aids set about the spring clean. To their horror they found, nice and snug, beneath the rushes of ages, several nests of snakes, which obviously felt they had found a very cosy retreat from the cold outside. Needless to say, all demands for the rushes to remain ceased at once.

The little town of Bala was one of those involved in the great religious revival, when as many as twenty-thousand people would crowd into the place to attend one of the religious assemblies. Providing hospitality for such a number must have been quite a strain on the townspeople but caught up in the great flood of religious zeal they no doubt thought it an honour to be chosen as hosts and managed somehow to both feed and house the multitude.

In former times, Bala was very famous for woollen stockings and gloves. Practically everyone in the town knitted, men and women. They knitted as they walked along and as they sat on their doorsteps chatting, or, as night fell, by the light of candles in their cottages. On fine evenings Tomen y Bala, a manmade mount of Norman or, some say, Roman origin, would be peppered with knitters, their needles click clacking away as they gossiped together until the sun went down. One might almost say that the stockings of Bala were by Royal Appointment, for it was well known that the monarch himself, George III, always wore them to ease his rheumatism.

Bala was, and is, famous internationally for its sheep dog trials. These are held each year in August. They began in 1873 when a local land owner, Robert Lloyd Price of Rhiwlas Bala, wanted to show that his collection of upwards of a hundred sheep dogs had within it dogs that would outclass those of a neighbouring farmer whose dogs were well known for their expertise. In order to prove his point, he organised the first sheep dog trials. Alas, it was humble pie for him, for the farmer's dogs won. However, he was a good sportsman and the trials continued and grew until today they are internationally famous. Lloyd Price's grandson Colonel Kenrick Price, carried on the tradition and special centenary trials were held on the Rhiwlas estate in 1973, while his great grandson became president of the International Sheep Dog Trials Society.

That indefatigable traveller in Wales, George Borrow, visited Bala twice in the eighteen fifties, on both occasions he stayed at the White Lion Royal Inn. On his first visit, he managed to severely ruffle the feathers of Tom Jenkins, the waiter, who also appeared to be the stand-in-manager

Borrow supposed that the ale he was served had come from Llangollen. Scandalised by the very idea, the waiter launched into a violent diatribe about the inhabitants of Llangollen. 'They are all drunkards', he thundered, 'and nobody can live among them without being a drunkard'. He finished up by adding that ale like that which George Borrow was drinking 'could never be brewed in that trumpery hole Llangollen'. Borrow, wiping his whiskers must have felt a trifle chastened, nevertheless he had to admit that 'The Bala ale was indeed good, equal to the best that I had ever drunk, rich and mellow with scarcely any smack of the hop in it, and though so pale and delicate to the eye, nearly as strong as brandy'.

On Borrow's second visit to Bala, he stayed at the same inn where a 'little freckled maid' served him some of the famous ale. He complained that it was 'very different from that I drank in the summer when I was waited on by Tom Jenkins'. The little freckled maid told him that it was the last in the cask and there would be no more for six months. Disappointed, he drank porter instead and went to bed. Breakfast, however, put the stuffing back into him. 'What a breakfast', he wrote. 'Pot of hare, ditto of trout; pot of prepared shrimps; dish of plain shrimps; tin of sardines; beautiful beef-steak eggs; muffin; large loaf and butter, not forgetting capital tea.'

About forty years after George Borrow stayed at the inn, in the year 1898, Arthur Bradley came trotting along in his trap and he wrote of the White Lion Royal in Bala, that it was 'Still one of the best inns in Wales.' The inn still stands in the High Street in Bala, though now it is dignified by the name of Hotel. It is a handsome black and white building, very welcoming and spacious, and has a very friendly and helpful staff but, alas, not a freckle in sight.

iii. *First catch your turtle. (See page* 121*)*

Chapter 10

Chirk, Llangollen & Vale Crucis Abbey

DINAS BRAN

Broken ruin; bracken; rain,
Raw cold wind,
Rank weed grows; crows complain,
Ancient stones that mosses stain,
Naught but wreck; man's work is vain.

Douglas Pringle-Wilson

When Arthur Bradley was seven years old and was staying in the Border Country with family friends, one of the expeditions they arranged involved climbing to the top of a Shropshire hill and, in old age, he remembered standing on this hill top and looking out to where, on the western horizon, he could see 'Dim shapes of strange and weird contour'. A member of the party told him they were the hills surrounding the Vale of Llangollen. 'The mellifluous phrase', he writes, 'caught my fancy (and I saw a vision then and there, no doubt from some familiar picture on a wall or in a book, of this fairy tale vale with the sonorous name.' Over the years he visited the area many, many times until, in his own words, 'I knew it through and through', and, he tells us, he found the reality 'Much more beautiful than the picture of my dreams'.

The strange thing is that in spite of the vast changes that have overtaken the countryside in the past one hundred years, dear Mr. Bradley would still find Llangollen much as he remembered it and the Vale, that wonderful mixture of mountains, dark hanging woods, bright meadows, rushing streams and pellucid pools is still a land of heart's desire.

137

The route which I chose to visit Llangollen was the A483 from Welshpool. After about fifteen miles, having bypassed Oswestry, it joins the A5, part of Telford's London to Holyhead road. On the outskirts of Oswestry there is a rash of electric pylons which continues for some distance in the flat fields on either side. They are difficult to ignore but soon, about four miles along, we are nearing Chirk, the village on the banks of the Ceiriog. Bradley would not recognise the approach to this village now for it is very built up and, on the right, though mercifully set back, are the ugly buildings of a wood-chip factory.

However, the heart of the village is as delightful as when he trotted by. On the left two stone-built Victorian schools flank the road, one for boys and one for girls, but they are now a furniture and a carpet factory respectively. The metamorphosis has been blessedly discreet and the school bell still tops the roof in its little bell-cot though silent now and no longer calling the children to their lessons.

The Hand Hotel, with its important pillared porch and Georgian facade, dominates the main street and, skipping along beside it like a school crocodile on the coat tails of an impressive prefect, is a row of pretty Georgian-fronted shops, many-paned sash and bow windows glancing uncomfortably across the street to one of the concessions to modernity this village has made, a Tandoori restaurant. At the far end of the street facing down its length is a very attractive and substantial Georgian house and a lane, off to the left, winds past this to the church, a handsome Norman building, though the north aisle and the tower were added in the fifteenth century.

A short distance from the church, on the opposite side of the lane, is the entrance to the park on the Brynkinallt estate. The long drive leads through lovely tree girt parkland and over a small stone bridge, where far below, through a leafy curtain can be seen bright flashes of the Ceriog hurrying along from its source on the wide grouse moors above Corwen At the end of the drive, rosy-red, dreaming down the years, is an old brick- built Carolean mansion, for centuries the seat of the ancient family of Trevor. In wilder days should anyone living between the Dee and the Ceriog be unwise enough to cause trouble, it was only necessary to raise the cry of 'A Trevor! A Trevor!' to chill the blood and send the marauders packing.

The Duke of Wellington, when at Eton, would often spend his school holidays at Brynkinallt with his grandmother, the Viscountess Dungannon a member of the Trevor family and in the eighteen eighties Lord

Duncannon sent a letter to the Oswestry Advertiser recalling an amusing incident which took place on one of those holidays. The future duke was playing a game of marbles with the son of one of the farmers on the estate, when a dispute over the game turned into a fight. Young Evans, the farmer's son, was getting very much the worst of it, when, like an avenging angel, his sister arrived on the scene. She was carrying a wet towel and with it she set about the future duke, hammer and tongs. A flailing wet towel wielded by a young amazonian was more than a match for him and he beat a hasty retreat to his elder brother, who had been watching the fracas with a deal of amusement.

Evans and his stout hearted sister lived at The Vache, a farm on the Brinkinallt estate, and in later years she married a man named Randles, who took over the farm when her parents died. Lord Dungannon, in his letter to the Advertiser, tells us that the Duke's elder brother, the Earl of Mornington, never forgot the incident and, on each of his frequent visits to Brynkinallt, 'Never did he omit to ride or walk over to The Vache and leave Mrs Randalls a substantial proof of his recollection of her girlish encounter with his illustrious brother'. In later years Mrs Randles was quite a celebrity in her village for having routed the great hero of Waterloo with a good deal of pluck and a wet towel.

Retracing our steps a left hand turn in the main street leads to Chirk Castle, for many years owned by the Myddleton family. Thomas Myddleton was a merchant adventurer who sailed the high seas and, when he came home to rest on his laurels in 1595, he bought Chirk Castle which remained with the Myddletons until it passed to the National Trust in 1981. Magnificent ornamental gates to the castle stand facing the visitor at the end of the short road to the village. These were made by two brothers, Robert and Thomas Davies, between 1719 and 1721. The brothers lived at Bersham near Wrexham and were known as being among the finest iron workers in Europe. The gates are a splendid exuberance of iron flowers and foliage and birds and animals and they richly deserve to be known as the Davies brothers' masterpiece.

In 1282 one of that ubiquitous and acquisitive band of Mortimore Border barons, Roger de Mortimer, was granted the Lordship of Chirk and in 1295 he began the building of Chirk Castle. It is the only one of the great Edwardian fortresses of North Wales to have been continuously occupied since it was built. The interior is one of great elegance many times altered and added to over the centuries.

Sir Thomas Middleton was a well known Cromwellian general who, during the Civil War, found himself attacking his own castle, which had been occupied by the Royalists. After this unfortunate business, he decided his loyalties lay with the King. It is to be hoped he made his peace with his neighbours at Powis Castle for, during his flirtation with Cromwellianism, he and Colonel Mytton, attacked and took Powis.

On the outskirts of Chirk an aqueduct, built by Thomas Telford in 1801, carries the Llangollen Canal across the River Ceiriog scampering along in the valley seventy-feet below. Running parallel to the aqueduct is a railway viaduct and this was built about half a century later. Still on the A5 for Llangollen we passed a sign on which was written Afon Bradley, Bradley's River. This was very exciting for I knew Arthur Bradley was a great fisherman and had fished in most of the places he visited in his extensive wanderings. He also loved the rivers of England and Wales and indeed, had written at least two books on rivers. Could this mean that we had stumbled upon a river which for some reason, perhaps because he often fished its waters, or perhaps because he wrote about it, became known as Bradley's River?

Calling at the nearby farm, we had no answer to our knockings, however, as we walked away, a tall figure emerged from one of the farm buildings and came towards us. 'I was just giving the cows a wash when I heard you' he said, 'I'm Roger Morris, did you want to see me?'. I explained why we had called and was very disappointed when, shaking his head, he replied, 'I've farmed here all my life and my father farmed here before me but no I've never heard any reason for it being called Afon Bradley. But I'll tell you what' he added, 'David Middleton, now he'd be the man to ask, knows all about the area he does, wrote a book about the houses and farms around, if anyone knows he will, he lives at New Hall farm just around the corner. You go and call on him, he'd know'. Thanking him we left, but not for New Hall Farm. Mr. Middleton would have to be visited some other time for there were still a few miles to Llangollen and much to see there, before our picnic at Valle Crucis Abbey. One day I will find Mr. Middleton and hope to get to the bottom of this mystery for it would be such a joy to know that Arthur Bradley, who loved Wales so dearly, had a little river there named after him.

Nearing Llangollen the road runs steeply down hill and, away to the right, the nineteen great arches of the Froncysyllte aqueduct march dramatically across the skyline, carrying the Llangollen canal on their backs across the River Dee which hurries along one hundred and twenty-seven feet below them. The land on the right falls steeply down to the valley and that on our left rises in rounded heights. The occasional farmhouse can be seen set snugly in a little hollow on the green slopes.

Before the final lap down to the old town which is known as 'The Gateway to Snowdonia' a glade of tall trees borders the road on either side and ahead, crowning an almost perpendicular hill, over 1,000 feet above the town, is the ragged curtain wall of that once great stronghold, home of many a proud Welsh prince, Castell Dinas Bran. The streets in the centre of the town are bustling and busy and lined with small shops, some of them with gaily striped awnings, and at the very heart of things is the great medieval stone bridge, its five arches spanning the rushing Dee.

27   *The ragged curtain wall of Dinas Bran*

The bridge was built in 1131, and a little over two centuries later, in 1306, the Bishop of Saint Asaph, John Trevor, improved and enlarged it. Originally there were four arches but a fifth was added in 1861.

Llangollen bridge is one of the seven wonders of Wales. So goes the old quatrain.

Pistyll Rhaiadr and Wrexham Steeple,
Snowdon Mountain without its people,
Overton Yew trees, Saint Winifred's Wells,
Llangollen Bridge and Gresford Bells.

Hugging the bridge on the right hand side approaching the town is the Royal Hotel, a large, white-painted building its feet firmly planted in the Dee, so that the windows on one side look straight down onto the river. Once known as The King's Head, Royal was tacked onto the name after

28   *The large bow window in the Royal Hotel, Llangollen on the left (photograph by Anne Richardson)*

a visit to the hotel by Queen Victoria and the Princess of Wales, however, The King's Head and Royal Hotel proved a bit of a mouthful so The King's Head was dropped and it has been The Royal ever since.

One evening in the eighteen nineties Arthur Bradley, who had been fishing all day from a coracle at Llansarnffraid Bridge, decided to round the day off by dining at The Royal Hotel. A table was prepared in the large bow window overlooking the river and this he shared with two newly married people. With consummate tact the waiter laid their places at one end of the table and Bradley's at the other. He then served the soup, leaving a large tureen in the centre of the table should the guests wish for a replenishment. The honeymooners, no doubt indulging in a little flirtatious chatter, lingered over this course. Bradley finished before them and peacefully contemplated the trout rising in the river below the window. Leaning on the table with both his elbows, probably to get a better view he brought about such a calamity that he remembered it for the rest of his life, as no doubt did the newlyweds. The table consisted of four boards laid on a trestle and covered with a cloth and, as Bradley lent on it, up flew the honeymooner's end, up flew the soup tureen and the water jug and, doing a neat somersault, deposited themselves and most of their contents right in the bride's lap. 'The trousseau frock', writes Bradley, 'was a sight for the Gods'.

This dreadful debacle and the great embarrassment it caused him did not deter him from visiting Llangollen, for he came again many, many times. However, he tells us that the was 'never able to behold that particular window in the Royal Hotel without a shudder'.

I asked Sharon Edwards, who works in the hotel and was showing me round, if I might see the window where he caused such a stir. It was easy to find by his description and I was shown into a pleasantly furnished and comfortable hotel lounge. Far too superior for such things as trestle tables. Sitting in the window alcove, as he did, and looking down on the river swirling and curling round the dark, protruding rocks in its bed, I thought of the little bride and her ruined dress and imagined her flight to her room in tears and her struggles to get out of her flowing garment with its frills and furbelows and, no doubt, since the deluge was so monumental, her stays and countless undergarments too - all those buttons and ribbon ties and a distraught groom standing helplessly by! Poor Mr. Bradley would have been down below miserably watching the mopping up operations going on around him. Good Heavens what a nightmare! A modern bride would just shed a skimpy slip or change to a fresh pair of jeans but a hundred years ago it was a very different kettle of fish.

My little guide around the hotel told me that she was born in Llangollen and had lived there all of her twenty years; that she loved the place, the people and the scenery, adding vehemently, eyes shining, 'I absolutely wouldn't live anywhere else'.

We had decided to picnic near Valle Crucis Abbey which is about two miles out of the town. This enchanting ruin lies in a flat bottomed bowl the hills encircling it. Just before turning down the track leading to the Abbey, we noticed an old stone well in the bank. Probably put there by the monks for pilgrims to the abbey to refresh themselves. With refreshment of a different kind in mind, we drove on down the track, passing some farm outbuildings where the dismembered remains of a Gilbert Scott telephone box were leaning drunkenly against a barn, and on past a gable-end of the Abbey to a wide green meadow, bordered by a happily prattling brook. Here, under the shade of an ancient tree, we unpacked the picnic basket. Horrors! We had forgotten the bottle opener. Can there be anything more frustrating on a warm summer's day than to regard a bottle of cool, flintily-green wine and have nothing with which to open it? However, help was at hand. In the far corner of the meadow a brightly coloured tent had been pitched and some boys were busily unpacking their gear. Bearing the bottle I walked over to them. 'Sorry', they said, 'we haven't a corkscrew', but as I turned to go one of them called out, 'I'll see if I brought my scout's knife'. He had and a true scout's knife it was, with all sorts of implements, including a corkscrew, lying side by side. The bottle was opened in a trice and one young scout had done his good deed for the day.

It was a perfect place for a picnic. The boys, as soon as they had finished unpacking, disappeared on their bicycles to explore and the only sound was bird song and the bleating of sheep. It was just such a scene as the old Abbey, comfortably settled on the banks of the little river, had been witness to for nearly a thousand years.

Not far from the Abbey, in a nearby field is all that remains of a great stone cross known as Eliseg's Pillar. Originally in the form of a cross, it was erected in the ninth century in memory of Eliseg, Prince of Powys, by his great grandson. When the Roundhead soldiers, those destroyers of monuments, came to the Vale of Llangollen during the Civil War, they knocked the cross down and much of it was destroyed. In later years the remains were re-erected but now it stands only seven-feet high instead of the original twelve and the cross piece, along with most of the inscription, has gone. The place where it stands became known as The Valley of the Cross and it was from this that the Abbey Vale Crucis took its name. This monastery was founded in the twelfth century by another Prince of Powys, Madoc ap Gruffyd, Lord of Dinas Bran. When he died he chose to be buried in the Abbey which he had founded.

The monks were Cistercians, those great agriculturists and sheep farmers, and it was they who were responsible for starting the wool and flannel industry which until comparatively recently flourished in Llangollen. The Abbey was very well endowed, the monks owning, among other properties, a mill and a number of dairy farms. Both the monks and the lay brethren were expected to work with their hands. The forty-eighth chapter of the *Rule of the Order* states, 'at fixed times the brothers ought to be occupied in manual labour, and again at fixed times, in sacred reading' and in the early days of the Monastery the *Rule of the Order* was certainly obeyed.

The Cistercians built their abbeys in remote and lonely places and there was much hard manual labour to clear woodlands and prepare sites. The abbots too were expected to live and work as the brethren but gradually this changed, observance of the Rule grew lax and eventually many abbots became immensely powerful and, in many cases, despots. Their quarters grew to palatial size and grandeur and the abbot's table was very far from restrained.

The Abbots of Valle Crucis Abbey were no exception. The Welsh bard, Gutyn Owain, in the fifteenth century sang the praises of his uncle who was the then abbot, telling us that each day would produce a 'Banquet new' and that every day was like a Christmas Day. On one occasion, fearing that he might be overlooked when the invitations to another banquet were issued, and hoping to jog the Abbot's memory and remind him of his kinship, he serenaded him with a poem, the last verse of which ran,

> Nor kings nor barons can exceed
> The wine thou dost bestow so well
> My parentage is of thy stock
> Thy nephew chipped from off thy block

A more flagrant bit of 'tee heeing up' would be difficult to imagine.

Giraldus Cambrensis writes that, when he dined with the Prior of Canterbury in the twelfth century, there were sixteen different dishes and 'much sending of dishes from the prior to the monks, with ridiculous gesticulation in returning thanks, whispering, loose idle licentious discourse, herbs brought in and not tasted, numerous kinds of fish, roasted, boiled, stuffed, fried, eggs, dishes exquisitely cooked with spices, salt meats to provoke appetite and many kinds of wine'. Richard de Sudbury, the Abbot of Westminster, was even more lavish in his hospitality. Early in the fourteenth century at a feast he gave in Westminster Abbey there were six-thousand guests, and three-thousand dishes, eleven tuns of wine, thirty oxen, thirty-four swans, five-hundred capons, one-thousand geese, two-hundred sucking pigs, nine-thousand six-hundred eggs and seventeen rolls of brawn.

Valle Crucis Abbey lasted until the dissolution of the monasteries when much of it was destroyed. When Arthur Bradley visited the place in 1898, a retired clergyman, who was also an antiquarian, lived in a part of the Abbey with his wife. His enthusiasm for the building and its history enchanted Bradley but when many years later he returned he found the old man had died. His son was now curator and an old woman knitting stockings outside was the deceased parson's widow. Alas, there is no devoted parson and his wife to show one round now, just an impersonal young man, in a kiosk at the gate, selling postcards and souvenirs.

Valle Crucis is a magical place. Enough is left of the building to make it no great effort to imagine the days when white-robed, tonsured monks tilled the land and shepherded their sheep, or the times of the great feasts

29   *Valle Crucis Abbey from Arthur Bradley's book. Nothing has changed in a hundred years. Compare with the cover photograph by Anne Richardson.*

given by the Abbot of Valle Crucis, when even the Lord of Dinas Bran would join the throng of high-born guests at his table.

It was to Valle Crucis Abbey that they brought for burial Iola Goch, Lord of Lledryd and one of the greatest of Welsh bards.. His passionate odes against the English stirred the Welsh in their cause, during the time of Owain Glyndwr. Born in 1315 he was still writing poetry as a very old man in 1402 and, in his declining years, he went to live in Owain Glydwr's palace of Sycharth, where he continued to write. He has left us a wonderful record of the domestic life and the great splendours of Owain's palace.

That lover of the good life, the Abbot's bardic nephew, also lies buried at Valle Crucis Abbey. Alas, the desecration and damage following the dissolution of the monasteries was very thorough and left no trace of their graves; but the spirit of the place and the people who knew it drifts around the crumbling walls. At dusk, when the long shadows fall across the soft, green turf in the roofless nave, it can seem the most natural thing in the world to wonder 'was that the wind soughing in the trees, or was it the faint echo of a harp and the haunting voice of one of those bards who spent their days in song at Valle Crucis long ago?'. It is the most natural thing in the world that is, as long as you avert your eyes from the field on the left, as you approach the Abbey down the track, for this is filled with caravans and mobile homes. Admirable things in their place but here, standing cheek by jowl, white roofs gleaming, to within a handful of yards of the Abbey walls, very definitely not in their place. How could this have been allowed to happen? How, with so much open countryside around, could this one particular field, once part of the green frame setting off one of the greatest and most evocative treasures of the land of Wales, be used in this way? Oh! Llangollen, how could you?

Rearing up behind the town to a height of almost a thousand feet is a conical hill, surmounting this, silhouetted against the skyline, are the ragged remains of the curtain wall of a once mighty mediaeval stronghold, Castell Dinas Bran. When Arthur Bradley first saw it he wrote, 'I know of no inland mediaeval fortress anywhere in Britain, so proudly and superbly placed'. The climb up to Dinas Bran is very steep indeed and, in days gone by, it was possible for the not so sprightly to hire a donkey from a yard near the station, and go up in style, however, now-a-days it is 'Shank's pony' or stay below.

No one knows exactly when the castle was built, though we do know that in the thirteenth century Gruffyd ap Madog Maelor inherited it from his father, Madog ap Gryffyd Maelor, and that he endowed Valle Crucis Abbey where both father and son lie buried. By the sixteenth century the castle was well on the way to decline because when Leland saw it he wrote that it was a 'battered ruin' and, in those days he tells us, there was an eagle's eyrie in some rocks below the castle, and each year some unfortunate person would be lowered in a basket to collect the young. This was quite a hazardous undertaking, because, apart from dangling from a great height, the nest robber was, not unnaturally, fiercely attacked by the parent birds and he had to resort to wearing a basket over his head to protect him from tearing talons and beaks. I would not think there were many volunteers for this particular chore.

The history of Dinas Bran was not always battle-torn for there are gentler stories of its past, such as the tale of Myfanwy Fechan (Vaughan) who lived there in the latter part of the fourteenth century. Proud and lovely, a daughter of the great house of Trevor, she ensnared the heart of a bard, Hywel ap Einion Lygliw, so that he was obsessed with love for the unobtainable beauty. His best known poem sang her praises and bemoaned his fate as the unrequited lover. 'Oh! white one, oh! bright one,' he sings, 'like new fallen snow upon Aran'. In several verses he begs her to pity him but when he knows it is hopeless he finishes;

> I still am thy bard, from morn to morn bringing
> To Dinas Bran Palace
> Lay after lay thy bright beauty forthsinging;
> Till all the earth's echoes are ringing;
> 'Myfanwy!'
>
> (*Translation by* Alfred Perceval Graves, MA)

Myfanwy's great beauty and grace certainly fired the imagination for another bard of the period. Gutyn Owain also sang her praises in a long and melancholy song and he ends his ode on an even more desperate note;

> Ah, bid me sing as well I can,
> Nor scorn my melody as vain,
> Or neath the walls of Dinas Bran,
> Behold me perish in my pain!

Even as late as the nineteenth century the lovely Myfanwy could set men's pulses racing, for the great Welsh poet, Ceiriog (John Hughes), achieved fame at once by winning the prize in 1858 at the Llangollen Eisteddfodd with his love poem *Myfanwy*.

Far below the castle and stretching for some miles north is an extraordinary limestone escarpment know as the Eglwyseg Rocks. Thousands of years of wind and rain have formed them into great terraces, which have a remarkable sculptured look. Although it was a warm day, there was a stiff breeze when I first saw them and the flying clouds caused ever changing shadows on the face of these great stepped formations, so that their colours varied in the shifting light from tawny streaked with purple to rosy-gold and misty-grey and, for a short time, while the summit was caught in the bright sunshine, it gleamed pearly-white. Eglwyseg means 'Ecclesiastic' and perhaps because this grandly beautiful escarpment with its dark shadowed gullies and bright changing colours does sometimes give the impression of a great cathedral hewn by nature out of the rock, it was so named.

The lane running along by the meadows below Eglwyseg is bordered by hedges tangled with honeysuckle and dog roses with here and there a flourish of foxgloves trumpeting their way above the waving grasses and ferns. We followed it for about six or seven miles until it became a rather more than bumpy track. So we left the car to wander in the heavily wooded land bordering a wild moorland. Quite suddenly, we came upon a small Elizabethan manor house, half hidden by a screen of ancient trees. I had found this place once before, some time ago, during my various peregrinations round Llangollen but in those days it was empty and desolate, bramble and thorn making the approach difficult. This time we found the land around had been cleared and the little manor looked pristine and cheerful with a front door invitingly open.

Plas Uchaf, for that is the name of the place, has a long and fascinating history. It was built during the reign of Elizabeth I, in the year 1563. Elizabeth herself is said to have stayed there on several occasions and there is a strong tradition that during one of the visits she gave birth to a child. The poor little scrap is said to have been promptly put on the fire. Plas Uchaf would certainly have been a very good hiding place during the latter days of a confinement. If the unfortunate child had been the product of a king's indiscretion, ah! then that would have been very different. He would have simply been given the prenom 'Fitz' along with a number of titles and a lot of property and when he was old enough a good marriage would have been arranged, in short, everything would be as 'Merry as a Marriage bell'. To choose a queen for an unmarried mother, as Lady Bracknell would have said, could only be considered careless - no titles, no estates, just a premature death.

At the time of the Civil War, Oliver Cromwell's brother-in-law, Colonel John Jones, lived at Plas Uchaf. Many Parliamentarians, however ready to fight for the right to be ruled by Parliament, did not agree with the removal of His Majesty's head in order to facilitate this. Colonel

Jones, alas, was not one such, in fact, he was one of the signatories to the King's death warrant. In due course, when the Restoration came, one imagines he retired from the limelight and made all speed for his remote fastness, Plas Uchaf. To no avail however, for he was captured and sentenced to be hanged, drawn and quartered. Pepys, in his diaries, writing at that time when on his way to or from somewhere, recounts, 'I have just past the smoking quarters of Colonel Jones'.

Long after Colonel Jones met his grisly end, George Borrow, that dear old nineteenth century traveller, who, armed only with his umbrella, wandered far and wide into places remote, lonely and sometimes sinister, came upon World's End and Plas Uchaf. He had stowed his wife and step-daughter into a rented cottage on the banks of the Dee and using it as a base set off to explore the area and North Wales. In George Borrow's day the manor house, Plas Uchaf, was occupied and he met the man who lived there and had a long chat. Plas Uchaf, he was told, was so called because it was the highest house in this wild valley. The other two homesteads were Plas Canol, the Middle One, and Plas Isaf, the lowest one.

Arthur Bradley also visited World's End and Plas Uchaf in 1898. He was shown over the house and remembered the 'rich panelling of the walls, the old oak stairs, the quaint furniture, the carved bedsteads and deep windows letting into the low oak-raftered room a dim light'. He noticed too a number of old portraits from the Civil War period on the wainscoted walls. Among them was an original of Cromwell by Lely and one of Cromwell's mother, all relics of the days before Colonel Jones, Cromwell's brother-in-law, was executed. Bradley also found many things, 'unmistakable relics of the Civil War, scattered around'. Where are all these treasures now, one wonders?

Before the Tudor Manor was built a house existed on the same site. It belonged to Cadwgan, Prince of Powys and South Wales. The place was his Hafod or summer dwelling place. Cadwgan's eldest son, Owain was a wild and impetuous youth always causing his father much trouble and eventually bringing about his death. In the year 1106 Cadwgan decided to hold a great feast in Cardigonshire to which every one of consequence was invited. It was while his father was busy hosting his party that Owain committed an act of extreme folly bringing about the downfall of his father's house.

The young man had heard a great deal about the beauty and charms of King Henry's ward, Nest. Her husband was Gerald of Windsor, Constable of Pembroke. Owain, with a party of young hot-blooded friends, raided Gerald's castle and carried off Nest and her children. Gerald just had time to escape down a drain. Owain took Nest to his father's virtually inaccessible house at World's End. The subsequent furore was enormous for King Henry entered the fray, Nest being his ward, and Gerald of Windsor the husband he had chosen for her. Owain fled to Ireland and Henry, unable to find him turned his wrath on Owain's father Cadwgan. Poor Cadwgan, who was completely innocent of any wrong doing, was stripped of his estates by the King and what the King did not take many a Marcher Lord moved in and filched, knowing it would be with the King's approval. Cadwgan was, eventually, killed in one of the many battles that broke out in Wales because of Nest's abduction.

As time went by Owain seems to have been forgiven and, indeed, in his more mature years we find him fighting for King Henry in a Welsh revolt. However, one man could not forgive him, Gerald of Windsor. Gerald was also fighting in the battle. When he realised one of the knights fighting alongside him was Owain, he was determined to avenge his wrongs. He left the battle and gathered some friends around him. Waiting their opportunity, they waylaid Owain and killed him.

The beautiful Nest was grandmother to the even more famous Geraldus Cambrensis or Gerald of Wales. In 1188 Geraldus together with Archbishop Baldwin, journeyed through South and North Wales in order to preach the Cross. Geraldus wrote a book on their travels called *The Journey through Wales*. It is really in the form of a journal and gives a wonderful picture of life in Wales at that period. Geraldus must have heard the stories of his grandmother's abduction and enforced sojourn at the World's End, and perhaps he was curious to see the place and visited it? Who knows? We do know however, that, after the second world war, quite a number of famous people stayed at Plas Uchaf, the old manor house at the World's End. Eventually, the manor was once more used as a shooting lodge and one of the guests of the then owner was Sir Winston Churchill.

During the second world war efforts were made to deflect the German bombers on their way to blitz Liverpool. Fires were lit on the moors around Plas Uchaf as decoys. In some cases it worked and there are still craters on the moor to show where bombers' crews had been deceived into thinking the burning city lay below and had unloaded their bombs. Plas Uchaf was not damaged, that was left to the attentions of vandals who stripped the place of all its panelling and anything they could remove. They hacked out the heart of one of the most historic properties in the land of Wales. They even took the stone inscription over the entrance 'What shall war but endless wars breed' together with the names of various Welsh kings killed in battle.

The old manor has new owners now and has been restored, although of course all the internal wood is new. I suppose the exterior timber framing has been sandblasted because it is no longer black, as in all the old prints and photographs of Plas Uchaf. This gives the place an East Anglian look, for here on the Welsh March and in Wales timbers are almost invariably black. The flat lintel over the door has been replaced by an ogee arch, perfectly in keeping, of course, with the twelfth or thirteenth century and on into the fourteenth century and fifteenth century. I have seen timber-framed houses in Suffolk with such an arch over the doorway but, as yet, not in the March and Wales. I must keep my eyes open in the future. One thing the vandals were unable to despoil was the great stone fireplace in one of the rooms and this has what appears to be a rather timeworn little stone mouse carved in one of the uprights.

Looking down the years what a long cavalcade of people must have sat before that fireplace from Colonel Jones in hiding from the Royalists, toasting his toes and planning ways of outwitting them to Winston Churchill, perhaps in a haze of cigar smoke reliving his days in the Boer war or recounting episodes from the last great conflict between Great Britain and her allies and the Germans and, in the shades, Nest and Cadwgan's tempestuous son, Owain, and a host of others who came to this still sequestered corner, The World's End.

Of course, the undisputed queens of Llangollen are two Irish women, Lady Eleanor Butler and Miss Sarah Ponsonby, or 'The Ladies of Llangollen' as they became known.

Eleanor Butler was born in 1739, her father, Walter Butler, was head of the Roman Catholic branch of the Ormonde family. A slight blight had been cast on this otherwise illustrious family by James, the second Duke of Ormonde. He served at the court of James II and played a large part in snuffing out the Monmouth rebellion but he was, however, a turncoat and changed his allegiance, at the Battle of the Boyne, to King William. Later, Queen Anne seems to have been unperturbed by this behaviour and left him in peace. Not so George I. When he came to the throne the Duke of Ormond was required to forfeit his estates and relinquish all his honours because of his past treachery and his Jacobite sympathies.

Eleanor Butler's father became, de jure, sixteenth Earl of Ormonde in 1766 and in 1791 her brother John's right to the title was recognised. Eleanor was educated in a convent in France. The family coffers being rather bare and Eleanor no beauty and unlikely to marry into a moneyed and landed family, it was decided that she should enter a convent. Decided by everyone except Eleanor, that is, she did not share her family's enthusiasm for this way of solving a problem and had no intention of being incarcerated in a convent for the rest of her life. In spite of great family pressure, she successfully resisted over a period of many years, their efforts to consign her to such a fate.

Not far from the great, gloomy castle of Kilkenny in which the Ormonde's lived was the village of Inistogne. Here, at Woodstock, a comfortable Georgian house standing high on a hill, lived Sarah Ponsonby. Sarah, although descended from a landed family, had no inheritance.

30   *Plas Newydd, Llangollen*

She was orphaned very young and her father's cousin, Lady Elizabeth Fownes, and her husband, Sir William, gave the young girl a home.

Sarah first met Eleanor Butler when she was thirteen years old and

Eleanor sixteen years her senior. In spite of the great age difference, they became life long friends. When Eleanor was thirty-nine years old and being even more pressurised by her family to enter a convent, and Sarah was twenty-three and constantly having to repulse the amorous attentions of her uncle, Sir William Fownes, they made up their minds to run away and spend the rest of their lives together. Their first attempt was thwarted and they were hauled back to their outraged families. However, they persisted in their demands to be allowed to leave and set up house together and, eventually, after many discussions, arguments and threats, it was realised that they were determined on their chosen course. Perhaps with the thought of a possible scandal looming over their heads, if they restrained them by force, their families agreed to their leaving.

Accordingly in May 1778, together with Mary Caryll, one of the Ponsonby housemaids, they left Ireland never to return. After two years of wandering in Wales they came to rest at Llangollen. Here they rented a small cottage, Pen-y-Maes. It was situated on the side of a hill overlooking the little town. They changed its name to Plas Newydd (New Hall). This does seem a rather optimistic gesture, but in the light of the future additions and improvements made by them it was not an optimism misplaced. The cottage grew and flourished under their care as did the garden, part of which wandered down a romantic ravine. They were blissfully happy in each other's company and devotedly looked after by the faithful Mary Caryll and a few other servants. Their dress was somewhat eccentric both of them favouring riding habits with starched cravats and tall beaver hats.

With the coming of the Holyhead road, Llangollen became a convenient stopping place on the route for Ireland and many inns sprang up to meet the coaching demand. This, as Arthur Bradley puts it, 'unearthed the ladies', and soon no one of consequence journeyed that way without paying them a visit. They may well have escaped from the world of fashion but the fashionable world certainly sought them out, as witness a typical entry in their journal for 1821. 'Sunday August 5th. My Lord of Rhagatt, Mr, Mrs, Miss and Mr Augustus Morgan in the morning, then Lord Ormonde and Lord Thurles, then Lord Maryborough and Lord and Lady Burguish to luncheon, then Lord and Lady Ormonde and Lord Thurles to dinner, then Lady Harriet, Lady Anne, Lady Louisa, Mr Walter, M. James, Mr Richard and Mr Charles Butler to supper. Prince Paul Esterhazy for a short time in the evening and Lord and Lady Ormonde slept in our state apartment'. If that leaves you breathless, how about Mary Caryll in her kitchen! The Duke of Wellington was a frequent visitor but as he often stayed with his grandmother, at nearby Chirk, this was not surprising. The Ladies thought him 'a charming young man, handsome, fashioned tall and elegant'.

Many literary lions found their way to Plas Newydd, among them Anna Seward, the 'Swan of Lichfield', Sir Walter Scott, Madame de Genlis, the French authoress, and many others. William Wordsworth arrived with his family in 1824. They stayed for tea and Wordsworth composed a poem while walking in the garden and sent the Ladies a copy. In it he referred to their pride and joy, their now quite splendid Plas Newydd, as a 'Low roofed cott on Deva's banks'. This was poetic license to the point of gross inaccuracy. Feathers were seriously ruffled and he was not asked again. Furthermore, Eleanor Butler, stung to the quick, declared she 'could write better poetry herself'.

Another poet who came to Plas Newydd was the Reverend Leonard Chappelow who lived near Diss in Norfolk. He was so overcome at the thought of meeting the Ladies that he wrote to Mrs. Piozzi (Hester Thrale, Doctor Johnson's friend) telling her that the night before meeting them he had rehearsed the whole occasion in a dream. He too wrote a poem for them. It is one in which the Ladies themselves reflect on their idyllic abode and delightful way of life.

> For us the deep recess of dusky Groves
>
> The fall of waters and the Song of Birds,
>
> And Hills that echo to the distant herds,
>
> Are Luxuries excelling all the Glare,
>
> The World can boast and her chief Favourites share.

There are several verses in the same vein. No raw edges there and in consequence the Reverend gentleman was permitted to scamper over from his vicarage in far away Norfolk to visit the Ladies as often as he wished and enjoy, as he puts it in his poem, 'Converse sweet and brilliant wit, the music of the mind'. Mrs. Piozzi and the Ladies had long wished to meet and it was Mr. Chappelow who introduced them, to their great mutual satisfaction. Brynbella, the Piozzi's house, was only about fifteen miles from Plas Newydd and the Piozzi's often broke their frequent journeys to Bath by visiting the Ladies en route.

Even though they teetered on the edge of a financial abyss most of the time, their life at Plas Newydd was perfection itself. The days flew past occupied in planning and planting their garden, supervising the gothicising and beautifying of their house, reading aloud to each other, painting and walking, and entertaining their numerous interesting visitors.

Alas, the waters of this serene and delightful situation were sadly rippled when Mary Caryll, the servant who left Ireland with them and who had devoted her life to furthering their comfort, after various periods of sickness, died in 1809. Before her death, Mary had spent her life savings on purchasing the field called Aberadda, which the Ladies leased from the vicar for their livestock. This field Mary left in her will to Sarah Ponsonby. She was buried in the churchyard of St. Collens, the parish church of Llangollen, and the Ladies had a three-sided memorial stone erected over her grave, near the church porch. Here they planned to join Mary when their time came. Mary's epitaph composed by Doctor Dealtry reads

> Patient, industrious, generous, kind,
> Her conduct left the proudest far behind,
> Her virtues dignified her humble birth,
> And raised her mind above this sordid earth.

Eleanor Butler died in the summer of 1829 aged ninety. Two years later Sarah Ponsonby followed her beloved friend to the grave. The three women, Eleanor and Sarah and Mary, sleep one each side of the three-sided memorial stone which the Ladies erected when Mary Caryll died.

Early in the nineteen thirties, just over a century after Sarah Ponsonby's death, the one time medical officer of Holloway Prison, a woman named Mary Gordon, was visiting her friend. the wel-known psychoanalyst Carl Jung. While there she had a strange dream. She found herself wandering among the ruins of Valle Crucis Abbey, which she had not seen since she was a young girl. Her dream made such an impression on her that she recounted it to Jung, who insisted that she revisit the Abbey where he felt the meaning of her dream would be made clear.

Doctor Gordon was a woman of seventy-three years and what is known as a 'down to earth and no nonsense' sort of person, both in manner and appearance. She has been described as 'rather stocky with short cropped grey hair'. She was certainly not the sort of woman given to fantasising, one can almost hear snorts of derision accompanied by 'Poppycock', and 'Balderdash' issuing from her sensibly tweed clad figure at the very idea of anything supernatural and yet she found her dream so disturbing she decided to take her friend's advice to re-visit the Abbey

She booked a room in Llangollen and set off for Valle Crucis but although she spent many solitary hours in the Abbey, hoping the meaning of her dream would be made clear, she was to be very disappointed. There were no revelations spiritual or otherwise. However, she had arranged to stay for a few days and decided to make the best of a bad job by visiting some of the other places of interest in and around Llangollen. Her first choice was Plas Newydd. At that time the house of the Ladies stood empty and desolate and was sadly in need of care.

Doctor Mary climbed the hill out of the town, crossed the garden and entered the house. At once she had an overpowering feeling that she was not alone and that two unseen presences were with her, but they chose not to manifest themselves, and after a while she left. The following day her visit to Llangollen ended. The feelings she had experienced in Plas Newydd made such a great impression on her, that during the following months she read everything she could lay her hands on about the Ladies.

Eventually she returned to Llangollen and once more set off up the hill to Plas Newydd. She wandered round the house but had no sensation of other presences and after a while, again disappointed, she left. However, instead of returning to the town at once, she decided to have another look around the garden, which had once been such a joy to the two Ladies. She chose a path leading up the hillside and, as she turned a corner, she came upon two figures seated together on a low bank. They were unmistakably Eleanor Butler and Sarah Ponsonby. Writing about it later she remembered that they were quite motionless and she felt she must have disturbed them from sleep. Quietly she introduced herself and after a brief conversation it was arranged that the three of them should meet in the house at nine p.m. that evening.

This fearless seventy-three year old woman kept the rendezvous. Once again she plodded up the hill to Plas Newydd. It was an extraordinary situation, an elderly, heavily respectable, very down to earth doctor keeping an assignation with the ghosts of two women who had died a hundred years before. On arrival at Plas Newydd, she found it locked for the night, the custodian no longer there. Undeterred, she walked round to the back and broke in through a window, after which she sat calmly waiting in the library. So unconcerned was she, about a situation which would have been for most people spine chilling at the very least, that she dozed off. She woke with a start, and there they were, Eleanor and Sarah. Eleanor sat beside her on the sofa and Sarah chose a chair. The three women chatted away together for several hours until dawn broke and then, as swiftly and quickly as they came, they vanished. And the unflappable Mary Gordon clambered up over the cill and out of the window and presumably arrived at her hotel with the milkman.

With such a galaxy of savants and wits foregathering at Plas Newydd, when the Ladies were alive, there must have been hundreds of sparkling and fascinating conversations such as those described by the Reverend Leonard Chappelow in his poem, but I hardly think the one Doctor Gordon had with the Ladies would rank with them for we are told it consisted in a great part of talk on the education of women and marriage in the twentieth century.

Mary Gordon wrote a book about her experiences called *The Flight of the Wild Goose*. She used some of her royalties to have a plaque erected in memory of the ladies in Llangollen Church.

Much has been written about the Ladies of Llangollen and a book on them by Elizabeth Mavor was published in 1970, it is an absorbing and fascinating read. In her book Elizabeth Mavor writes, 'There occurred in the summer of 1774 a minor literary tragedy. On the 5th of July, Doctor Johnson, in company with Mrs. Thrale and her daughter, set out on a tour of North Wales. On his return home two months later he passed by Llangollen just four years too early to meet the celebrated Ladies'.

Elizabeth Mavor is right - a minor literary tragedy indeed. Had the great lexicographer stumped up the hill to Plas Newydd to astonish them all with his vast learning, how the ball of conversation would have bounced back and forth, his brilliant mind and Eleanor's stringent wit striking sparks off one another, with here and there a little divertissement from Mrs. Thrale, and a quiet smile of encouragement for her 'Beloved' from Sarah Ponsonby. Although he was unable to visit the Ladies, Johnson did, however, leave his impressions of the Vale of Llangollen. 'All the blessings of Nature,' he wrote, 'Seemed here to be collected and its evils extracted and excluded'.

For those who would know Wales, it seems to me, this is where they should go for the very essence of that fair land has been distilled and infused in the lovely and romantic Vale of Llangollen. Sad, indeed, am I to leave it.

31   *Carving from Plas Newydd - Adam and Eve*

Chapter 11

Earthquakes, Landslides, a Shropshire Parson & Stapleton

One Monday afternoon, about three years ago, I was sitting in the kitchen sorting seed packets and fantasising about a proverbial 'blaze of colour', when I heard a deep and prolonged growling noise. Looking up, I saw the cooker gently sashaying towards me. I watched in horrified fascination as it advanced and, with what seemed like a skip and a distinctly Mae West wiggle, came to a halt about two-feet out from the wall, stretching its flexible pipe to the limit. The deep growling continued for a moment or two a, while I had a vaguely unstable feeling, almost a sensation of floating. Another moment and all was quiet again. It was then that the thought flashed through my mind that something untoward must have happened to the calor gas cylinders outside. Rushing out, I found the cheerful, red twins standing side by side like two Victorian pillar boxes, as meek and mild as could be, not a sign of trouble there. As I pushed the skittish cooker back into place, I reflected that were it not for its little foray I might well have supposed that I had imagined the roaring noise and the floating feelings.

However, on the news that evening I learned that the cause of the disturbance was in fact an earthquake, which had been felt from Edinburgh to Southampton and, as earthquakes go, one of no mean size, for it measured 5.4 on the Richter scale. According to a spokeswoman from the British Geological Society, who came down from Edinburgh to investigate, the quake was equal to one which took place in 1984 on the Lleyn Peninsular in Wales making it jointly, with that one, the biggest earthquake in Britain on their records. Experts traced the epicentre to Guildon Farm at Clun, about five miles from where I live. They then pinpointed it to a grassy hill, pastureland for sheep and owned by the Gwilliams family. It seems it was caused by a fault in rock hundreds of millions of years old, lying about nine miles beneath the hill.

Guildon farm is farmed by the two Gwilliams brothers. They live in Lower and Upper Guildon Farms. Mrs Frank Gwilliams who lives in Upper Guildon Farm told me that she 'Heard a terrific rumbling and then the whole kitchen shook and it seemed as if the walls were moving to meet each other and the table started jumping about. At first I thought I must be having some sort of a turn, then my two children came rushing into the room crying "a lorry must have crashed into the back of the house", we ran outside but found all was well, it was then I thought I wonder if there's been an earthquake? When my husband came home and we told him what had happened, he said he'd been out in the fields in the landrover and felt nothing. It was the same with my sister-in-law who lives at Lower Guildon Farm, just below the hill. She and her children felt terrific vibrations and plant pots were falling off the shelves, but when her husband came in, he said he had been working on the tractor and heard nothing. The men working in the sheep-pens heard it though and they rushed into the open, fearing the corrugated iron roofs would collapse on them. In spite of what our husbands said, we were determined to listen to the news and we heard that there had indeed been an earthquake'.

The hill at the centre of this disturbance is called The White Hill and across the valley a similar hill is the Black Hill. Frank Gwilliams told me that he did not know why the White Hill was so called but he would hazard a guess that it might be because after a period of dry weather, with sun is shining on it, it looks silvery white .

A few days after the earthquake, scientists from The British Geological Society came down from Edinburgh and placed thirteen monitoring stations at various points about six miles from the epicentre in order to keep tabs on any further movement. Information gained in this way is radioed to the Long Mynd and from there to Edinburgh to be analysed.

About twenty miles north of Clun at Stapleton, one of the villages in the lanes between Bishop's Castle and Shrewsbury, a friend of mine had a narrow escape during the earthquake. Her husband remarked, 'Jo would have been killed had she not been in bed with 'flu. She had intended that afternoon to wade through a pile of paperwork on her desk, which was standing near a chimney breast. However, feeling unwell she went to bed instead. The earthquake brought the chimney breast down onto the desk and all around were great lumps of debris. This must be one of the rare occasions when having 'flu has been a blessing!

Wales and the Border Country are not strangers to landslips and earthquakes. Over the years people have left some fascinating records of them. In 1571 at Much Marcle in Herefordshire there was a tremendous landslip. Camden writing of it forty years later says 'The hill called Marclay rose, as it were, from sleep, and three days together, shoving its prodigious body forwards with a horrible roaring sound, overturning all that stood in its way, advanced itself to the great astonishment of the beholders to a higher station by that kind of earthquake I suppose which naturalists call Brasmatia.'

Another writer, in an old book entitled *Admirable Curiosities Rarities and Wonders of England,* gives a more specific account going into such technicalities as to how large a hole it left in its wake. 'Marclay Hill', we read 'began to open up itself in the evening and this hill with a rock made at first a mighty bellowing noise and then lifted up itself to a great height and began travelling carrying along trees which grew upon it, and sheepfolds and flocks of sheep abiding thereon. In the place where it was moved was a gaping distance 40-feet wide and 300-feet long. Passing along it overthrew a chapel, removed a yew tree in the church yard from east to west, thrust before it highways, houses and trees, made tilled ground pasture and pasture into tillage.'

The famous nineteenth century geologist, Sir Roderick Murchinson, records that the chasm left was 400-feet wide by 520-feet long. This is somewhat larger than the measurement given in the old book, making one suspect that holes like fish tend to grow with the telling. However, Sir Roderick's reputation was such that his figures are more likely to be the correct ones.

Tradition has it that two bells were dug up from the chapel that was overthrown and that sometime during the last century they were hung respectively at Stoke Edith House and Homme House. There was quite an extensive correspondence about these bells in the *Hereford Journal* from September 30th 1893. Colonel E. Money Kyrle of Homme House told the *Hereford Journal* that there was a bell at Homme House which was certainly believed by the family to have been dug from the ruins of the chapel at Much Marcle sometime towards the latter half of the eighteenth century. This bell was taken to his grandfather as the then Lord of the Manor. He added the bell was still in use and was rung to call the workmen in from the Park. Any rival claim to chapel-bell ownership was successfully quashed when, in 1898, someone climbed up to examine the bell at Stoke Edith, only to find the date 1690 clearly incised on the bell rim. As this date was much later than the landslip, it could not have been one of the chapel bells.

In May 1773 there was an enormous land slip between Buildwas and Ironbridge in Shropshire. The Reverend John Fletcher, the vicar of nearby Madeley, wrote a vivid description of what he referred to as 'this dreadful phenomenon'. This was found in a dilapidated little book, by a certain Mamie Whitford. 'When I cam to the spot', wrote Parson Fletcher, 'the first thing that struck me was the destruction of the little bridge that separated the parish of Madeley from that of Buildwas, and the total disappearance of the turnpike road to Buildwas, instead of which nothing presented itself to my view except a confused heap of bushes and huge clods of earth tumbled over one another.' He clambered about over what were once fields of crops and were now churned up into great mounds, some of them several yards high with vast hollows between. 'The desolation', he writes, 'appeared to me inexpressibly dreadful. Between a shattered field and the river, there was that morning a bank on which besides a great deal of underwood grew twenty fine, large oaks this wood shot with such violence into the Severn before it, that it forced the water in great columns a considerable height, like mighty fountains and gave the overflowing river a retrograde motion.'

After telling us of various calamities to buildings and fields, he goes on to say, 'The Severn, notwithstanding a considerable flood which at tha' time rendered it doubly rapid and powerful having met with two dreadfu shocks, the one from her rising bed and the other from the intruding wood, could do nothing but foam and turn back with impetuosity.' The river, out of its bed, was rising at such a rate as to cause great alarm a' Buildwas, but luckily, Parson Fletcher tells us, 'It got a vent through the fields on the right, after spreading far and near and over the grove tha' had so unexpectedly turned it out of its bed which it had enjoyed fo' countless ages. Sharp was the attack but the resistance was yet mor' vigorous and the Severn repelled again and again was obliged to seek ou' its old empty bed. The moment it found it again it precipitated itsel' therein with a dreadful roar, and for a time formed a considerabl' cataract then with considerable fury began to tear and wash away a fine rich meadow opposite the grove and in a few hours worked itself a channel three-hundred yards long through which a barge from Shrewsbury ventured three or four days later.' What terror this mighty river, rampaging and roaring around like a herd of rogue elephants on the loose, must have struck in the hearts of those who lived in or near its path.

The parson who wrote this spirited account was born on September 12th in 1729, on his father's estates in Switzerland. His real name was Jean Guillaume de la Flechere, which was later anglicised to John Fletcher. He was educated at the University of Geneva and, when he left, he came to England in order to learn the language. He travelled to Shropshire and took a post as tutor to the two sons of Mr Hill, the M.P. for Shrewsbury, and so began his life-long, love affair with the Border Country and Wales. Although he returned to Switzerland to visit his father at various times, he made Shropshire his home. A few years after becoming tutor to the Hill boys, at the age of twenty-eight, he was ordained and he obtained the living at Madeley in Shropshire. He was growing increasingly interested in Methodism and spent much time with John Wesley and, indeed, it was Wesley's wish that when he died John Fletcher should succeed him and carry on his great work. This was not to be, however, for John predeceased him, dying from tuberculosis at the age of fifty-six.

John Wesley was deeply distressed by the death of this man whom he so respected and had grown to love and he wrote a moving biography of him. In it he says, 'within four score years I have known many excellent men - holy in heart and life - but one equal to him I have not known - nor do I expect to find another such on this side eternity.' John Fletcher's fame during his lifetime for his piety and powerful preaching has travelled down the years and in August 1985 the parish of Madeley arranged many events to commemorate the two-hundredth anniversary of his death.

Far away in California, the genealogist and historian, John Bowater, heard of this forthcoming commemoration and, knowing that I lived in Shropshire and might be interested, sent me a fascinating package containing various items to do with this remarkable parson. Among the contents was an original letter, written and signed by him, to his friend William Perronet, also Wesley's biography of him and an engraving signed by Fletcher. In the engraving he would appear to be preaching, standing before an open book, presumably a Bible. A cheerful touch is a horribly grinning skull on which his left hand rests. Was this a

novel idea for congregation control? John Fletcher pulled no punches
when preaching. At Atcham church near Shrewsbury, for example, he
addressed the parishioners as 'Ye adulterers and adulteresses.' This
undoubtedly woke them up, and seeing such grisly evidence of man's
mortality before them would certainly dampen down any excesses.

32   *Parson John Fletcher*

Wesley's book, although extremely informative, is absolutely devoid
of any humour, surely one of God's most precious gifts. Obviously, this
is a sentiment with which Wesley would disagree, for when giving his
readers the text of a letter from John Fletcher's friend, William Perronet
he is disturbed by its tone and writes, 'There is something in the beginning
of the letter which is a little humorous, but this the candid reader will

easily excuse.' Wesley tells us that in 1768 the Countess of Huntingdon, who had long admired Fletcher's preaching, asked him to be the director of an establishment she had founded in Wales. Trevecka, as it was called, was to be a place where young men could be trained for the ministry. He accepted her offer but remained Vicar of Madeley, visiting Trevecka as often as he could. John Fletcher had for some time shown symptoms of tuberculosis and the frequent long journeys over arduous terrain often in dreadful weather to Trevecka, did nothing to improve his health.

On one occasion, when crossing a bridge on horseback, it collapsed just as he arrived at the middle of it. His mare's forelegs were in the river, but the rest of her was still supported by part of the bridge. He managed to get off her back and unfasten the saddlebags. He felt the best thing to do was to somehow get the rest of her into the river and hope she would swim ashore, but heave and push as hard as he could, she was not to be budged and remained 'lying as if dead' with her forelegs dangling in the river. The remaining part of the bridge was making an ominous cracking noise, so Parson Fletcher decided the time had come to abandon ship. Somehow he managed to clamber and scramble over the broken bridge to the bank. The moment he set foot on the ground, the mare came to life and wildly plunging and kicking caused the rest of the bridge to collapse into the river taking her down with it. There were some anxious moments but, eventually, she surfaced and swam towards the shore.

In view of this sort of diversion on his journeys into Wales, it was perhaps as well that, after a few years at Travecka, he found it necessary to resign as Director of the Seminary. His resignation was not due to his failing health but was on a matter of principle. The Headmaster of Trevecka had been sacked because he did not believe in the Absolute Doctrine of predestination and insisted that all men, through Jesus Christ, could be saved. John Fletcher shared his views, feeling that his dismissal was most unjust, and he therefore resigned his post.

Fletcher had suffered from tuberculosis for many years but during his remissions his energy was enormous. He travelled great distances along the Border and in Wales, preaching and evangelising, and tended his flock in his Madeley Parish with great care but his illness progressed until, at one period, his doctors advised him to refrain from speaking lest it bring on the dreaded spitting of blood. For a man who so burned with the fierce desire to exhort people to follow the Lord, this surely could not have been more frustrating. It was during this sad time that he stayed with a Mr and Mrs Greenwood and, when he left them, Mrs Greenwood must have been not a little surprised to receive a letter from him thanking her for her 'Kind attention to a dying worm'.

Soon after leaving the Greenwoods, he journeyed to Switzerland in the hope of a cure. While staying with his father, he was joined by his friend, William Perronet, who wrote a letter home describing their journey through France. In the letter there is a delicious snippet of social history in France at that time which is well worth quoting. 'Though it was wartime', he writes, 'yet we did not meet with the least incivility, either here or in any part of France; but the badness of the inns makes the travelling through this county very disagreeable. The rooms in general are so dirty as to be fitter for swine than men. Each room both above and below stairs is provided with two, three or four beds, and they are so high as to require steps to get up to them; for there is on each bed, first a monstrous canvas bag stuffed with a huge quantity of straw, over this is a feather-bed, and on this as many mattresses as the host can furnish, but the worst is the sheets are not damp but downright wet. At table everyone is furnished with a spoon and fork but no knives, and in general they are not needful for both flesh and vegetables are so stewed down as to be properly termed spoon meat'.

France was not the only country to be so distinguished by its inns at that time, for in 1790 John Byng recalled in his Journal that, 'when travelling in Montgomery my blankets stank so intolerably that I was obliged to sweeten them with a quarter of a pint of brandy'.

When John Fletcher returned to England, his health was so much improved that when he met a Miss Bosanquet, whom he had known twenty-five years before when she was a girl of fifteen, he found he was still attracted to her. Being in a position to ask her to marry him, he proposed. They were married soon afterwards and Wesley tells us that John Fletcher said to the friends who had joined him on this glad day for breakfast, 'The postillions are now ready to carry us to the church, in order to see our nuptials solemnised, but death will soon be here to transport us to the marriage of the lamb'. It is to be hoped that his bride did not hear of this pronouncement by her intended, true she was not in her springtime, but she could hardly be said to have one foot in the grave and such predictions could have been a mite unnerving.

Mary looked after John so well that for over a decade he was restored to health and they lived happily together in Madeley where he busied himself in his Parish, and founded a school and several Sunday schools. Unfortunately, the old enemy returned in full force and in 1792 on

EARTHQUAKES, LANDSLIDES, A PARSON & STAPLETON

September 12th, John Wesley's Parson 'sans pareil' slipped quietly away. But now, we must leave earthquakes and landslips which led us on to Parson Fletcher and return to Stapleton, for we scarcely put a toe in it before being diverted to Much Marcle.

Although Stapleton lies barely a mile from the busy A49, the village ignores this unwelcome intruder, which has taken the place of an old turnpike road on its eastern side, leaning instead to the west where a maze of winding lanes wander among the meadows and woodlands. At the heart of the village is the Church of Saint John the Baptist, and what an extraordinary building it is. It is said to be unique in England. The first record of a church at Stapleton was in the year 1291 and it was then a chapelry of Condover. According to the *Victoria History for the Counties of England,* the nave and chancel are thirteenth century, the tower and vestry being added in the nineteenth century. It would be necessary for a priest to wear stilts in order to wash the communion vessels in the piscina for it is situated, way above one's head, in the south wall over the chancel. A possible reason for this extraordinary position is that the building was originally two stories, the upper being used as a church and the ground floor as an undercroft or a store. This would mean the piscina would be the perfect height for any priestly chores. It is supposed that the two floors were made one in the latter middle ages.

Another theory is that a church was built in the twelfth century on top of an existing Norman church, the original church then serving as a crypt. Many other ideas have been advanced as to the usage of this lower story. One suggestion is that it was a fortress, presumably a place where the villagers could gather and barricade themselves in during the interminable border battles. Another is that it was a lodge for a forester and his dogs. Perhaps this last is not so far off the mark for Wild Edric is known to have had a lodge in Stapleton. Edric was the Saxon Earl of Shropshire who held out against the Normans for a considerable time, joining with the Welsh in a bloody battle with the Conqueror and his men. He was finally defeated by the first of the Mortimer clan. Being a realist, Edric then swore allegiance to King William and joined him in his battle with the Scots. The manner of his death is a mystery but it is said that he is sometimes seen riding a white horse, his wife at his side, leading a band of warriors in a wild gallop over the moors on the Long Mynd, a range of giant hills near Stapleton. His appearance is usually on the eve of a great conflict and, when Arthur Bradley came to the area, he was told by his friend, Miss Jackson, who with Charlotte Burn wrote a book of Shropshire folklore, that she had met a young woman who told her that, just before the Crimean War, she and her father had been on the Long Mynd together when they heard a blast from a horn and Edric leading his ghostly cavalcade swept by. The girl described Edric as having 'Short, dark curly hair'. She said he wore a green cap with a white feather, a short green coat and cloak, a horn and short sword hanging from a golden belt. The lady with him was dressed in green and her yellow hair was long and hung to her waist, around her forehead was a band of white linen and she wore a dagger in her belt. She told Miss Jackson that her father had seen the same thing before the battle of Waterloo.

Nicholas Dunn, in his excellent booklet *Stapleton and its Church down the centuries,* leans to the theory that the ground floor of the church was a place for the rector to store the produce of his glebe. He also points out that the two-story arrangement can only have lasted one hundred years or so because the priest's doorway, in the south wall, which leads into the chancel rises above the dividing line between the two floors and the architectural style shows that the doorway was in position around the year thirteen-hundred. The church was restored in 1790. On the wall is a black painted tablet, with gold lettering recording that it was 'Repaired and new pewed' in the rectorship of the Reverend Edward Powys (1790-1819). During the incumbency of the Reverend the Hon. E R B Feilding, the little wooden bell-cot was removed from the roof and a rather unfortunate looking tower erected to take its place.

The more recent restoration was in 1866-67, when the Reverend C W A Feilding was Rector. A London architect was employed and two thirds of the cost of the project was provided by the Rector and his connections. There were many exciting discoveries during this restoration; when the old plaster was stripped off the walls, slit windows and a long hidden Norman doorway in the north wall emerged. Much work was done including the replacement of a hideous brick vestry, the product of the 1790 efforts, by a combined organ chamber and vestry. The pews, choir stalls, pulpit and lectern all date from the 1866-67 restoration. The huge candlesticks have a very sombre teutonic look, which is not surprising as they were made in Nuremberg in the fifteenth century. A delightful and very rare treasure is a fragment of needlework which is framed and hangs on the south wall. This is said to be the work of Mary, Queen of Scots. Nicholas Dunn tells us that it once belonged to the 'Historic Scottish family of Grant', though how it came to be in this old church in rural Shropshire is not known.

In the churchyard, which on one side looks across a green sward to an oxbow pool formed by an old stream, there is a curious mound referred to by some authorities as a tumulus and by others as a motte. The Rector, the Reverend Robert Payne, Major Mark Harwood-Little, who lives in the Old Rectory, and I scrambled up the steep, bramble covered sides and found on the top, overgrown with tufty grass and more brambles, four graves. We were able to clear the undergrowth away on three of them and revealed that they were the graves of a former rector, the Reverend Charles Feilding and his two wives. The fourth grave was too buried in greenery to uncover in a short space of time.

The white-walled rectory alongside the churchyard was built in 1827 to replace a former one. The ground floor of its predecessor was constantly awash, in inclement weather. The Harwood Littles who live there cherish it and have brought it back to life. There are certainly no pools on the ground floor now. It was in this Old Rectory that the chimney came through the roof during the earthquakes. Over the porch is a shield which probably held the arms of the Feilding rectors, they being kinsmen of the Earl of Denbigh.

At the turn of the century, the curate of a Birmingham suburb left the Midland metropolis and, with his wife and two children, came to live in his old house as rector of the parish. Three-quarters of a century later in 1977 one of his children, Miss M Haseler, wrote a few pages recalling life in the village when she was a child. She was seven-years old and her brother was five when they first arrived in what, to them after the busy city streets, was a veritable wonderland. With the help of the gardener, who had worked on a farm in his youth, her father decided to 'Try his hand at farming on the nine acres of Glebeland'. A pig and a few sheep were purchased and the old gardener enjoyed the days he went to sell or buy sheep at the Dorrington market and, writes Miss Haseler, 'He invariably came back "market peart"'.

This venture into farming was by no means an unqualified success. The Rector one year, determined to enter into the spirit of the thing, decided to make his own cider. He hired a cider-making machine. An old blind horse, attached to it by a beam, walked round and round in a circle until every scrap of juice was expressed from the apples. Alas, they were not cider apples. When the Rector proudly trotted out to the fields to try the resulting beverage on the men helping with the hay making, they were not impressed. One of them, with exquisite politeness, in order not to hurt the Rector's feelings, said that it was 'Better 'n water'.

The old half-timbered barn, the stables and the kitchen garden, with the north wall covered with fruit, all formed an enchanted land for the two children. Then there were the Shropshire Yeomanry, mostly sons of farmers, who would come riding through the village resplendent in their uniforms. Down by the brook the clog makers would camp in the summertime and cut blocks of alder to be made into clogs in Lancashire. In the winter, when the snow lay thick as it used to do in those long ago winters, there was 'gorgeous tobogganing' on Wayford Hill. A particular excitement was the arrival of a hurdy-gurdy and how they loved the performing monkey sitting on it. Gypsies, pedlars, tramps and, of course, the annual visit of the threshing machine, all mixed up in an exciting rag bag of memories for the Rector's daughter as she looked down the years. The most interesting of the callers she found were the tramps. They worked their way from workhouse to workhouse by doing stone breaking or sawing wood or some such. No doubt there were some good tellers of stories to small children among them, for tramps before the second world war were almost invariably true 'Gentlemen of the road'. 'What an idyllic existence!', she writes, 'No rates, no taxes, no ties, no responsibilities, but not so idyllic as those child-hood years spent in Stapleton a long time ago'

About a mile from the village is the Old Moat Farm. Time was when this ancient house, built on the site of a Saxon stone dwelling, was known as Moat Hall. Curiously, the name does not derive from the fact that there is a moat, now dry, around the place, but because it stands on the site of an original 'mote' or 'moot', the meeting place of the Saxon elders. The Hall and the land were held by the Stapletons, from the reign of King Stephen until 1455, when a certain Edward Leighton married Elizabeth a co-heiress of Sir John Stapleton. She brought Moat Hall and its land with her to the marriage. In 1614 the place was still in the hands of the Leightons, but Robert Leighton sold it and by 1699 it had ceased to be a manor house and had become a farm. The house then passed through several different families until it came by marriage to the Oakleys In 178 Richard Oakley built the timber-framed malthouse. However, the Oakley removed to Montgomery in 1850 and, after various other occupants, the house is now the home of Mr and Mrs Mottram who farm the land. It is a mixed farm, arable and animals.

This remarkable old house is built on a massive stone plinth, about fifteen-feet above the level of the ground, and thought to be all that is left of the former Saxon dwelling. At one time the moat was filled with water but now it is dry and in its grassy bed grow gnarled and venerable appl trees. Over the moat there used to be a drawbridge leading through an arched gateway, and in Tudor times a timbered gatehouse was built over the gateway but, alas, it was demolished in the nineteen forties. The great black oak timbers were taken to build the lych gate at Stapleton Church. Miss Haseler tells us in her reminiscences that 'The men constructing it (the lych gate) said that sawing the old oak was like trying to saw cast iron'.

Through the gateway and to the right is the entrance porch, supported by huge timbers. A great oak door, iron-studded, leads into the house. Much of the oak panelling in the house has gone. Richard Oakley, whose family lived at the farm for many years, wrote a fascinating booklet on the old house. He says it went to form cupboards and pedestals for displaying antiques in galleries some years ago. But, in spite of this, there is no denying the charm of these low ceilinged rooms. The beautiful oak doors still remain and scraps of linen fold panelling give a taste of what has been.

In the drawing room, at the centre cross point of the magnificently moulded and reeded ceiling beams, is a beautifully carved Tudor rose surrounded by acanthus leaves. Surprisingly this embellishment is relatively modern. It was the idea of the then occupier who had it fashioned by Carver Hill, who lived at nearby Pulverbatch in the eighteen hundreds. The carving is so crisp and elegant that one feels that a latter day Grinlin Gibbons was hiding his light beneath the hills of the Marchland. When Richard Oakley saw the place and wrote about it, it was standing empty and forlorn and likely to fall into ruin. Happily it has been rescued from such a fate.

Turning to look back as we left, I thought of the days when men had ridden through that gateway, pennants flying, to repel another patch of border strife, or of the days when all had not gone well, returning, helter-skelter across the drawbridge, through the arch to safety, as the gate clanged behind them. Days that are long gone and the beautiful half-timbered gatehouse with them, but the rambling old farmhouse seems quite content to settle down among the Shropshire hills and meadows and dream on its proud past, when it was the manor house of the Stapletons, whose great baronial lords of the area.

iv. *Pop back into the dining room for a few top-ups. (See page 39)*

Chapter 12

Lines of Communication, Evancoyd, Old Radnor & New Radnor

I was much looking forward to another week of wandering in Wales, this time with Old Radnor and New Radnor in my sights. Accordingly I scampered into the village of Leintwardine early one Monday morning, all 'bright eyed and bushy tailed' as the Australians say (or is it the Americans?) in order to gather up a few goodies for a picnic. As I emerged from the village shop, I found, that as so often happens, the 'Best laid schemes o' mice an' men gang aft agley' for a large diversion to my plans in the shape of a tall stranger was walking towards me. 'Can you tell me', he said, as he drew level, 'if this Leintwardine Watling Street is still part of the old Roman Watling Street?' 'It is indeed', I replied, 'but it is only a very small part. Watling Street, as you probably know, runs from Dover in the south-east, up one side of England and down the other, to Caerwent in the south-west. Its rather like a huge horseshoe'.

'They were great on their communications, those Romans', he said. 'Not only the Romans', I replied, 'Long before they came to Britain the Bronze Age Trade Routes were well established. Routes like the Clun-Clee Ridgeway stretched from the Long Mynd, only a few miles from here, for about forty-five miles to Cleobury Mor timer in Worcestershire. The people using those old trade routes came from as far afield as Egypt and Central Africa'. My pompous little homily on the bronze age was cut short as we leapt for the pavement and the little, red post-van shot past. 'There goes your twentieth century line of communications', he said wryly, adding: 'I live in California and in the days when the West was young, we Americans formed some pretty good lines of communications ourselves. In fact, I dare say that the Oregon Trail and the Santa Fe Trail are as well known today as, say, your little old Clun-Clee Ridgeway.' He had fallen into step beside me as I walked to the car and when we reached it I suggested he come back to the cottage and join Geoffrey and me for a glass of cider and tell us more about those wildwest trails.

Sitting on the sun warmed stones of the well-head, a jug of cider between us, the drone of bees in the honeysuckle, and the gentle faces of the Herefords gazing at us from the fields beyond, we listened to his quietly, pleasant drawl as he unfolded a story of fierce determination, enterprise and daring, a story of the days when Wells Fargo began its stage and banking service in America and of the brave and colourful men who rode the routes.

It was in 1832, he said, that Henry Wells and William G Fargo got together to launch their venture, a banking express business to serve the great Californian gold rush. They opened their first offices in the roaring, rumbustious town of San Francisco and, as soon as they were established, they set up agencies all along California's main gold producing area - The Mother Lode. This was a strip of land winding along the foothills of the Sierra Nevada. One of the main services they provided was the transportation of gold from the mines to San Francisco, where they exchanged it for money. The gold balance scales they used were so efficient that miners declared they would register the weight of a pencil mark on a piece of paper.

They also provided a stage-coach passenger service and a pony express service for the United States mails. The coaches used by Wells Fargo were built by the Abbot Downing company in New Hampshire. They could carry nine passengers inside and six more on top. At one time the service was so flourishing that a single order for replacements, contained a request for thirty new coaches. A ride in one of these red and yellow painted affairs was by no means a comfortable experience. In 1860 one bruised passenger ruefully described the journey as a ride with 'Fifteen-inches of seat space, with a fat man on one side and a poor widow on the other, a baby in your lap and a band box over your head, and three or more persons immediately in front of you leaning against your knees'.

There was always the constant hazard of highwaymen and scalp hunting Indians and even the danger of marauding bears, who had been known to terrify the horses causing them to rear and overturn the coach. Each coach left the station with a driver and a messenger, who was armed with a double-barrelled shot gun and a pistol known as the Wells Fargo Colt. This was a gun especially designed in 1853 for Express guards, whose job it was to protect the gold shipment and the mail and, incidentally, the passengers. The drivers of the six-horse teams and the messengers or guards, who rode with them, were the heroes of the day and were responsible for the transportation of countless millions of raw gold hidden in the treasure-box beneath the driver's seat.

As colourful in a different way were the highwaymen who waylaid the coaches. One of these, Charles Bolton, or Black Bart as he was know, chalked up the enormous figure of twenty-eight successful stage-coach robberies. He had the irritating habit of leaving a piece of mocking verse in place of his ill-gotten gains. He was eventually captured in 1883 by Wells Fargo's chief detective, James Hume.

Wells Fargo also ran the western leg of the famous Pony Express Service, which was started to bring regular communication between the east and west coast, along a central overland route. Eventually, Wells Fargo ran their own Pony Express over the Sierra between Placeville and Carson City. The Pony Express riders had a hard and extremely dangerous job. They rode for long hours on bad roads and often in dreadful weather and were constantly at risk from Indian encounter. An advertisement of the time for Express riders ended on a very chilling note. It offered twenty-five dollars a week for: 'Skinny, wiry fellows, not over eighteen. Must be expert riders, willing to risk death daily. Orphans preferred'.

Following the Californian gold rush came the Great Silver Rush of the Comstock at Virginia in Nevada. This was in 1859 and the Wells Fargo agency in the boom town of Virginia City became the richest of all its many agencies. Eventually, in 1905 the Wells Fargo and Company's bank in San Francisco merged with the Nevada National Bank also in San Francisco. The new bank was known as the Wells Fargo Nevada National Bank.

Only one year after the announcement of the amalgamation of these two banking concerns, much of the great city of San Francisco lay in smoking ruins, and the huge block of the Wells Fargo Nevada National Bank was a burned out shell. It was shortly after five a.m. on April 18th, 1906 that a major slippage occurred along the San Andreas fault. Much of San Francisco straddles this fault and the city was violently shaken. Following the earthquake came the horror of fire, which raged uncontrolled through the major part of the city's business and financial area.

However, by 1915, San Francisco rebuilt, beautiful and shining, was once again rich and bustling. So much so that in that year the Panama Pacific International Exposition was held there. Since those days the Wells Fargo Nevada National Bank has gone from strength to strength. The name has changed from time to time and today it is simply Wells Fargo & Co.

It was growing chilly, a little wind had sprung up and we pulled on cardigans and collected glasses to take into the house. 'What a fascinating story', said Geoffrey, as he walked with the American to the gate. 'You know the history of Wells Fargo so well it must interest you a great deal'. 'Yes', was the reply and he was smiling as he walked off up the lane. The Americanism, 'You can say that again', floated back to us, followed by a distinct chuckle. About a month later, I received a package from America. Inside was a booklet from the Wells Fargo Bank History Room, together with a card which said simply, 'Thank you for a very pleasant morning, Gillman Haynes, Senior Vice-President, Wells Fargo Bank'.

The following day with picnic on board, we set off as planned to visit New and Old Radnor. I chose the route via Knighton, turning left soon after passing the school, and at the top of a long incline taking the right hand turn onto the B4351 for Whitton, Evancoyd, Evenjobb, Burlingjobb, delicious names, and, finally the two Radnors.

The narrow road winds between hedges woven with dog rose and honeysuckle, above drifts of Rosebay Willowherb and meadow- sweet. Here and there a stretch of fencing or a field gate reveal fine, sloping pastures with fat, grazing sheep. It darts over a cross-roads, known as The Beggars Bush, because the story is that Charles I in his wild flight across Wales used a nearby cottage in which to disguise himself as a beggar. Then past a little village school; on over a small, stone bridge where a wayside cottage waves an astonishingly bright, pink-painted door at the passer by; through the hamlet of Maes Treylon with its stone barns and old farmsteads, and its nice, familiar, old fashioned telephone box; up a steep incline, not quite in the class of Bradley's 'Kill horse' heights, but one which might be, as he puts it, 'A strain on the collar'; until soon, on the right, it comes to the lodge at Evancoyd. A profusion of moon-faced shasta daisies mingled with blowsy, old fashioned roses beckons at the gates. Opposite, a wild hop has scrambled up a telephone pole disguising this twentieth century interloper with a screen of green rusticity.

Often in years gone by, we have turned in at the gates of Evancoyd, and driven along the drive to the old mansion, embossomed in trees in one of those exquisite dips between the hills, so prevalent in this part of Wales, to be greeted by the warm welcome of Major Lewis and his wife, Hillary. Although he was not born at Evancoyd, his father, a Derbyshire parson, having bought the estate, removed his family there when Jackie Lewis was eleven-years old, Jackie always seemed to me to be the very model of the old type Welsh country squire. Passionately fond of his estate, a devotee of country pursuits, firm in his opinions, his friendships and loyalties, and a warm and generous host in the old style.

A summons to dine at Evancoyd was one to be obeyed with the greatest pleasure, for once through the door it was a journey back in time, down the wide and chilly hall, past the old chests and the fishing and hunting impedimenta and on into the great drawing room with the wall of long windows, looking across the wide drive and over a dingle where shrubs and flowers and colourful weeds formed a tangle of delight, and past the small lake from which Hilary, the family fisherman, would catch the trout we enjoyed at dinner, to the green and heliotrope slopes of distant hills. At the far end of the room, a roaring fire created a cosy ambience where the guests wisely foregathered. Wraps and stoles and even 'long Johns' under enveloping skirts were the order of the day in the old country houses of that time and, indeed, still are where central heating has been resisted, either because of the damage it does to lovely old furniture, or because of the horrendous cost of installation and subsequent upkeep.

Pre-dinner drinks at Evancoyd were always Jackie's 'Special'. This was a somewhat lethal cocktail he had learned to mix in his army days. It required a good deal of shaking which Jackie did with flair, all eyes following his expertise. The recipe was Jackie's secret but it obviously contained large dollops of gin. By the time we went into dinner, the dining room seemed positively cosy, not to say almost too warm, and any rubicund noses were not all due to room temperature. In the dining room where old portraits gazed down on the long mahogany table, its polished surface gleaming in the soft candlelight, favoured guests were given the chairs on the side near-est the fire. This was not an unmitigated blessing, for if the meal went on for long, as it often did, part of one's anatomy became extremely well toasted.

When the time came for the ladies 'God bless 'em' to depart for the drawing room, leaving the men to their port, there was a hasty gathering together of wraps and stoles and a brisk sprint down the arctic hall and across the drawing room to the delicious comfort of the fireside circle.

Young moderns brought up in what I and many of my friends find the distinctly stuffy constant warmth of centrally heated houses, can never know the bliss of alighting on a warm spot after a flight through near zero temperatures.

Long years ago when I was young and we lived in an old Queen Anne House, we never left a room in the winter time without donning cardigans and woollens galore, and thus, fully booted and spurred, yes hideous fur-lined boots were often part of the equipment, scooted across the hall to a pool of warmth in another room. Those were the days when an elderly family friend, arriving on a visit, greeted me with 'Dear child, will you enquire if my sheets are well aired'. 'Dear child' all of twenty-five years, assured her that indeed they were, but we never saw her downstairs without her fur coat and mittens during the whole of her visit. If all this seems rather bleak, it wasn't at all and the contrasts were so invigorating.

But those days have gone and the evenings at Evancoyd are no more, for Jackie has been dead these many years. The old house was sold to young people and, no doubt, exudes warmth in every corner, but it cannot exceed the warmth of the laughter and companionship on those convivial evenings when Jackie and Hilary held court.

How I am wandering! But now we are past the great trees bordering the grounds of Evancoyd and, on our left, high above the road is the little church of Saint Peter where Jackie sleeps, and facing it, across the road, a little way up the second drive to the old house, is a low-roofed cottage with the surprising name of The Dragon's Den. This has nothing to do with the Welsh monster, although the Radnor Forest looming near is reputed to have been one of the favoured lairs of those fiery beasts. The dragon referred to here is Hilary, a most undragonlike person. Wittily anticipating what she felt certain members of her late husband's family might be calling her, she spiked their guns by thus labelling her cottage. The road winds on through the little villages of Evenjobb and Walton, past a spattering of pretty cottages until it joins the A44 for Rhayader, turning right here and a short way along right again and we are in New Radnor (Maesyved). The 'new' is relative for it refers to the thirteenth century when New Radnor came into being to replace Old Radnor, two or three miles away, and which had taken the force of so many fierce battles that it was on the point of expiring. The town grew up beneath the hill which soars above and on which stood a great castle built by Philip de Breos sometime in the eleventh century. The castle remained with the de Breos family until 1240. In that year it passed by marriage to the

178

Mortimers, those proven experts at selecting useful brides well able to replenish their coffers.

The castle was constantly attacked and besieged and in the thirteenth century, during a period of fifty years, it was captured no less than four times. Llewellyn the Great took it twice, King John once and then it fell to Llewellyn the Last. Finally, in 1401, along came Owain Glyndwr. Never one to do things by halves, he captured the castle and relieved the entire garrison of sixty men of their heads. In 1843, when the foundations were being dug for the New Radnor Parish Church, the workmen came upon a huge pile of human bones. Some distance away was another pile, this time of skulls.

The determination with which the castle was so frequently attacked was because it was the guardian of one of the most important gateways between England and Wales. After Glyndwr's ministrations, the castle limped along quietly with no notable battles until 1644, when it was garrisoned by the Parliamentarians against the Royalists during the Civil War. However, this was its last flourish and from then on it fell into decay. Little now remains but a few grassy mounds to show where a once mighty fortress withstood six-hundred years of battering.

In 1536 Radnorshire was made a county under 'The Act of Union' and New Radnor became the county town. Some time after the Civil War, however, this honour was transferred to Presteigne, but since 1889 the administrative centre has been at Llandrindod Wells. Under Prime Minister 'Chubby Chops' Edward Heath, a juggernaut was let loose in Britain, and in spite of great wails of protest, began mowing down the old counties and bundling others together into new ones. Radnorshire, Brecknockshire and Montgomeryshire were lumped into one and given the joint name of Powys. Llandrindod Wells was made the County Town.

The church in New Radnor is new and was built in 1845 on the site of two previous churches. It was to one of these, soon after Ash Wednesday in 1188, that Baldwin, Archbishop of Canterbury, and Geraldus Cambrensis came from Hereford before setting off on their tour of Wales in order to recruit men to fight in the Third Crusade. Rhys ap Gruffydd, Prince of South Wales, was the then owner of the castle. He was related to Geraldus, being the nephew of Nest, Geraldus's grandmother and he was waiting to greet them on their arrival. A number of other knights and local people had gathered round and the Archbishop, obviously not one to miss an opportunity, began preaching to them at once. In his sermon he urged them to fight for the cross. It was necessary to have an interpreter, but his words lost none of their fire thereby, for Geraldus tells us that he, himself, was the first of many to come forward. 'I threw myself at the holy man's feet', he writes, in his marvellous account of their journey through Wales. 'And', he continues, 'devoutly took the sign of the Cross... I acted of my own free will, after talking the matter over time and time again, in view of the injury being done at this moment to the Cross of Christ."

One of those present, who followed his example, was Rhys ap Gruffydd himself. However, when Rhys returned to his castle, his wife Gwenllian, the daughter of Madog ap Maredydd, Prince of Powys, was not at all happy about her Lord's decision. She watched him for two weeks keeping her peace. He rushed hither and yon making his preparations, gathering together pack animals and sumpter saddles to transport the multitude of things he required for such a journey. In between organising all the provisions, he was active in raising funds and prevailing on other knights to join him and take the Cross. However, by this time Gwenllian had had enough and she decided to put a stop to the whole affair. This she did, according to Geraldus, 'By playing upon his weakness and exercising her womanly charms'.

We must not judge Gwenllian too harshly, for Rhys would probably have been away for some years, that is if he ever came back at all, for many did not. In those turbulent times, had he been fortunate enough to return, he might well have found his family had been put to the sword and his castle either destroyed or the domain of another man. Then there was the little matter of chastity belts. These iron contraptions were often bolted on to women by the local blacksmith, so that their wandering husbands could be sure that their wives behaved themselves during their absence. I remember seeing one of these endearing little pieces of the blacksmith's art in a museum many years ago, and they must have been appallingly uncomfortable to wear.

Entering New Radnor from the A44 on the South Eastern side, one is confronted at once by an enormous memorial. It is a stepped edifice culminating in a spire and is seventy-one feet high. Some people have likened it to an Albert Memorial and others to an Eleanor Cross. For me, the Albert Memorial wins, but only by a short head. It was erected to commemorate Sir George Cornewall Lewis of Harpton Court near New Radnor. Sir George was a member of one of the oldest Radnorshire families. The Lewis's were at Harpton in the sixteenth century and remained there until 1911 when, there being no direct heir to the estate it was inherited by a kinsman Henry, later Sir Henry Duff Gordon. The front part of Harpton Court, which was Nash designed, was demolished after the Second World War, but the Tudor part at the rear was in good condition and remains occupied to this day. Sir George Cornewall Lewis shone in the world of politics. He was M.P. for the Borough from 1855 until his death in 1863, and for a time he was Chancellor of the Exchequer.

I have been lent a delightful booklet written by Pauline Jobson, who is the widow of a doctor who practised in New Radnor for many years. It is crammed with fascinating facts and anecdotes about the little town in days gone by. The families of Lewis and Duff Gordon produced benevolent squires and in Pauline Jobson's book we read of the jollifications when The Old Radnor and New Radnor W.I.s held their annual tea party there. 'The ladies took tea (always china tea - not popular) in the great hall, what was popular was the enormous swing large enough to take twelve women'. Once a year the Sunday School children, too, all aboard a char-a-banc would arrive at 'The wrought iron gates of the big house. There they joined children from the neighbouring parish; then walked up the long tree-lined avenue, each one carrying a mug, for tea, bread and butter and plum cake. Tea taken in embarrassed giggles because Jenny Neighbours would leave her teaspoon in her mug!'

Another little snippet from Pauline's book concerns 'Poor old Mrs Dai, who curtsied and called me ma'am. She always wore black and was never seen without her black beret'. Mrs Dai, when sick refused to go to the hospital in Knighton because the building had once been the workhouse and, although thoroughly refurbished, it still held that stigma. Pauline Jobson visited Mrs Dai on her death bed and she writes, 'She still wore her jacket and beret, a wisp of grey hair growing through a hole on the top. But like many of her generation, she preferred to die at home. The disgrace and reputation of the workhouse was not forgotten'.

Remembering the wartime in New Radnor, Pauline tells us that even places as remote as New Radnor experienced great changes. When the Americans arrived in the little town she recalls, 'They introduced chewing gum, jitterbugging and they had their own band. Jitterbugging was a loud primitive dance, danced so energetically it seemed to rock the building. Harold Pugh, then a lumper of a lad, was in the men's club with his Uncle Jack. Uncle, looking at the ceiling, said: 'The floor will stand it lad, but I doubt the walls will'. 'On the whole', she says, 'the military were well received by the local people, at times there were difficulties. Sir

Henry Duff Gordon's keeper and gardener, complained of excessive poaching and of vegetables disappearing from the kitchen garden. Sir Henry had a word with the commanding officer. The officer, full of apologies and to make amends, invited him to dine in the mess. One reads of disasters in British history, of battles lost because of lack of communications. There was obviously no communication between the commanding officer and the cook. Sir Henry was served with pheasant.'

One last little story from this delightful booklet concerns the period just after Dunkirk, when most of the country was in fear of an invasion by the Germans. A local man, George Williams, was sent with two others from the Old Radnor Unit to guard a cross-roads near Trewern. Writing of this time, Pauline remembers that, 'An old gentleman living near came wandering down the road and said, "What be ye doing boys?" "We're to stop the Germans coming" was the reply. "Oh let the buggers come, we be here first.", came the response.' One must applaud an attitude of such superior indifference so reminiscent of those mighty border barons who once straddled the area glaring down from their castle strongholds and daring anyone to knock them off their lofty perches because they were there first.

Pauline Jobson has moved from The Laurels, which was a doctor's house for over a hundred years, and now lives in the stables of the old place, which she has converted into a very attractive cottage. Now that parsons have such large parishes and so little time in which to keep diaries and records of their times, or are too trendy to wish to do so, it is such a blessing that people like Pauline Jobson set down their memories of the old days, for these will be a treasure house for the generations yet to come.

The town of New Radnor is an attractive hotch-potch of old houses and inns and at the far end of Church Street, almost the last of the houses on the right hand side, is Mrs Bart's cottage. This cottage has not changed a whisker since Bradley trundled up to it at the turn of the century and asked his artist to draw it, for there it is in his book exactly the same as in David Mitchell's photograph, which I have used in this book. Mrs Bart, or Mrs Bartholomew, her real name, had lived there all her life and she was then about ninety. Recently she moved and the place was let. It still has a gentle, faded shabbiness about it as in Bradley's book, and mercifully it has not been built on to or 'tarted up' and long may it remain so

Old Radnor, Maesyved - Hen, which is about two and a half miles distant, is really just a gathering of houses, farmsteads and an ancient inn around a church. But what a church! It stands high on a rocky outcrop

33 Mrs Bart's cottage, New Radnor. How little has changed between the 100-year old drawing from Bradley's book and today's photograph.

on Old Radnor Hill, 840-feet above sea level, and the outlook from the old graveyard across the wooded valley to the distant hills is indeed, as Bradley puts it, 'One to linger over'. The present church is dedicated to Saint Stephen and was built in the fifteenth and sixteenth centuries on the site of two former religious buildings. It has a massive embattled tower with a stair turret at one corner, this used to contain an iron cresset housing a beacon. A light shining from that turret must have been visible for miles around and certainly from New Radnor Castle. This broad and sturdy defensive tower with its arrow slits for the use of archers undoubtedly provided a splendid refuge for parishioners during the turbulent days of the Border Wars.

Edward III in the fourteenth century, pronounced that in future all beacons should be 'High standards with their pitch pots'. The beacon on the tower of Saint Stephen's church certainly complied with the height part of this directive. In 1588 when the Armada was sighted in the Channel, beacons fired their warning from height to height all over Britain, and no doubt the pitch pot at Old Radnor church blazed forth. To a people nourished on tales of the might of Spain and the horrors of the inquisition, how those lights would have curdled the blood.

However, it was not always at times of impending disaster that beacons were fired. In 1897 for example, at the Diamond Jubilee of Queen Victoria, there was a display of unprecedented brilliance. It was decided, after much pontificating among the higher echelons, that directives be sent to all local bodies in charge of beacons, to the effect that at 9.55 p.m. precisely, on June 22nd, 1897, a detonating rocket would be discharged from the Malvern Hills as a five-minute warning, to those responsible for beacon baskets and bonfires, to stand by for firing at 10 p.m. No doubt this caused a great topping up of pitch pots, including that in the stair turret of Old Radnor church. Malvern was given the honour of getting things going because it was considered to be the highest point near the centre of Britain. It must have been an incredible sight, all those leaping lights which ever way one turned, simultaneously pricking the night sky. The public took great interest in beacon fires and 'Beacon Spotting' was quite the rage, people wrote to the *Times* proudly telling their score. One gentleman announced in the *Times* that from the Quantock Hills he had counted one-hundred beacons on the Somerset side of the Bristol Channel and twenty-five in South Wales.

But we must back now to Old Radnor and its church. Happily, Saint Stephen's Church has escaped the fate of Saint Mary's Church in New Radnor which was virtually demolished in 1843. Of the church built to replace it, in the Gothic style, W H Howse, the historian, lifts a trembling pen and records, 'It is difficult to write temperately about the new building which is no more gothic than the village pump'. The mos astonishing thing in Old Radnor church is the font. There it stands, four square, a massive lump of greenish-grey igneous rock on four elephantine legs. How it was ever moved into place is a mystery. Archaeologists state that this font is certainly no later than the eighth century, and may well have been much earlier, some have even suggested that it might be prehistoric. It is the oldest font in the county, and very probably in the country. At all events, thanks to its sheer size and weight, it can never have been in danger of sharing the fate of so many fonts in Georgian and Victorian times which ended up as bird baths or flower troughs in local gardens. Most of the glass in Old Radnor Church is clear but there is a small stained glass window in the North Chapel, commemorating Saint Catherine and her wheel, which is late fifteenth century. In fact Radnorshire has very little mediaeval glass and I understand that only the churches at Old Radnor and Presteign have any at all.

What the church lacks in old glass, it more than makes up for with magnificent wood carving. The fifteenth century rood-screen is one of the most beautiful in the county and stretches across the full width of the church. The carving is thought to be the work of the Gloucestershire School of Wood Carvers, but, with all due humbleness and many salaams, I wonder if this is so. As I understand it, the fact that there is a small piece of a similar rood screen in Cirencester Parish Church is one of the main reasons for coming to the conclusion that the Gloucestershire wood carvers did the work, and yet in Radnorshire, a county poor in stone but rich in oak, the wood carver's art is known to have reached a very high standard. Is it not possible, therefore, that the Old Radnor screen was the work of men of Radnorshire and not Gloucestershire? And might not the Gloucestershire screen have been their work too? This is heretical talk and, before I am drummed out of the regiment, we will move on to other things, the organ case for example.

This case, dating from the fifteenth century, is said to be the oldest in the country. It has the same rich, crisp carving as the rood-screen. Both screen and organ case were at one time painted and richly gilded, but this was stripped off in the restorations of 1856 and 1882. However, the woodwork, though now a discreet brown, glows with polishing and is beautiful to see.

One of the squires of nearby Harpton Court, Sir Franklin Lewis, insisted that he be buried in Radnor church yard, looking down the valley to his beloved estate. In 1724 seven-hundred men followed the funeral cortège of the then Squire Lewis of Harpton, when he was being brought to Old Radnor church for burial. This huge number was made up of his family and friends and tenants, surely a testament to his benevolence and popularity. Fifty years later, however, when his descendant, Squire Thomas Lewis died, a huge monument was set up in the classical style in what was once the Lady Chapel. In order to accommodate such an enormous edifice, the east window of the chapel was blocked up. Benevolent no doubt, but a strong whiff of the feudal lord here.

The road which winds past the church widens into a broad grassy square, on one side of which is a long, low, stone building. This is The Harp Inn. The inn was restored in 1971 by The Landmark Trust and mine host is now Stephen Cope. As they only church in Wales to be dedicated to Saint Stephen is the church at Old Radnor, Stephen Cope feels it must be some sort of an omen that he should come to The Harp. He loves the place and has not plasticised it. Charles I spent a night at The Harp and the local tradition is that he complained about the food. After the Battle of Naseby, the King set off on a wild and harrowing march over the Welsh Hills, reaching Chester on September 23rd, 1645. Charles and his men were in a desperate state, keeping away from any roads and struggling on over steep, trackless hills and through densely wooded valleys, and all this with the black cloud of their recent defeat hanging over them.

When they reached Old Radnor, they were worn out and it was decided to spend the night at The Harp. The Woolhope Transactions quote an account of this written not long after. 'He (King Charles) slept in a low, poor chamber and on his arrival the good wife did her best to entertain her visitors but, troubled with continual calling for victuals, and having, it seems, but one cheese, comes into the room where the King was and very soberly asks if the King had done with the cheese for the gentlemen without desired it'. From this it would seem that it was the quantity rather than the quality of the food that caused the complaints and, in any case, to complain seems extremely churlish for who would expect to find, when opening their door, the King of England and the rag-tag and bobtail remnants of his defeated army on the threshold? The poor woman, scampering from room to room with her single cheese, is to be pitied not blamed.

The Harp was built in 1462 so was already two-hundred years old when Charles and his men crossed the great flagstones, which still cover the floor. The 'low, poor chamber', in which he slept, is now a pretty bedroom with old beams, a latched door and a wonderful view over

186

Radnorshire. The bar of the inn, with high backed settles, round tables and stools and its deep-silled window looking across the square, and over the valley to where the Whimble - that old mountain about which the local saw, runs 'When Whimble wears his cloudy cap, let Radnor boys beware of that' - thrusts his sugar loaf crown above the Radnor Forest, must look much the same as when those weary men staggered in. The Harp was certainly well placed for the King's lookouts to spot any approaching danger, and perhaps, therefore, Charles was able to sleep a little easier in his 'low, poor chamber'.

These two sequestered villages, Old and New Radnor, lie on the edge of the great Radnor forest. Once the hunting ground for the mighty Marcher Lords and still a wide and lonely moorland, much of it on the flanks of great hills and mountains, fretted with little streams, and clothed here and there with the dark green cloak of the Forestry Commission plantations. The villages slumber now and are havens of peace, but 'Turn but a stone' and the past leaps out and we are back in the days when those who held the two castles held the key to one of the most important gateways to Wales, and battles raged almost continually around them. New Radnor was nevertheless, in spite of the efforts of Owain Glyndwr, still a place of consequence in 1603 and Camden when writing of the Radnorshire towns says, 'The greatest of note is Radnor, the chief town of the county, called in British Maesyved, fair built but with thatch- ed houses as the manner is of that county. Formerly, it was well fenced with walls and a castle, but being by that rebellious Owain Glyndwyr laid in ashes, it decayed daily, as well as Old Radnor called by the Britons Maesyved - Hen.' Owain Glyndwr has much to answer for but even more has Lord Grey of Ruthin who set Owain on his wild path of destruction.

v. *Wells Fargo country agent weighing the gold - after an illustration
in the Wells Fargo history book. (See page* 174)

Chapter 13

Lingen, Presteigne, More & Linley Hall

Old Radnor is but a handful of miles from Presteigne but, when I left the village, the shadows had lengthened and there was little time before dusk, so I decided my visit must wait for another day.

About a week later, when I eventually set off for this erstwhile County Town, of Radnorshire, I took the route from Leintwardine, passing through the village of Lingen, which lies on the edge of the Deerfold Forest, that old hunting ground of the Mortimers. In this forest is the Chapel Farm where that doughty old warrior, Sir John Oldcastle, friend of the King and an anathema to the bishops and high churchmen, was successfully hidden for close on four years, until his capture and martyrdom. Many other Lollards came to the Lingen area to hold their services in the Chapel Farm and to 'lie low' in this remote and tolerant corner. Before the advent of Lollardism in these parts, Robert de Lingen founded a nunnery in the forest, but only a few sad stones remain to show where the Limebrook Priory, as it was called, once stood, and where those naughty nuns of long ago caused the Bishop of Hereford such headaches over their merrymaking.

The village itself is a delightful place, stone and timber-framed cottages border the long village street overlooked by the Church of Saint Michael. This church was almost entirely rebuilt in 1891 but it is said that the pews, which are sixteenth century, came from the church at the Limebrook nunnery in the Deerfold forest.

Near to Lingen is Willey, a somewhat spread-eagled hamlet reached

189

through a tangle of lanes. For peace and beauty and magnificent views, this area is hard to beat. I once, some years ago, turned on the wireless to hear the unmistakable voice of Brian Johnson doing one of his 'Down Your Way' programmes. He could hardly speak for laughing. It seems he was at Willey and attending the village fete. 'Mrs Woolley', he gasped between laughs, 'has just won the Willey welly wagging competition'.

Back on the road to Presteigne, we are soon passing the entrance to Kinsham Court. Byron, like Shelley and Wordsworth, seems to have been attracted to Wales and the Border County, so much so that he leased Kinsham Court at one time. The fact that the London to Aberystwyth coaching road ran close by, on its way to Central Wales via Presteigne, made it reasonably easy for people who wished to do so to visit the border country and Wild Wales. Florence Nightingale spent part of her childhood at Kinsham Court. Did she, like many small girls of her period, play at 'Doctors and Nurses', bandaging up her 'wounded' dolls in the nursery at Kinsham, far away from later years when in her makeshift hospital in the Crimea make-belief became grim reality?

Not far from Kinsham Court is another fine old house. This is The Broad Heath. Set well back from the road, almost hidden by trees, it is just possible to catch a glimpse of it in passing. Parts of the house and the ornate Italianate well-head in the garden were designed by Clough Williams Ellis. For many years, until his retirement, a much loved family doctor lived at The Broad Heath. I have mentioned him before in connection with Knighton. Doctor John Garmon was truly a doctor of 'the old school'. We have all heard the phrase 'a good bedside manner', alas, few doctors possess it now-a-days but John Garmon had it in abundance. His tweed clad figure, carrying his doctor's bag, had only to enter a room, with his cheerful greeting, 'Well, well and what have you been up to my dear', and the patient, who had a few moments before been convinced of his or her imminent demise, experienced a remarkable revival and felt fifty per cent better. I know many, many people who mourn the day that he retired. I doubt if we shall be fortunate enough to see his like again.

Presteigne teeters on the very border between England and Wales. The boundary between the two countries is marked by the shallow, fast-flowing River Lugg and the little town is settled on its south bank. An old packhorse bridge spanning the river leads on to Broad Street, one of the town's two main streets. Like most other Border towns, Presteigne's distant past was very violent and war torn, in addition, in the fourteenth and fifteenth century, it suffered the ravages of the Black Death. More troubles were to follow for in the sixteenth and seventeenth centuries there were several calamitous outbreaks of the plague. The severity of this infliction can be judged by the fact that in 1593 out of three hundred and eighty-five deaths recorded in the church register, three hundred and fifty-two had the dreaded 'P' for Plague beside the entry. During the third outbreak in 1636 the magistrates for the County of Hereford were so concerned that a warrant was issued for 'The charitable relief and ordering of persons infected with the Plague'. Sums of money were to be collected, from various places listed on the warrant, to help the people of Presteigne. The amounts ranged from ten shillings a week from Brampton Bryan to two shillings a week from Willey. John Price of Combe was to receive the money and distribute it, and if any person refused to pay his share it would be to 'His peril'.

In spite of this disaster and the fact that it led to a decline in the cloth industry, hitherto one of the mainstays of the town's prosperity, Prestiegne prospered. Thanks to the fact that New Radnor had lost its castle during the Civil War, and consequently its position of County Town, Presteigne was even able to assume that mantle and kept it for over four hundred years, until at the turn of the century, Llandrindod Wells took on the role.

Presteigne today is a delightful town. The two main streets are lined with houses of varying periods, from Tudor to Victorian, and several smaller streets of considerable charm lead off them, such as Saint David's Street dominated by Saint David's House, with its pleasant nineteenth century stone overcoat hiding the sixteenth century timber-framed house beneath. Most of the smaller houses on the right hand side of this street were built to replace houses destroyed in a disastrous fire in 1681. Harper's Lane is another little offshoot from the main streets. At the end of this lane lives Graham Hoyte, a retired tea planter, who now plants flowers galore so that his little garden overflows with colour. There are many people 'From off', as they say in these parts, who have been seduced by the charms of this little border town. Potters, artists and writers abound and the small shops are filled with evidence of their expertise.

About halfway down Broad Street is the Shire Hall, a most impressive building with classical arcades and a pillared porch reminding us of Presteigne's illustrious past as County Town. A little further on, on the opposite side, is one of the entrances to the church. At the approach to the church gate, the pavement widens out to a piece of land known as The Scallions. A scallion, in my youth, was a spring onion and I fear I always imagined that at one time or another this piece of land had been an onion patch. Not so, I now learn, from those who know better, that scallions is probably a corruption from the Norse 'Scallwegg' meaning 'The way of the skull'. Either way, odiferous or grisly, light relief is at hand for opposite The Scallions is a much more fragrant nomenclature. Neatly painted on an archway between some cottages fronting the street is a sign directing us to The Garden Cottage. Through the arch, down a little path between gardens, and we arrive at a little grey, stone Welsh cottage, with an arch of cream roses around the door and a rustic seat beneath a gnarled, old, apple tree. Here lives another one of those people that make Presteigne special, Daphne Ransome the lace maker. Daphne spent much of her adult life in Singapore and came to live in Presteigne after her husband's death On summer shiny days you may see her through her open cottage door, sitting with her lace pillow on her lap, bobbins flying through her deft fingers, creating pieces of cobwebby delight. How many towns can boast a lace maker I wonder?

The Welsh name for Presteigne, Llanandras, is derived from Saint Andrew to whom the Parish church is dedicated. This church and that of Old Radnor are considered to be the finest churches in Radnorshire, if not further afield. Most of Presteigne church dates from the fourteenth and fifteenth century, but evidence of an earlier church on the site can be seen in traces of Saxon and Norman work in the walls of the aisle and the tower. A certain John Beddoes in 1565 founded a grammar school in Presteigne and he agreed to continue funding it, if a curfew was rung every evening. The rent from a meadow was left to continue paying for this and the curfew bell rings every evening as if has done for over four hundred years.

Being suitably sited as a staging place on the London - Wales coaching route, Presteigne was at one time a very busy coaching town with several flourishing inns, the magnificently magpied Radnorshire Arms was one of them. This building dates from 1616, and for over one hundred and fifty years was a private house. However, in 1779, at the height of the coaching period, it became an inn. Members of the Woolhope Club, who visited the Radnorshire Arms at the turn of the century, reported that during alterations to the building a small secret room was found. It was thought to be the hiding place of a Royalist, for Presteigne was staunchly Royalist during the Civil War. King Charles knew the area well and must have often hunted there in happier times, for he owned a hunting lodge nearby. We know he stayed at The Harp at Old Radnor and he is said to have stayed in Presteigne twice after the battle of Naseby. How dispirited and utterly exhausted Charles and his men must have been after that defeat, struggling on over the Welsh Hills, keeping clear of the main routes. When they finally crossed the bridge over the Lugg into the friendly town of Presteigne, they had been on the March from 6 a.m. to midnight. The little room in the Radnorshire Arms was panelled. Some of this must have been removed for the Woolhope gentlemen reported that,, behind the panelling, were found two or three small volumes. One, alas, having been much gnawed by rats. The Radnorshire Arms still has several beautiful panelled rooms, but the secret room is now a large cupboard leading off the Conference room and is now used as a storeroom for spare tables and chairs.

The oldest inn in the town is the Duke's Arms in Broad Street. In 1652 it was the Headquarters for the Committee set up by Cromwell to seize Royalist estates. This must have endeared it to the locals, but no doubt the honour was unsolicited. A somewhat more salubrious item in its past is the fact that it was from the stable yard at the Duke's Arms that the last mail coach in Britain sallied forth.

Among the old gravestones in the churchyard is one in memory of Mary Morgan. Mary was a very pretty, sixteen-year old girl employed as a member of the kitchen staff at either Newcastle Court near Presteigne, or at a castle near Glasbury. There seems to be some contradiction over her place of employment, but perhaps she was on the staff of both these places at different times. Mary had a lover, some said he was a fellow servant and others that he was the son of her employer. Eventually the girl became pregnant and on September 23rd in the year 1804, she delivered the baby herself in her room. She must have been in a wretched condition, when we consider the shock of the birth under such conditions with no friend to support her; the knowledge that she was abandoned by the father; that she would most likely lose her job, because having an illegitimate child was a dreadful disgrace; and that many a deceived girl in those days was shown the door not only by her employer but by her parents too. In her anguish this child, for child she still was, killed her baby with a penknife.

The death was soon discovered and Mary was arrested and sent to Presteigne gaol. Five months later, in April the following year, her trial took place. Mary was found guilty and sentenced to be hanged. Two days after the trial, they brought the terrified girl in a cart to Gallows Lane and hanged her at the crossroads. An eye witness said she was 'More dead than alive' when they lifted her from the cart. The judge at the trial, a Mr Justice Hardinge, was said to be in tears as he pronounced sentence of death on Mary. Why am I reminded of The Walrus and the Carpenter in *Alice Through The Looking Glass?* Before pronouncing sentence, he made a nauseatingly pious and pompous address giving his reasons for exacting the extreme penalty.

Mary was buried in a corner of the rectory garden which later became incorporated in the churchyard. A friend of Judge Hardinge had a sickly, sycophantic inscription inscribed on Mary's gravestone. The poor child was, according to him, 'roused to a first sense of guilt and remorse by the eloquent and humane exertions of her benevolent judge, Mr Justice Hardinge'. One of the jury was the son of Mary's employer, the very man who was suspected by many as having caused her dreadful predicament.

There is a tradition, though unverified, that a man attending the trial was so horrified by the sentence of death on Mary that he made a great effort to save her, riding day and night and changing horses frequently, in an effort to get a reprieve from London in time to prevent the hanging. It is said that he arrived back in Presteigne just two hours too late to save her life. Another tradition is that Judge Hardinge was so affected by her death, as well he might be, that he visited her grave whenever he was in Presteigne. No doubt to shed crocodile tears. Eleven years after his cruel sentence, the Judge was in Presteigne while on circuit when he suddenly died. The people of Presteigne erected their own stone in memory of Mary Morgan, on it was inscribed, 'He that is without sin among you, let him first cast a stone at her'.

My book is nearing its end, but before I run out of space I must make one more visit to a corner of the border country that is unrivalled for its historical interest and charm, the Clun and Bishop's Castle area.

Quite near to Bishop's Castle, about two miles distant, surrounded by green fields and winding lanes is the little village of More. The church is plumb in the middle of the village, on slightly rising ground, and the village street wanders in a circle right round it. On one side is an old farmhouse and farm buildings and, next to it, an ancient dwelling with post and span timbering - where the timbers stand in rows, upright with only the width of a beam between them. This type of building used considerably more wood than the chequerboard type of timbering. It was forbidden during the reign of Elizabeth I, for those were the days when the defence of our islands depended on ships made of English oak and, what with the ravages of the charcoal burners and the enormous amount of timber used for fuel, certain economies were needed. Further round the street, facing the lych gate, there are a few other attractive cottages and here those which are timber-framed are in the permitted chequerboard style. After these a little lane wanders off somewhere and on the far side of this an immensely high stretch of old brick wall follows the perimeter of the churchyard, surely at one time guardian of a splendid kitchen garden. Now we are full circle and back to the farm and at the top of another lane, this one leading to Linley Hall, for centuries the home of the Mores.

The church which is dedicated to Saint Peter, was almost en-tirely rebuilt in 1845, though the transept and gated pews are circa 1640. It has an airy simplicity with few tablets and modest memorials, in keeping with the rather puritanical background of some of the later Lords of More, for the Mores were one of the few great families in the Border Country to espouse the cause of the parliamentarians. The scant remains of a Roman villa were found some years ago in the More Park and some pieces of the black and white pavement from this are around the font.

The Lord of More was Constable of the King's army and kept his very extensive lands on condition that he provide two hundred footmen to join the King on any occasion that the English were battle bent and crossing the border into Wales. He also had the doubtful honour of leading the English van, and carrying the royal standard himself. As a recipe for a short life this could hardly be bettered.

From a list in the church of the past rectors, we learn that there have been six Mores, beginning with Roger and Adam who were between 1220 and 1230. Mores have also been patrons of the living since the fourteenth century, interspersed from time to time with the King. In 1301 the King had this distinction during the minority of William de la More, and in 1349 it was again the King who was then Custos of the land and heir of William de la More, yet again in 1392 the King pops up as Patron and heir of John de la More.

Under the organ pipes, facing down the aisle to the alter is a brass tablet in memory of Sir Jasper More, KB, DL, MP, who died a few years ago, but more of him anon. Over this tablet is a painting of the More arms, done by a friend of the family, the Clun artist, Alison Peppe.

The main drive to the Hall is a mile long and sweeps majestically through an avenue of oaks, but the lane from the village arrives there just the same if not so splendidly. It finishes in a T-junction facing a moderately low stone wall, behind which at a distance across a green mead, stands Linley Hall, a stone mansion designed in the Classical style in 1742 by the architect Henry Joynes. The late Sir Jasper More used to say that it 'Was built by correspondence course' since the architect, who was then almost sixty years old, instructed the local builders on what to do by letters from London, where he had the time consuming job of Surveyor of Kensington Palace. He must have been a very able man for he was Vanbrugh's assistant in the building of Blenheim Palace. He must also have been a man capable of giving very clear and precise instructions because the quality of the workmanship at Linley is excellent and the local builders who carried out the work were obviously men of great talent.

The main entrance to the Hall is on the east side under a large Venetian window, and opposite the entrance is a delightful lake, tree girt and aflurry with water fowl. In the late eighteen nineties Jasper More's grandfather was forced to let the house. This was because the agricultural depression, which began in 1873, coupled with the fact that the lead mines on the east were forced to close down because of foreign competition, caused a financial disaster to loom. In spite of great efforts to keep the ship afloat, including the selling of Larden and Shipton, two other More estates, and the sale of much family silver, and even the felling of the great trees on the 'Forty Acres', nothing could save the situation. After Linley was let and the other estates sold, life for the More's changed completely, as Jasper More put it 'It was inevitable that my grandparents led separate lives'. His grandmother moving from Shropshire farm to Shropshire lodging-house, from Shropshire lodging-house to seaside rooms, then perhaps to some great house where old friends remembered her. The More family did not return to Linley until 1954 although Jasper More had as he put it himself, 'dossed down there' for some considerable time. There was no electric light, everything when darkness came was by candlelight and very dilapidated oil lamps.

Emma Bullock, a friend of the More's who lived with them at Linley, told me that at that time, on opening the door to the house, the stench from the paraffin oil was as so strong as to make one feel sick. The huge vaulted basement was over-run with rats and Sir Jasper soon had a nodding acquaintance with them, remarking in his book that during the long, evenings 'I would venture down the carpetless stairs (carrying a candle), meeting with a rat on the way, and explore the extraordinary basement'. The saga of the war against the rats is long but two years later with the help of 'The Man to Match the Hour', Mr Morgan, it was won.

At last with electricity installed, water supplies sorted out and rats evicted, Clare More was able to join her husband and together they battled on for ten years restoring the house, the stable block and the other buildings, so long neglected, and getting thousands of acres of Shropshire borderland back into shape. The story of how they achieved this colossal task, against enormous odds, is told in a sparklingly entertaining way in Jasper More's book *The story of Two Houses*. The other house in question was Westport in Ireland and belonged to his uncle Ulick.

The interior of Linley now, after all those years of effort, is one of great elegance but one of the most fascinating things in this house is the Roman pig of iron. This is kept in one of the great vaulted rooms in the basement, a room that was at one time the kitchen of Linley. The pig of iron was found in the old lead mines on the estate. It is about two and a half feet long and six inches high. It is in perfect condition and the words IMP HADRIANI AUG are inscribed in letters about one and a half inches high along its length.

The dining room has a cool air of uncluttered symmetry. Every room in the place, following Henry Joynes's plans, had to be symmetrical, doors and windows all following this rule. There is a portrait, among the many ancestors on the walls, of a man in a full bottomed wig, who seems to be looking a little askance at his surroundings. This is General Samuel More. It was he who in 1643 gathered together the men of Hopton Castle and the villages around and arranged its defence during the Civil War. I have written elsewhere about this epic stand of the Cromwellians against the Royalists attackers, and of how all the defenders, with the exception of General More, were massacred. At the far end of the wall on which his picture hangs is that of his father, so different in appearance from his son. Papa looks a pale aesthetic man. His garment is trimmed with a beautiful lace collar of the type so frowned upon by the Cromwellians and so favoured by the Royalists.

A very interesting story to do with the private life of Samuel More was unearthed after a great deal of painstaking research by Donald F Harris in 1992. When Samuel More was a young lad of seventeen years a marriage was arranged between him and his cousin, Catherine, who was eight years his senior. Catherine was the daughter of Jasper More of Larden, another great More estate. The marriage which took place on February 4th, 1611, was obviously, one of convenience, being seen as a way of combining the two More estates of Larden and Linley. It was not a very auspicious way to start married life and not helped by Catherine being so much older than Samuel. Very soon after the wedding Catherine took a lover, or indeed, she may have already had one at the time of the marriage. Her paramour was a man called Jacob Blakeway. His parents were tenants of the Mores and had thirty acres, meadow, pasture and arable land. Jacob was three years older than Catherine and, as a young woman of twenty-five years, she could well have found her teenage husband of the arranged marriage very callow by comparison with the older man.

However, Samuel seemed to be quite unaware of his errant wife's transgressions, in spite of the fact that she had four children by her lover, Blakeway. I suppose she passed them off as Samuel's and he, being so much younger than Catherine, was naive and trusting enough to believe everything she told him. Nevertheless, the time came when the penny dropped. Ellen, the eldest child, was eight years old, her brothers, Jasper and Richard, were six years and five years respectively and the youngest child, Mary, was four years old, when Samuel realised they were not his. There followed a great deal of litigation and counter litigation but, finally, in 1619 Samuel managed to obtain a divorce and the four children were declared bastards. Catherine appealed but the appeal was dismissed and nothing more is known of her.

Surprisingly the children were not given into the care of their mother and her lover, instead, it was arranged that they should go to America on the Mayflower. Whether or not this was against their mother's wishes we do not know, but surely, unless she was a quite unnatural parent, it must have been a time of great anguish for her. Presumably Samuel More must have had some affection for them since, for several years, he had thought they were his own children. We do know that they were put in to the care of people who 'Were rich from land or trade, honest and religious people' and that these people were to be their guardians for the voyage and when they arrived in America.

There were thirty-four children on board the Mayflower with them, all going to start a new life in America. Alas, eight year old Jasper never landed in that country for he died of a fever, while the ship was anchored off the coast. Little Ellen followed soon after him. Mary died the first winter ashore and only Richard survived. He grew up to become a ship's captain. He was no doubt a bluff sea-faring man with possibly 'a wife in every port', all the same it is surprising to learn that, when he was seventy-years old, he was accused of lasciviousness and gross indecency. He publicly apologised for his misdoings, some might say he was a 'chip of the old block', although in the intensely puritanical climate of Salem, where he lived and is buried, at that period even a modest peccadillo would be heavily censured and he would certainly not not need to to go to the lengths of sprinkling illegitimate children around to qualify as a sinner. Strange to think that this old ship's captain, product of a union between a member of the great house of More and the son of one of the humbler tenant formers on the estate, was one of the Pilgrim fathers. Samuel More married again and when he was nearly fifty years old he organised and took part in the brave defence of Hopton Castle.

After the second world war, when Jasper More came back to the border country, he and his wife, Clare, had to make a decision. Should they live in her huge but comfortable house, ten miles away, and demolish Linley, or should they rescue Linley and turn it into a smaller and more manageable house than Netley Hall? They made their choice. Linley was saved. So this far-away corner of Shropshire has one of the most delightful country houses, standing in grounds of great beauty and serenity, and little more than a bowshot from its minuscule and very attractive village.

vi. *What awful luck to be a duck. (See page 211)*

Chapter 14

Christmas Miscellany

Heap on more wood, the wind is chill,
But let it whistle as it will,
We'll keep our Christmas merry still.
W.M. Thackeray

Earlier this year they tarmac'd our lanes, at least that is what I suppose it is. The men arrived with their machines, spreading a layer of thick tar on top of which they poured cart-loads of chippings, which were then rolled in, so that the old, rutted surfaces in varying shades of gentle brown are no more and, in their place, battleship-grey ribands flaunt their way along between the green verges. Where the lanes meet the village street gleaming white lines have been painted on them so that our village of less than fifty people would seem to be a very metropolis. However, I suppose we should be thankful that the lanes are too marrow to have pavements and concrete curbs bestowed upon them.

Robert Louis Stevenson, in a beautiful and evocative poem to his wife, written when they were leaving these shores on the schooner Equator, reminds her in the first verse of the old rutted lanes she is leaving behind. It goes:-

Long must elapse ere you behold again
Green forest frame the entry of the lane-
The wild lane with the bramble and the briar,
The year old cart-tracks perfect in the mire,
The wayside smoke, perchance the dwarfish huts,
And ramblers' donkey drinking from the ruts.

201

At least the rutted lanes would still be there if they ever returned from their tropical island, but for us I fear they are gone for ever. No longer does the solitary snipe, I often surprised on my walks, peer into a little pool between the ruts, or the family of hedge sparrows splash around in it enjoying a morning bath, and even the rabbits and squirrels, which would scamper across from hedge to hedge, seem reluctant to put a tentative paw on the stark surfaces. As for Peppi, he hates the chippings that are so unkind to his little pads and for a long time, until they had been flattened into the surface, he stuck firmly to the verges too disgusted to bother to start up a pheasant or bark at a tractor. I have walked the lanes a thousand times and come to no harm, and yet, almost as soon as this most inappropriate surface was laid, I slipped on an imperfectly covered patch of tar and badly sprained my ankle.

One cold and damp day, having at last recovered from this mishap, I set off, together with Peppi, up Twitchen Lane, fulminating against those purveyors of progress as I trod the steely surface. After a while I became aware of an agitated bleating. It seemed to come from the hedge hiding the steep bank leading up to the fields, which are several feet above the level of the lane. At first I took no notice but the bleating became so insistent that I hurried along to the field gate in order to investigate. This I found firmly chained and padlocked, sheep rustlers being by no means unknown in these parts. I managed to squeeze through a gap between gatepost and hedge and then walked back along the field to the place where I had first heard the bleating, which had now ceased.

A movement in the brambly thicket at the foot of the bank attracted my attention. I peered down and there, lying on its back with its legs in the air, looking like a large ball of wool, with knitting needles sticking out, was a fat sheep. Slipping and slithering down the incline towards it, I managed by hanging on to a blackthorn trunk to use my free hand and my feet to roll it over, whereupon it started to scramble up the bank. Suddenly it rolled back again. It was then that I saw that it had somehow got itself firmly entangled in several, long, whippy brambles. They were wound tightly round its middle and neck, and were so deeply embedded in the wool that only the root ends in the ground were visible. The poor animal was being slowly strangled, no wonder the bleating had ceased.

At first, I struggled to pull the brambles, which were as fat as a thick finger, out of the ground but this proved impossible. However, my efforts had created a little slack in them and, by bending and twisting them back and forth, I finally broke them, one by one. During this operation the ram, for such its two little horns proclaimed it to be, had ceased to struggle and was lying quietly on its side issuing periodic strangulated squeaks. I was wearing an ancient sheepskin coat and a pair of very battered walking shoes and I suspect he thought I was an elderly ewe with foot rot and posed no threat. Having broken the last bramble, the next thing was to get him up the bank again. This was quite a problem as, not surprisingly, all his 'get up and go' seemed to have 'got up and gone'. However, with a great deal of shoving and pushing I managed to get him upright and then with much wobbling and staggering and more man-handling from me, he made it to the field. The brambles still held him in a vice, their broken ends sticking out like porcupine quills, as he tottered unsteadily away to his waiting harem. The flock had been standing at a respectable distance, no doubt because of Peppi, who had been darting back and forth barking encouragement during the entire proceedings.

Back at the cottage, I telephoned Michael Williams, the farmer, and told him of his ram's unwelcome neck collar and stomach girdle, and he set off with shears to rectify matters. It was later, when recovering from my exertions, with a cup of coffee, and bemoaning a pair of ruined gloves to Geoffrey, that it dawned on me that I had actually rescued a ram caught in the thickets! A truly biblical situation, so it was somehow very satisfying to know that, in spite of the march of civilisation with its cars and aeroplanes and tarmac'd lanes, rams are still caught in thickets just as they were over two thousand years ago.

And now it is wintertime again, and very soon Christmas will be upon us. I remember an old man of ninety-three years telling me, shortly before his death, that his earliest recollection was the bowl of oranges his grandmother would place, on Christmas Eve, in the bar parlour of the inn she and his grandfather kept. He said that all down the years he never smelt an orange without remembering that old panelled room, the leaping fire, the shining pewter, and that bowl of golden munificence, and feeling himself a small boy again on Christmas Eve.

For me it is sugar mice which unlock the memory of long ago Christmases. Driving home recently I stopped at a village shop near Hereford to buy a loaf of bread. Carefully weaving my way around the stands of newspapers and postcards, I reached the counter and there, among the bootlaces and biscuits, the glacier mints and toffees, was a tray full of the little creatures. Fat, evocative, and quite irresistible, they snuggled side by side, in meek, submissive rows. I picked a pink one up by his little waxy tail, remembering as I did so the innumerable skirmishes in the past with my siblings over who should have the pink ones. They must have tasted the same as their despised white brethren but they always seemed so much more delicious. No childhood Christmas was ever complete without its share of sugar mice hanging from the tree, along with the silver balls and the gaily coloured birds with spun glass tails.

There were always candles on our Christmas tree, like twists of coloured barley sugar they stood, erect and expectant on the tips of the branches awaiting the long, lighted taper that, touching them like a fairy wand, brought the whole thing to shining life. Mercifully, Christmas was not advertised in the shops from mid-August on, in those days, and the proclamation of the coming event burst upon us, as if by a pre-arranged signal, in the first week in December.

Oh, those halcyon days! There were the ritual visits to pantomime and circus, and the exciting shopping expeditions, and from four o'clock onwards everywhere was a fairyland of blazing light and every shop window had its snowstorm of cotton wool through which could be glimpsed a multitude of Christmas goodies. In the weeks before Christmas, we children were busily occupied making our Christmas presents. Breakfast eggs were carefully eaten so that the shells could be painted and stuck into plaster of Paris to form little 'Posy Pots'; fretsaws flew to and fro cutting round pictures stuck on ply wood to make calendars; and cotton reels were glued, one on top of the other, topped by a metal cap and painted a brilliant red or virulent green, to serve as 'elegant' candlesticks. Of course, there was always the ubiquitous pipe rack, with its whirls and twirls, a masterpiece of the fretworker's art.

What happened to the wealth of things that emerged from our labours, gifts for various aunts and uncles, I do not know, for I never recall seeing them in use.

One of the pleasantest of the old Christmas customs was surely the bringing home of the Yule log, or Christmas brand, as it was known in Shropshire (usually pronounced 'bron' or 'brund'). Numerous artists have left us pictures portraying the event, sometimes it is a patient shire horse that is shown dragging the great baulk of wood along snow streaked, rutted tracks, and sometimes stalwart villagers are depicted hauling away on stout ropes. Whichever method was used to transport the great trunk to manor house or farm, it was always an occasion of much jollity and in Shropshire, at least, journeys end meant a convivial drinking of ale, served in huge tankards for those who brought in the Christmas brand.

If a horse had been involved in the operation, it was his last chore for some time, for among the old Shropshire taboos was one which stated that a horse must not be used for ploughing during the twelve days of the Christmas season. A Shropshire woman reminiscing in 1883 on her childhood, remembered that in 1845 in an old farmhouse, called The Vessons Farm, and situated at the northern end of the Stiperstones, there was a kitchen where the ancient flagstones were badly chipped and battered in a wide path leading from the door to the hearth. She was told that the damaged area was caused by the horses' hoofs when the Christmas brand was being dragged in. If nothing else, this must be a testimony to the size of the kitchens in some of the old Shropshire farmhouses.

In the Border Country, the Yule log was usually of oak or holly and, occasionally, of crab apple. Up until the turn of the century, it was customary to light it on Christmas Eve and keep it burning throughout the twelve days of Christmas. In the 'good old days', when this custom was commonplace, even the humblest cottages had great wide hearths on which to rest quite sizeable Christmas brands, but in twentieth century Britain few, indeed, are the houses with such generous fireplaces. This is in part due to the fact that from the middle of the nineteenth century onwards, it became fashionable to insert those extremely practical Victorian ranges into the old inglenook openings.

Many of the owners of these ancient hearths were so anxious to step into the modern world, that the work was often carried out with indecent haste, as must have been the case when workmen restoring a cottage belonging to a friend of ours, uncovered a whole rack of clay pipes still in situ behind the thick plaster on the chimney breast.

What happened one wonders? Did Mrs Claypipes nag an unyielding husband about the 'mod cons' of Mrs Jones up the lane? Until the day when Mr Claypipes, being safely ensconced in the Plough and Harrow, she had a quick job done in his absence, ingle-nook was reduced, kitchen range in place and the plasterer sloshed over the pipes in his panic to be off before Pater Familias returned. Whatever the reason, many generations later, it gave our friend a splendid name for his 'butt and ben', for his white wicket gate now proudly proclaims 'Claypipes' in shiny black paint.

Years ago, when we first came to the Border Country, we bought three sixteenth century timber-framed cottages and turned them into a long, low, family house. The middle cottage had an enormous stone chimney breast straddling across more than half of the room and serving a grate of modest size. The other two cottages had chimneys in their end walls. Sadly, we decided the stone chimney must go for with it in place the seating arrangements were novel indeed. It was a case of either frying in front of the fire, where, even with the chairs pressed against the far wall, there was a space of only three-feet between oneself and the flames, or freezing to death in one of the long alcoves formed at the sides of the great jutting edifice. Evenings spent thus resembled an extended game of musical chairs, as every so often the occupants of the room swopped freezing for roasting and vice versa. We consoled ourselves at the chimney's demise, however, by thinking of the fine inglenooks we were sure would be revealed when we opened the remaining fireplaces.

Alas! No such delights awaited us. With the plaster and rubble removed, we found one chimney breast was of stone and had an iron bar inserted where we had expected to find a beam. The other was of brick and had a brick arch to support the chimney. Nevertheless, an inglenook we were determined to have and, with this end in view, we set about modifying the brick fireplace. The old kitchen range was taken out but we left the great iron bar, which swung out from the side wall, to hang over the grate. We were told by Mrs Slater, the neighbouring farmer's wife, that this great swinging bar was called a sway, although she added that, in some parts of Shropshire, it went by the name of a chimney crane. 'When I was a child on our farm up above Rhayader', she said, 'there was always a big, black kettle hanging from the sway over our fire, so that we always had hot water ready for use. There was a big, iron, stewing pot too, and my mother would cook anything you can think of in that pot; porridge, potatoes, apples, stew, anything, and the smells were delicious'. We decided the 'sway' must stay.

During the restoration of the cottages, a number of rotting timbers had been removed but many of these had long sections of hardwood in them. A length of oak from one of them was inserted above the opening that once enclosed the range, and in place of the range itself we put a dog grate. We laid the first fire, lit it and settled down to enjoy the leaping flames. The only thing leaping was us! With smarting eyes we fled for the door. Without even a decent interval, the smoke curled and billowed into the room. 'Must be the wind', gasped Geoffrey, the tears streaming down his face. 'But there is no wind', I choked, not a blade stirring, 'perhaps its the cold chimney'. 'More like a bird', he spluttered, staggering after me into the garden. 'That chimney needs sweeping. I'll get on to Tom Galliers and see what he suggests'.

206

The faithful Tom duly arrived armed with a holly branch. He climbed up on the cottage roof and thrust it down the chimney. There followed a brisk exchange of grunting and shouting between Geoffrey on the ground and Tom on the roof and, at last, after several forays down the chimney with the holly branch, a shower of soot and lumps of old brick and twigs along with the remains of a bird plopped onto the hearth. 'That'll do the trick', pronounced Tom, red from his exertions. We lit the fire again but it was no good. The chimney might not have existed, not a wisp of smoke issued from it, instead great billows poured from the cottage windows.

We consulted the 'experts' who had gathered round the gate, alarmed that we might be on fire. The general consensus of opinion was that what we needed was a 'Good 'ood', and the best thing we could do was to find ourselves a tinsmith and get him to 'knock one up'. Tinsmiths it would seem, are a rare species. After making several fruitless enquiries, we were on the point of settling for a less demanding form of heating, when one cold grey day as we hurried for the car after a morning's shopping in Ludlow, we heard the rhythmic 'clink - clank' of metal on metal. Intrigued, we followed the sound up a small alley, past a blacksmith whose glowing coals gleamed through an open doorway, to another entrance, also open, from which the sound was coming. We peeped in and there, big and genial, surrounded by a vast array of fenders and fireirons, pots and pans and countless other things awaiting his expertise, was Mr Chapman, master-tinsmith. We told him our problem and he agreed to make us a hood. We gave him the measurements of the fireplace and he said he would bring the completed hood, or canopy, as he preferred to call it, in a week's time, and fit it into place.

On the day he was due, the rain streamed down and churned up the mud in the lane. My heart sank as I thought of the state of the floor, after several trots had been made back and forth to his van. I need not have worried. Mr Chapman arrived with a role of immaculate dust sheets tucked under his arm. These he placed carefully on the floor before neatly laying out his tools and bringing in the hood. He worked steadily for several hours and, when he had finished, a beautifully made black, steel canopy was in place over the dog grate. The moment of truth had arrived. Geoffrey put a match to the kindling and the carefully placed logs. The wood hissed and crackled and burned as merry as a marriage bell with never a puff of smoke into the room. The grey swirls made straight up the chimney throat as if drawn by a magnet.

As we sipped our coffee, in front of the dancing flames, Mr Chapman told us of some of the hearths he had doctored so that the fires burned bright and clear. 'All over the country, I would go', he said, 'even as far as Aberystwyth'. 'Have you always lived in Shropshire?', I queried. 'Bless you no,' he replied, 'I was born in London on the Old Kent Road, and I did my apprenticeship there. Seven years it was, and I was paid three shillings and ninepence a week. The ninepence kept back for my tools. My mother had to find fifty guineas to apprentice me to a master-tinsmith. She was a widow and it was very hard for her but she managed somehow. In nineteen twenty, when I finished my apprenticeship, I could earn seventeen shillings and ninepence a week. The ninepence was

34 *Mr Chapman, master-tinsmith*

still kept back to repay my tools. I went to work in a small factory which supplied Woolworth's. We made twenty-four gross of kettles each day and Woolworth's took all our output, selling them sixpence- halfpenny a kettle. They kept threepence-farthing on each kettle themselves and paid our factory the other threepence-farthing. We'd make kettles for three months and then switch over to baking tins for three months'.

'But how is it Mr Chapman', I said, 'that you came to live in Ludlow?' 'Ah, well', he replied, 'it was the war you see. I was in the army and we were posted to north of Shrewsbury. While we were there I went down to Church Stretton and there I met my future wife. When the war was over she didn't fancy going to London to live, so I decided to look for work in Shropshire. Ludlow was the place we chose. Off I went to the labour exchange and asked if they had any work for a tinsmith. "A tinsmith", said the young man behind the counter, "what's a tinsmith?" That set me thinking and I decided that if the Ludlow people didn't know what a tinsmith was, here was a chance for me to start up on my own and shew them!' He smiled. 'I've never regretted it', he said. 'I'm a real Shropshire countryman now. It's much more relaxed here and you live longer, of that I'm sure'. He gathered together his dust sheets, gave a final pat to the hood and departed, leaving two very satisfied customers sitting one each side of a spanking fire and hoping that he would live forever.

The houses of the Border Country were decorated at Christmas time with ivy and holly and, of course, there was always a bunch of mistletoe - all the bounty of nature for even the mistletoe grows freely in the March land. Many of the old superstitions and beliefs linger on in the area and Mrs Slater told me that it was still the custom in certain parts to give it to sheep after lambing. From time immemorial it has been used as a remedy for apoplexy and Mrs Slater remembers as a girl seeing Mistletoe tea being given to someone who had just had a fit. 'Up until recent times', she said, 'it was the custom to cut a mistletoe bough and bring it into the house on Christmas Eve, where it would be hung in the kitchen for twelve months. Then it would be taken down and burned, and a new bough put in its place'. This was considered a very powerful talisman and protection for the whole household. Sir Walter Scott begins one of his poems with the following verse:-

> The damsel donn'd her kirtle sheen,
> The hall was dressed with holly green,
> Forth to the wood did the merry men go
> To gather in the mistletoe.

In the old channel port of Deal, when the icy wind whistled through the streets swirling scurries of rain in our faces, we children would chant a

harmless parody of his words. It went like this:
>The damsel donn'd her mackintosh
>Her rainproof hood and stout galosh,
>Forth to the shops did the damsel go
>to try and get some mistletoe.

The mistletoe buying expedition usually took place on Christmas Eve when, having hung the last trail of ivy from the cornice, and fixed the last piece of holly in place, someone would cry, 'Oh, we've forgotten the mistletoe'. It was easy enough to forget for, although Christmas trees and evergreens abounded, the only mistletoe in the town was usually an insignificant bunch to be found hanging over the sprouts and potatoes in Mr Chittenden's grocery shop. 'The lad'll get you some', he would say in response to our request, and the 'lad', who must have been all of seventy years, would clamber onto an orange crate and break off a small sprig. The price was always the same - exorbitant - one shilling and sixpence,or seven and ahalfpence in today's money.

I remember those days when I am wandering in the lanes of the Border Country, and see the ancient apple trees in the orchards hung with great balls of green mistletoe, suspended from the bare branches for all the world like Chinese lanterns. I remember too our incredulity when, just before our first Christmas in the March, we found in our porch a bunch of mistletoe, gift from dear Mrs Slater. It was so vast it would have decorated every house in Deal.

The Border, and particularly Herefordshire, has always been famed for its luxuriance of mistletoe and for many years exported quantities of it to less favoured counties. As long ago as 1868, it was recorded that one-hundred and fourteen tons of mistletoe left Hereford by train for Manchester, Liverpool, Birmingham and London, and the diarist, Parson Kilvert, writing in 1871 from his Clyro parsonage in Herefordshire, notes, 'The mistletoe men are going about gathering mistletoe boughs for the London market'. It became the accepted practice for the engine drivers and the guards on the trains to export the mistletoe from the county themselves, and during the early part of December they did so by almost every train. This must have been a very welcome Christmas bonus when pay was far from generous.

By Candlemas Eve, all the Christmas greenery had to be taken down for it was believed that to leave it longer would mean a death in the family before the following Christmas. This belief was especially strong in the villages of the Clee Hills. Sometimes, when the holly and ivy came down, it was replaced with bowls of snowdrops, or Candlemas bells as they were called, and still are, on the Welsh border. This was rather a strange custom because at any other time of the snowdrop season these delightful little heralds of spring were considered very unlucky flowers. Many Shropshire and Herefordshire people would not have them in the house.

It was the policy of Cromwell and the Puritans to suppress Christmas altogether and in 1642 all the churches were ordered to close on Christmas Day, while shopkeepers were told that they must remain open. This caused an uproar and many people were injured in the subsequent riots. The Roundhead soldiers were ordered to deal harshly with anyone infringing the new laws and all Christmas celebrations ceased or were driven underground.

This banning of Christmas lasted two decades until the return of the monarchy and even then it was some time before things were back to normal, for the new generations only knew of the old ways from hearsay. Ironically, just as people rediscovered the joys of celebrating Christmas, the authorities produced a new calendar and a new day was chosen for Christmas Day. This caused great consternation but nowhere so much as at Glastonbury where, for centuries a thorn said to have sprung from the staff of Joseph of Aramathaea, burst into bloom at midnight on Christmas Eve. People waited with bated breath on January sixth, which was the date on which the old Christmas was due to fall, praying that the thorn would oblige. Happily it did. Parson Kilvert, writing in his diary in 1879, records, 'Monday, Epiphany, Old Christmas day, last night the slip of the Holy Thorn which John Parry of Dolfach grafted for me last spring in the Vicarage lower garden, blossomed in an intense frost'.

In Mediaeval times, there was a great deal of feasting and jollification over the whole of the Christmas season, which lasted until twelfth night. At a nobleman's table it was customary to serve a boar's head with a rosy apple in its mouth. This would be followed by a gilded peacock, the brilliant tail feathers still in place. In later years the goose was the bird for the table, and in the sixteenth century the turkey, imported from Spain, was the fashionable bird. However, the roast beef of old England still held pride of place, as it had done for many years in countless homes where boars and peacocks were a little hard to come by. Parson Woodforde records in his diary for Christmas 1794, 'A very fine sirloin of beef roasted and plenty of plum puddings for dinner'. Obviously a man of some prudence, he added a footnote, 'Took some rhubarb going to bed'.

All in all, Christmas is no time of rejoicing for the feathered fraternity, their plight being pithily summed up in the following light-hearted doggerel, origin unknown.

'Now Christmas cheer
Is almost here,
What awful luck
To be a duck.

Past English monarchs certainly celebrated the Christmas season in style. In 1248 Henry II invited the poor to fill Westminster Hall, where he feasted them for a whole week on such delights as Dellegrout and Karumpie. But the prince of all party givers was surely Edward IV. In 1482 in his palace at Eltham, he feasted more than two-thousand people each day of the Christmas season. Did his mind drift back, I wonder, to a Christmas two decades before, when as the young Earl of March, he travelled from Ludlow Castle to spend Christmas at Shrewsbury Castle. This was the time of the Wars of the Roses and he had spent several weeks energetically rousing the men of the Border Country to fight for his father, the Duke of York. The Christmas festivities at Shrewsbury came to an untimely end when a message arrived that his father and brother, the seventeen-year old Duke of Rutland, had been killed by the Lancastrians and their heads were gracing the Micklethwaite gate in York. Filled with horror and a burning desire to avenge their deaths, Edward left Shrewsbury and gathering his forces together, defeated the Lancastrians at the Battle of Mortimer's Cross near Wigmore. After the battle he joined up with his cousin, Warwick, and together they rode to London where, on March 4th 1461, he was proclaimed King by the citizens as he entered the gates of the city.

A very important day around Christmas time for the Shropshire poor was December 21st, Saint Thomas's day. Every year, each Shropshire farmer reserved a sack of wheat to be distributed among those less fortunate than himself. This was known as the 'Wheat Dole'. The farmers' wives and daughters would dispense this beneficence on Saint Thomas's day, ladling it out in pints and quarts according to need. The poor of Clun somehow managed to get a double dollop of the 'Dole', securing a portion of wheat for themselves and one of barley for the pigs. This would seem to confirm what has been said about Clunites in the past. For example, Arthur Bradley, when writing of them, tells us 'They were noted for the eye they kept on the main chance, no one it was said, who

212

crossed the Clun Bridge was ever the same again, in other words he was dangerous in a deal'.

Over the years the generosity of the Clun farmers was so abused that the custom became a sort of marathon favouring the able bodied poor, who would scamper from farm to farm getting hand-outs at each, while the more frail among them could only stagger to one farmhouse. Aware of this sorry state of affairs, the farmers eventually joined together in sending all the 'Wheat Dole' to Clun Town Hall, where it was distributed fairly.

And now I have come to the end of my stories. This book, like my first one, is a kaleidoscope of people and places, and remembrances of times past in the Border Country and the land of Wales.

Looking out of the window, as I write, it is difficult to believe that the quiet meadows and the dark woods on Hopton Titterhill, which rises behind them, were once part of one of the most battle torn areas of Britain. But the grey ruins of Hopton Castle, that old Norman stronghold, standing desolate by its grass grown moat, remind one that 'Turn but a stone' and a thousand stories of the turbulent and romantic past on both sides of the border, which is the oldest frontier in Europe, come tumbling out, and I have barely touched the fringe.

Index

215

INDEX

About the author

Veronica Thackeray was convent educated and, in the spring of 1939, was sent to a convent in Germany to study. She managed to get out of the country a few days before the second world war began. She returned to England and married. Nine months later her husband, a bomber pilot, was killed in the battle for France. She became a member of the S.O.E. and was sent to Cairo to work for the Balkan Section.

After the war she remarried. Early in the sixties, with her family, she moved to the Welsh Border Country, fell in love with the area, and became fascinated by its people and history. She began to write articles for local magazines and her research formed the basis of numerous talks, given both in England and America. Her first book, *Tales from the Welsh March*, followed in 1992. It was well received by the press and figures prominently on bookshop shelves.

Tales from the
Welsh March

by Veronica Thackeray

'One of the first things that struck me about this naggingly beautiful
and restless landscape was that the earth itself seems to stir with the vast
scars of ancient times... There is still a rare, out-dated pleasure in driving
through places Miss Thackeray describes so appealingly in her meticu-
lous and absorbing book. I see her bouncing cheekily along the lanes in
her stylish, black Morris Traveller, noting down the whole panorama of
astonishing pleasures... What a happy achievement it is - a bumpy ride
perhaps for her, but an invaluable chart of adventure, past and present,
preserved for those who seek its guidance'. -

from the foreword by John Osborne

One hundred years ago , Arthur Bradley also bounced along the lanes
of the Border Country. He recalled his joy in *In the March and Borderlands
of Wales*. He wrote 'one looks upon the identical landscape one was
familiar with forty years ago and, to the eye, nothing has changed'.
Veronica Thackeray struck by that same unchanging landscape, set out
to travel the same beckoning lanes. Using photographs of today's scene
and the delicate drawings from Bradley's book, she compares many of
the same scenes one hundred years apart.

Of course, it is not only the landscape which thrusts itself into the mind.
The whole area clamours with the sound of sword on armour. Ruined
castles bear witness to the powerful Marcher barons and their unceasing
quest to seize power. All through the years, underlying all the drama of
the great events, are the people of the region going about their everyday
lives. As Veronica Thackeray jouneys through the Middle March and
the land of Wales, she fills her pages with anecdotes and stories about
them.

240 *pages*, 22 *drawings*, 31 *photographs*, 6 *sketches*, 210 x 145 *mm*.

Limp cover. £12.50

Saints and their Emblems
in English Churches

by Robert Milburn

Each figure of a saint in an old church, whether in stone or glass or on the carved screen, usually represents some particular person but they are rarely named and the interested visitor who is without a guide-book cannot easily identify them. St. George and the Dragon and a few others are well known but in medieval craftsmanship many other saints also had some emblem or object as a regular accompaniment in windows and carvings.

This is a book describing more than 250 saints, including all common and many uncommon ones, each of whom is connected in some way with at least one English church.It tells briefly who each was in fact or legend. Where there is an emblem by which the saint can be identified, it gives this informatiom. The commonest emblems are illustrated by line drawings.

The author, Robert Milburn, is an Honorary Fellow of Worcester College, Oxford and a Fellow of the Society of Antiquities. He was Dean of Worcester Cathedral, 1957-1968 and Master of the Temple 1968-1980. Other works by him include *Early Christian Interpretations of History* (Bampton Lectures) and *Early Christian Art and Architecture* (1988).

55 *drawings*. 321 *pages*. 210 x 145 *mm. Limp cover.* £8.50

Tyndale's Dream
A COMEDY OF SORTS

by John-Stuart Anderson

This three-act play, *Tyndale's Dream: a Comedy of Sorts,* based firmly on historical fact, deals with the extraordinary story of William Tyndale, a priest who devoted his life to the translation of the Bible into English and who was burnt at the stake for his pains. It is the story of a man of vision, a man with a dream, to whom everything outside his vision is slightly distorted and of little importance. This is the stuff of high tragedy but John-Stuart Anderson sees it as the story of an heroic man, steadfast of purpose but surrounded and thwarted by grotesque characters who, however despicable and comic, at last secured his downfall.

Its style ranges through rhythmic prose, blank verse, and pantomime doggerel. It encompasses scenes of book-burning at Cambridge, storms at sea, success, betrayal and finally death. *Tyndale's Dream* speaks for all who find themselves unjustly oppressed on account of the gifts they offer humanity - but who eventually conquer to attain immortality. It is a play which can be performed by almost any number of actors. The staging can also be highly flexible, though the author prefers simplicity in sets and costumes.

103 pages. 210 x 140 mm. Limp cover.

£3.50